City of American Dreams

HISTORICAL STUDIES OF URBAN AMERICA

Edited by Kathleen N. Conzen, Timothy J. Gilfoyle, and James R. Grossman

ALSO IN THE SERIES

Parish Boundaries: The Catholic Encounter with Race in the Twentieth-Century Urban North
by John T. McGreevy

Modern Housing for America: Policy Struggles in the New Deal Era
by Gail Radford

Smoldering City: Chicagoans and the Great Fire, 1871–1874
by Karen Sawislak

Making the Second Ghetto: Race and Housing in Chicago, 1940–1960
by Arnold R. Hirsch

Faces along the Bar: Lore and Order in the Workingman's Saloon, 1870–1920
by Madelon Powers

Streets, Railroads, and the Great Strike of 1877
by David O. Stowell

The Creative Destruction of Manhattan, 1900–1940
by Max Page

Brownsville, Brooklyn: Blacks, Jews, and the Changing Face of the Ghetto
by Wendell Pritchett

City of American Dreams

A History of Home Ownership and
Housing Reform in Chicago,
1871–1919

MARGARET GARB

The University of Chicago Press
Chicago and London

Margaret Garb is an assistant professor of history at Washington University in St. Louis.

The University of Chicago Press, Chicago 60637
The University of Chicago Press, Ltd., London
© 2005 by The University of Chicago
All rights reserved. Published 2005
Printed in the United States of America

14 13 12 11 10 09 08 07 06 05   1 2 3 4 5

ISBN: 0-226-28209-0   (cloth)

Library of Congress Cataloging-in-Publication Data

Garb, Margaret.
  City of American dreams : a history of home ownership and housing reform in Chicago, 1871–1919 / Margaret Garb.
      p. cm.
  Includes bibliographical references and index.
  ISBN 0-226-28209-0 (cloth : alk. paper)
  1. Home ownership—Illinois—Chicago—History. 2. Housing—Illinois—Chicago—History. I. Title.
HD7287.82.U62C64 2005
643'.12—dc22

                                                                    2005007798

For my parents

CONTENTS

LIST OF FIGURES

ACKNOWLEDGMENTS

With my first job out of college, as a police beat reporter for the City News Bureau of Chicago, I came to know Chicago intimately. A decade later, when I began to research the dissertation that became this book, I quickly realized that the city I knew so well had little in common with Chicago of the late nineteenth century. The stockyards, once the symbol of the mighty midwestern city and still vivid in the memories of some of my friends, were a wasteland of overgrown fields punctuated by piles of sheet metal and dilapidated sheds in the mid-1980s. Hull House, the settlement launched by Jane Addams and Ellen Gates Starr, had become a museum. Street names had changed, some streets—like Newberry Avenue, which now is covered by the University of Illinois campus—had vanished, highways had eviscerated neighborhoods and changed residents' sense of travel and distance, and new populations with different cultures, languages, and religions had transformed the sounds, smells, sights, and traditions of the city. Even buildings that survived a century of change were numbered differently; the street numbering system was reworked in 1909. I have detailed some of these changes in my notes. Without a doubt, the footprints of the late nineteenth century are everywhere in twenty-first-century Chicago. Yet, to paraphrase the English novelist Leslie Poles Hartley, the past is another city. The Chicago described in this study is the industrial city in the half century after the Great Fire.

Many people have contributed, in tangible and intangible ways, to the writing of this book. Eric Foner, my adviser and friend, offered his usual sharp comments and steady encouragement through the years of working on this dissertation and later book. His generosity and humor enriched my graduate career almost as much as his keen insight helped to improve this book. Elizabeth Blackmar read many, many drafts, always offering new insight and brilliant critique. She was for me, as for so many other Columbia

University graduate students, the model of a passionate scholar and teacher. I am grateful to friends, teachers, and colleagues who read all or parts of various drafts of the manuscript: Peter Marcuse, Alice Kessler-Harris, David Rosner, Iver Bernstein, Gerald Isenberg, David Suisman, Eliza Byard, and Andrea Friedman. Becky Nicolaides' generous reading added much precision and depth to the final manuscript, as did the comments of two anonymous readers for the University of Chicago Press. I thank my editor, Robert Devens, for his good humor, patience, and crisp commentary, and the series editor, James Grossman, for a careful reading and incisive critique of the manuscript. Thanks to Michael Koplow and Elizabeth Branch Dyson for their expert handling of an unruly manuscript.

At both Columbia University and Washington University I found friends and scholars who were in many ways crucial to the development of this project. My thanks go to Richard Bushman, Derek Hirst, Howard Brick, Sam Haselby, Rebecca McLennen, Tim and Anne Parsons, Nic Sammon, Lara Vapnek, Corinne Fields, Martin Kenner, Thea Hunter, Angela Miller, Paula Lupkin, Leslie Brown, Annie Valk, Robert Vinson, Walton Schalik, Danny and Seena Kohl, Henry Berger, and David Konig. Further back, for setting me on course to become a scholar, I thank Stephanie McCurry, Steven Hahn, Rachael Klein, Michael Bernstein, Michael Meranze, Gregory Rodriguez, and Richard Sugarman.

Librarians, archivists, and staff at the Chicago Historical Society, the Newberry Library, the University of Chicago library, the Richard J. Daley Library at the University of Illinois at Chicago, the Harold Washington Municipal Library in Chicago, Butler Library at Columbia University, the New York Public Library, and Olin Library at Washington University provided needed assistance. I received financial support for work on this book from Washington University and Columbia University. Parts of chapter 3 were previously published in "Health, Morality, and Housing: The 'Tenement Problem' in Chicago," *American Journal of Public Health* 93 (2003): 1420–30.

I have the good fortune to have friends in New York, Chicago, and St. Louis who provided shelter and sustenance (both intellectual and material) during the writing of this book. It is with great pleasure I thank them here. Sonia da Silva, Sarah Hanson, Gerry Cleary, Rich Cohen, Chris Kasamas, Miles Harvey, Rengin Altay, Tom Henry, Francesca Costano, Lee Guthrie, and Frank McGee offered steady support on my many research trips to Chicago. For their abiding friendship, I thank Willie Thaler, Stephen Drukman, Becky Rosenfeld, Efat Azizi, Will Warren, Becky Mode, Chris Erikson, Peter Sherman, Gillian Costello, Danny Weglein, and Amelia McDonnell-Parry in New York. Lois Anderson, who sadly did not live to see this project completed, provided generous financial aid. Betsy Farrell and Babs Davey, dear friends, gave me a summer of seclusion in Greenport and so much else, too much to list here. Mark Gregory Pegg offered editorial comment on every page, indeed nearly every word. His brilliant mind and elegant prose have enriched this book more than I care to admit.

My family, long ago, taught me that home is defined by warmth, laughter, love, and loud political debate. For all of that and so much more, I thank my brother, Charles Garb, my sister, Emily Garb, and my parents, Isaac and Joan Garb. Finally, my deepest thanks go to my daughter, Eva, who contributed absolutely nothing to the writing of this book, but brought the greatest joy into my life.

The American conception of home ownership was profoundly transformed in the fifty years after the Civil War. As the nation moved from an agrarian to an industrialized urban society, as immigrants from abroad and migrants from rural regions flowed into American cities, and as reformers sought to improve living conditions in impoverished urban neighborhoods, the ownership of a single-family house emerged as a symbol of what many call "the American dream."[1] The American celebration of a particular form of property—the single-family house set on a tidy yard—was neither natural nor inevitable. Rather, it was grounded in changing material conditions of housing and social relations of work in industrializing northern cities, and in struggles over the meaning, form, and function of the family home that divided wage laborers and salaried workers, immigrants and their native-born neighbors, tenants and municipal officials, and African-American and white home owners. The result, no less damaging for its having been unintended, was the emergence of cities sharply divided along class and racial lines, and the expansion of an urban poor who were increasingly shut out of the nation's housing markets.

This history of home ownership in Chicago begins and ends with street riots. The first, in January 1872, was a protest by immigrant wage laborers seeking to maintain their ability to purchase houses. It dramatizes the deep commitment to property rights by workingmen who would be among the first to link home ownership to "an American standard of living." The book concludes with the race riot of 1919, which in important ways was a tragic result of the reorganization of residential property relations that began in the final decades of the nineteenth century. By 1919, public health advocates, concerned about the spread of contagious disease in tenement neighborhoods, had urged families to seek single-family houses set on spacious yards and fitted with the new technology of indoor plumbing. Urban reformers, crystallizing a new more rigid definition of the function of the family home, had proclaimed the privacy of what later was called the nuclear family the key to protecting the morality and health of the nation. And builders, seeking to profit from the sales of single-family houses, had developed elaborate advertising campaigns to promote home ownership. All, in one way or another, argued that the single-family, owner-occupied house was a solution to a wide range of social problems. That the race riot in 1919 demonstrated that home ownership could not solve the nation's housing problems is obvious. Still, the ideal of home ownership endures.

A home is both a concrete object and an idea. Or to put it another way, I recognize that not all dwellings are considered "homes," and my aim is to analyze how one particular type of dwelling, the owner-occupied single-family house, came to embody the American ideal of the family home. Thus, both ideas and material conditions are central to this study. This book is about changes in the ways Americans conceived of and assessed the economic and social value of residential property. It chronicles a dramatic shift in the social function of property rights in housing, a shift from immigrants' uses of home ownership to augment household income and assert their status as Americans to the more modern middle-class version of property as a profit- and status-generating investment whose value was determined by the size, amenities, and location of the house, as well as the race and class of neighboring residents. That change, worked out in political struggles among land speculators, builders, wage laborers, and their more affluent neighbors, redefined urban neighborhoods and reoriented the social geography of Chicago. This book contends that struggles over property rights in housing fundamentally transformed living conditions and social relations in American cities.

––––––––

Property rights have long held a primary place in American political theory and society. In the agrarian republic, property owners claimed social independence and citizenship rights based on their ownership of property and control over household labor. Early nineteenth-century urban craftsmen asserted similar rights founded on their ownership of workshops, tools, and skills. In preindustrial America, the link between property and social independence was explicit: property owners used their property to produce income or necessities for their households. A house sat at the center of a farm or was attached to a craftsman's workshop. Until the 1820s, most states set property requirements for the vote, underlining the republican theory that a man who owned property and controlled the labor of his household would cast his vote according to the best interests of the nation.[2]

But the gradual disintegration of household economies, the rise of a permanent wage-laboring class that did not own mechanisms of production, and in broad terms, the massive shift from an agriculture-based to an urban industrial economy put property rights in housing in an anomalous position. Though waged and unwaged labor remained within urban dwellings, production in an industrial society was associated with manufacturing enterprises and transportation networks owned by the nation's captains of industry. Ownership of residential property, which was clearly distinguished from manufacturing sites, no longer provided families with the ability to generate income enough to sustain the household's independence. Cities with streets lined with cottages and brick two- or three-flat buildings a short walk or trolley ride from factories, shops, and offices appeared to strip the family home of its income-producing functions. A house set on a tiny lot on an urban street still had economic value. But its value seemed diminished or at least unclear when compared to pay packets earned in the clatter of workshops and, even more, to the remarkable earnings of businesses mass-producing commodities for exchange in national and international markets.[3]

In the antebellum era, no ideal better illustrated the reorganization of work and of city life than the family home. In scores of books, magazine articles, and advice manuals dedicated to guiding young people through the rigors of courtship and marriage and to recommend proper housekeeping techniques to wives and mothers, writers defined the home as a pastoral refuge removed from the rigors and competitive worlds of commerce and politics. Although many families employed servants and both waged and unwaged labor were needed to maintain a household, the ideology that came to dominate much of American culture designated the home as outside of market relations. The ideology of separate spheres, effectively providing a new version of gender order by distinguishing between men's world of work and women's world of domesticity, invested the family home with priceless emotional value. Though men and women rented and purchased dwellings, and wage laborers and their employers needed shelter, so long as the home represented an idealized refuge from market relations, whether a resident owned or rented his or her home was a matter of indifference to many urban dwellers. The family home, in theory, stood outside market relations; its economic value was obscured by its sentimental functions.[4]

In the years after the Civil War, the economic value of an urban house was further blurred by the growing use of forms of property that competed with landed property for capital investments. Most common were government-issued bonds and private mortgages or notes on loans, purchased by well-to-do families hoping to achieve a large return on investments in nonlanded property. Affluent families also established family trusts to manage their assets and produce income through investments in business, banking, land, and often railroads. Abstracted from direct ownership of tangible property, the trust became a form of property, which could generate income and pass wealth across generations. The rise of the corporation as the dominant mechanism for managing businesses also produced seemingly intangible forms of property (stocks, bonds, and a variety of commercial instruments), which could, as the enormous wealth of men like the banker J. P. Morgan, the steel magnate Andrew Carnegie, the meat packers Philip Armour and Gustavus Swift, or the railroad car tycoon George Pullman attested, yield enormous profits. As property in investment produced increasingly great wealth and grandiose styles of life, the purchase of a family home became, for those with income that stretched beyond daily necessities, just one of several options for investing surplus capital.[5]

In the final decades of the nineteenth century, jurists and legal scholars debated how best to represent property in law and public policy. Antebellum jurists had established that property rights included the right to the future value of the property (or to the profit from an investment); beginning in the 1870s the courts further strengthened the legal status of nonlanded property and reinforced investors' claims to future profits. In a series of decisions issued by the federal courts and the Supreme Court from the 1870s through the 1890s, jurists recognized, as John R. Commons noted, "that not merely physical things are objects of property, but the expected earning power of those things is property." Property was conceived in law and in custom as a series of abstract rights to the uses and future benefits of ownership. "Our concept of property has shifted," legal theorist Arthur L. Corbin wrote in 1922. "Incorporeal rights have become property . . . [Property] has become merely a bundle of legal relations—rights, powers, privileges, immunities." Responding to the stunning social changes spawned by industrialization and, at the same time, laying the groundwork for government regulation of property in the twentieth century, the courts gradually moved away from the historical conception of property as a tangible object and fortified claims of those seeking to enhance market values of all forms of property.[6]

This book chronicles a dramatic transformation in property rights in urban housing and traces that change on the city's social landscape. It bridges two distinct and rich strands of urban history: studies that have demonstrated significant rates of home ownership among the post–Civil War immigrant working classes[7] and those that have tracked the gradual expansion of middle-class suburbs in the late nineteenth century.[8] Home ownership in nineteenth-century cities was not equated with middle-class status. Nor was late nineteenth-century suburbanization necessarily a pursuit of home ownership. The aim of this study, then, is to analyze the ways urban residents struggled over and transformed the social value of property rights in housing in an industrializing city.[9] This study is inspired by the scholarship that demonstrates that property—those "bundles of rights" that expanded and contracted at different moments in the past—has a history. Property's meaning in custom and in law, and its intended social purposes, changed over time.[10]

The rapid expansion of home ownership rates in the twentieth century led many scholars and much of the American public to view home ownership as a homogenizing experience. The simple fact that large numbers of wage workers owned their homes would, by the mid twentieth century, obscure significant differences in resources, culture, education, and opportunities between waged and salaried workers. Ironically, the transformation in the social and economic functions of the family home occurred during a period when workers and their employers increasingly conceived of themselves as part of distinct classes with separate and conflicting economic interests. From the great railroad strikes of 1877 through the hundreds of strikes that followed World War I, late nineteenth- and early twentieth-century industrial workers engaged in regular and often violent battles over wages, hours, and working conditions with their employers. Yet the emergence of the single-family owner-occupied house as the American ideal of the family home, a social process that paralleled and intersected class conflicts around wage labor, served, in a sense, as the ideological unmaking of class in political and social debates. Expanding rates of home ownership among middle- and working-class Americans did not erase class differences, but the celebration of home ownership as the symbol of the American dream generated the appearance of uniform prosperity and of a classless society.

A study of home ownership reveals much of the complexity of class formation and of the murky and sometimes porous boundaries separating social groups. Language, ethnicity, race, and religion divided Chicago's populace. Those differences faded under the weight of class distinctions when it came to housing—whether to buy or rent, to live near a park or a factory, to install indoor plumbing or fight sewer construction—until, that is, just after the turn of the century, when the race of residents became the primary characteristic dividing Chicago's neighborhoods.

The terms "working class" and "middle class" have been muddied in contemporary usage, largely because of the ways Americans reconceived of the social value of ownership of a single-family house. In using these terms I am not ignoring the historical processes that shaped them. On the contrary, I recognize that class was fragmented, dynamic, and historically specific especially as class relations took new form in industrializing America. This study, without falling into a teleological trap, treats the class positions of the urban populace in terms that would have been recognizable to late nineteenth- and early twentieth-century Americans. Work, income, education, relationships with neighbors and relatives, participation in cultural activities and civic institutions, values, ideals, and access to ownership of the means of production were central to determining an individual's class. This social category, always conceived in relation to other classes, can be grasped only through the material and metaphoric existence of particular men and women in particular societies. Crucially, the ways people used their homes—from the most mundane problem of water supply to the apparent sophistication of acquiring multiple mortgages—and how they conceived of the value of owning houses, profoundly affirmed the class of communities and individuals.[11]

The postbellum working classes, an expanding and permanent group of wage laborers, were a diverse mass of skilled and unskilled men and women. They engaged in manual labor for hourly wages, ranging from the well-paid and highly skilled butchers in the packinghouses and skilled carpenters in the building trades to bakers, peddlers, household servants, and unskilled day laborers. Their ideals and aspirations were shaped both by the daily experiences of waged labor and the communities in which they lived.[12] Diverse in nationality and religion, wage laborers were overwhelmingly foreign born or the children of immigrants until after the turn of the century, when black Americans migrated in ever larger numbers to industrial northern cities.[13]

Immigrant working-class people left few explicit written accounts of their views of their homes and property, unlike more affluent urban residents, whose journals and letters, published articles, essays, and fiction offer a fuller record of their housing concerns. Though newspaper reports sometimes quoted urban wage laborers and the labor and the foreign language presses published articles and essays by working-class men, the voices of the immigrant working classes generally are absent from the historical record. Their views of property rights and of housing, however, are apparent in property records and in social investigations of the urban poor. In the pages of the city's property accounts, wage-laboring men and women left a vivid account of their uses of their property, their housing practices and aspirations. Wage laborers visibly pursued home ownership and used their property in ways that distinguished them from their more affluent salaried neighbors. Home ownership did not lift working-class households into the middle classes, but for many, home ownership was a mark of autonomy and dignity, a sign of the prosperity of "the working man."

The aspiration for home ownership was not imposed on the working classes; it was not a hegemonic force giving the illusion of social equality to the poor and working classes. Indeed, the home ownership ideal was inspired by the immigrant working classes and gradually transformed into a middle-class aspiration. Home ownership, then, was part of a constellation of symbols making up working-class culture and at the same time served particular economic purposes for working-class households struggling to survive in an industrializing city.

The late nineteenth-century middle classes, always an amorphous group, paid close attention to the design, decor, and location of their homes. Included were small businessmen, salaried office workers, and lower-earning professionals, often men who controlled some business capital and employed a few others in both their businesses and their homes. More financially stable were the lawyers, doctors, salaried business managers, and entrepreneurs who secured their status through education, family connections, and access to capital enough to maintain their households through all but the sharpest economic depressions. It was salaried workers—those who neither owned large corporations nor engaged in the physical labor of production—who after the turn of the century came to define themselves, in part, through the ownership of a particular type of house, the elaborate two-story owner-occupied single-family house fitted with the latest housing technologies and set on a manicured yard a distance from smoke-filled, fast-paced urban centers. For them, home ownership was associated with health and family privacy and with the potential for future profits on their investment in residential real estate.[14]

Yet even as more affluent families increasingly saw home ownership as a source of middle-class identity, working-class families continued to use their homes for income-producing purposes. Well into the 1920s and sometimes beyond, working-class families continued the practices of taking in boarders, growing vegetables in backyard gardens, and acquiring multiple loans on their property to generate cash in hard times.[15] Never unified or cohesive, the working classes' struggles for resources in housing, the expanding conflicts between African-American and European-born wage laborers, between the skilled and the less skilled for access to and control of residential spaces, are central to the history of home ownership.

Ultimately, the persistence of the working-class aspiration for property in housing and the massive expansion of the city's residential real estate markets to include middle-class home owners conceal the calamitous underside of the American infatuation with home ownership. The gradual acceptance of home ownership as an emblem of American identity stratified the working classes. It divided those who had the resources to purchase a single-family house from those who no longer could afford home ownership. Property rights in housing, the ability of wage workers, typically regularly employed and often unionized, to purchase single-family houses separated them from the less skilled, lower paid, often nonunionized workers. By the late teens and through the rest of the twentieth century, the expanding American fixation on home ownership meant that those at the lower rungs of the working classes, the unskilled and the poor, were increasingly left out of the American dream.[16]

———————

In the nearly half century from the Great Fire through the Great War, Chicago developed into a major industrial center, home to thousands of immigrant laborers and expanding working-class neighborhoods. By the time of the fire in October 1871, industrialists had already begun to transform the city from a commercial center for western farmers to the nation's leading industrial producer. Out of the rubble left by the flames grew a city whose economy was linked through capital, commodities, and transient labor to the rest of the nation and to Europe. In the final decades of the nineteenth century, Cyrus McCormick's farm implement factory, George M. Pullman's rail works, and Chicago's steel, lumber, and stone-cutting plants produced more than a third of the nation's industrial commodities. The packinghouses of Gustavus F. Swift and Philip D. Armour processed the packaged beef and pork served on American tables.[17]

Drawn by opportunities for employment, both native-born and immigrant laborers flowed into Chicago. Between 1870 and 1900, the city's population doubled every ten years, hitting over two million at the turn of the century and reaching nearly three million in 1920. More striking were the dramatic changes in the ethnic and racial character of the city's inhabitants. A handful of New Englanders and midwesterners had established the town in 1833. By 1870, German, Irish, and Scandinavian immigrants outnumbered native-born residents. In the decades following the fire, Eastern European Jews, Italians, and Poles wrangled for living space in already densely packed neighborhoods, seeking housing within walking distance of jobs. In the late 1890s, African-Americans began to migrate from the south to the Midwest's industrial center, forming small but growing neighborhoods on the south and west sides. By the early twentieth century, Chicago was patchwork of ethnic and racial groups.[18]

Late nineteenth-century Chicago was the nation's center for labor organizing, the site of some of the bloodiest labor conflicts, and the home of leading Progressive Era reformers. As the Knights of Labor and later the American Federation of Labor struggled to sustain unions, workers fought for the eight-hour day, higher wages, job security, and improved working conditions.[19] Many of the nation's leading reformers of the Progressive Era, that vast and nebulous movement for improving urban society, were inspired by Jane Addams, who with Ellen Gates Starr founded Hull House, the social settlement in a Victorian mansion on Chicago's west side, in 1889. Volunteers at Hull House and the half-dozen other settlement houses opened in its wake established the social survey, with its carefully charted maps and graphs detailing all elements of urban life as the model for "scientific" investigations of working and living conditions in immigrant neighborhoods. They also helped found the University of Chicago's famous School of Civics and Philanthropy, which institutionalized the new field. Outside the settlement houses, the city's middle classes and elite formed dozens of reform organizations dedicated to improving health, eliminating corruption in government, fighting gambling, prostitution, and child labor, and scores of other causes. Sometimes working together, at other times in direct conflict, Chicago's middle-class reformers, labor leaders, and political radicals profoundly influenced social reform work and labor organizing in other northern cities.[20]

Industrialization, immigration, class conflict, and struggles over property rights in housing occurred in slightly varied time frames but similar patterns in most northern cities. In Boston, Philadelphia, Detroit, Pittsburgh, and St. Louis similar and equally dramatic changes in the circumstances of work and housing generated parallel transformations in the social value of home ownership and of the social landscapes of those cities. This study, then, tracks those changes in a particularly large and turbulent but generally representative city.

To write a history of home ownership is to argue against much of the prevailing popular wisdom. It is to argue that the desire for home ownership is not a natural part of the human condition, nor is the aspiration for ownership of a single-family house an inevitable consequence of American political ideology, of industrialization, or of government programs and tax breaks designed to encourage home ownership. There is no linear narrative to the history of home ownership, just as there was no single actor driving this process. Approaching the problem of home ownership from several perspectives—those of home owners, builders, municipal officials, and urban reformers—this study explores the interconnected and often overlapping forces that transformed the social meanings of property rights in housing. The following chapters, circling around the problem, analyzing housing in its material and ideological forms, provide a chronological—though frequently overlapping—history of property rights in housing, a history of that peculiarly American obsession: ownership of a single-family house.

CHAPTER ONE

Equal Rights, Equal Property

"Equal rights and equal property." The words rang through the crowd gathered at the corner of Market and Illinois Streets in Chicago on a Monday evening in mid-January 1872. Men of German, Scandinavian, and Irish stock from the city's North Side, they stood on the sidewalk; and as their numbers grew, nearly three hundred filled the frozen streets. Most were home owners, skilled laborers and mechanics whose houses were among the thousands destroyed by the Great Fire the previous October. Reconstruction had begun almost immediately and by mid-January the commercial district, nine square blocks on the western shore of Lake Michigan, was being rebuilt. Already a handful of new brick houses were scattered along the streets north of the Chicago River, signs of the city's widely touted revival and of the faith of eastern bankers in their investments in Chicago's industries. But as the city struggled to recover from the devastating fire, reconstruction was marred by a public conflict over building materials. Faced with a threat possibly more ominous than another fire, the men gathered in "the memory of the great fire, for the love of their homes and their little ones" to demand the Common Council protect their rights to build or buy wood frame houses. Without assurances that the men could rebuild in wood, many, unable to afford new houses of brick, believed they would find home ownership beyond their means. Home ownership, the men argued, secured their economic autonomy in the industrializing city and signaled their hard-won status as independent Americans. European immigrants, ironically, were among the first Americans to claim urban home ownership, property rights in a single-family house set on a city lot, as the symbol of the "American standard of living," as the American dream.[1]

On the evening of January 15, the Common Council was scheduled to vote on an ordinance designed to protect Chicago from another conflagration

Built-up area
Parks and cemeteries
Area burned in fire
Boundary of 1872 "Fire Limits" building restrictions
LAKE VIEW
LAKE MICHIGAN
Belmont
Clark
Lincoln
Milwaukee
Chicago River
Elston
Fullerton
Lincoln Park
CITY LIMITS
North
Humboldt Park
Division
AREA DESTROYED BY FIRE
Chicago
CHICAGO
LaSalle
FIRE LIMITS
Central Park
Madison
Business District
Temporary City Hall
Ashland
Halsted
Crawford (Pulaski)
Kedzie
Western
State
12th (Roosevelt)
Newberry Avenue
Douglas Park
Ogden
FIRE LIMITS
N
ONE MILE
22nd (Cermak)
Lumber District
31st
Illinois & Michigan Canal
39th (Pershing)
Stock Yards
CITY LIMITS
Mason (47th)
47th
HYDE PARK
55th (Garfield)
Western
Halsted
Michigan
South Park
63rd
Maps by Chicago CartoGraphics

1. Map of Chicago (1872), showing area burned by fire.

by banning wood frame construction within the city limits. The city's immigrant wage laborers found this proposal particularly disturbing. The *Chicago Daily Tribune* (now known as the *Chicago Tribune*), the voice of the city's business-oriented Republican Party, had proposed the fire limits legislation just weeks after the fire; with the election of *Tribune* owner, Joseph Medill, as the city's mayor, the *Tribune* remained its strongest proponent. Though Medill had run on a fusion party ticket, which combined Democrats and Republicans under the banner of the Union-Fireproofer ticket, his election had hardly proved a mandate for the fire limits ordinance; by early January, Medill's supporters in the Common Council remained short of votes needed to pass the legislation.[2]

The men standing on Market (later renamed Orleans) and Illinois Streets that January night claimed the proposed ordinance threatened their rights to the "liberty and equality" assured by home ownership. They agreed, of course, on the goal of preventing another conflagration. But by requiring masonry foundations on all new buildings, the ordinance would, they believed, increase the cost of residential construction, narrowing, if not eliminating, wage laborers' ability to build or buy their houses. Hand-painted banners sprinkled among those gathered on Market Street carried phrases like "Don't vote any more for the poor man's oppressor," "No fire limits after this calamite [sic]," and "Leave a home for the laborer." One man carried a banner made of wood shavings on which was written "No shaving the poor."[3]

Yet while the protesters were concerned with home ownership, the evening's demonstration generated equally strong support for the ordinance from men who had a starkly different conception of the value of residential real estate. In the weeks following the demonstration against fire limits, smaller, less boisterous gatherings were held by the city's home builders and land speculators, business owners and professionals who fought just as vociferously for a citywide fire limits ordinance. Many of the ordinance's proponents, men who looked to residential real estate with the expectation of profitable returns on their investments, believed that setting the fire limits coextensive with the city boundaries would stabilize real estate values and so make their investments more predictable.

By placing the issue of home ownership at the heart of the debate over rebuilding the city, those who battled the fire limits ordinance exposed a key spatial element in the city's class and ethnic relations: struggles over proprietary claims to domestic spaces, and ultimately residential neighborhoods, were as central to the development of industrial cities as were conflicts over working conditions in industrial plants. In January 1872, as the nation rested on the cusp of a rapid shift from an agrarian to an urban-industrial economy, as a growing class of waged laborers sought to stake a claim on urban property and politics, the struggle over the meaning of property rights in housing was just beginning.

———

Carrying torches and shouting slogans, the North Side protesters headed south to Division Street, where they were met by hundreds more, "some with dirty, streaming wide-awake lamps, some with transparencies fearfully and wonderfully put together." Men, and a few women, from the West and South Sides joined the marchers as they headed down La Salle Street toward City Hall. "Down with the nabobs," they chanted. "The buzzards," one man told a reporter, "they want to crush us laborers. They know we can't build of brick." To the protesters that cold January night, the fight over the ordinance divided the city's "working men" from the more affluent proprietors and professionals.[4]

The march ended with a crowd of about two thousand on the steps of City Hall. Men from all districts in the city had joined the marchers and after halting for a few minutes outside, they pushed past the great wooden doors of the building and surged forward into the council chamber. Within minutes the room was so packed that reporters feared some might suffocate. Several aldermen climbed onto their chairs to get a better view. What they saw was chaos as men and a handful of women and children pushed and shoved and yelled. "Everybody in the room was talking. All of the Aldermen were out of their seats, and gathered in little knots discussing the situation and gesticu-

2. "Chicago in Ruins." *Harper's Weekly,* November 4, 1871.

lating violently. The lobby," the *Tribune* reported the next day, "was in a fearful ferment." Banner after banner was pushed into the room. "There seemed to be no leaders, and no spokesman . . . The crowd was very boisterous, some of them infuriated." While the sergeant at arms tried to calm the crowd, the protesters "claimed they wanted nothing but 'homes for their families.'" The *Tribune* commented, "If they could get the 'rights of the poor man' they all seemed ready to die content."[5]

Finally, former Alderman James Conlan, whose district included many of the North Side mechanics protesting that night, rose and urged the crowd to go home. In a speech barely heard above the clamor, Conlan announced that they had come "as law-abiding citizens and all they wanted was, simple justice." They came, he said, "from the North Side, which was the home of the artisan and the mechanic. If persons wanted fancy dwellings of brick, let them have them. But let the fire limits on the North Side be where the people wanted them." Then the crowd called for Anton Caspar Hesing, editor of the German-language *Illinois Staats-Zeitung.* Hesing rose to speak.[6]

Noise and shoving mounted, cut suddenly by the crash of breaking glass as a brick flew through the window behind the crowd. "There was a moment of fearful silence. Then came another and another crash. The first scattering shot became a storm of missiles." The crowd rushed toward the door. "The masses of human beings surged backwards like a great wave, carrying everything before it and some leaped over the desks, others crept under them: some pressed against them, sweeping them from their fastenings." The janitor began turning out the lights and despite some yells, the people left the room, passing down the front stairs, "still muttering, and still discussing and still cursing the fire ordinance." By midnight, the streets around City Hall were dark and quiet again. Only one injury from the melee was later reported; a police lieutenant hit in the face with a brick suffered a bloody cut and a lasting scar.[7]

The protesters had made their point. Though the newspapers over the following weeks urged the city's aldermen not to yield to "mob" rule, the council finally approved fire limits legislation that marked a jagged line through the city, clearly distinguishing the neighborhoods of the wealthy from those of the laboring classes, blocks of well-to-do tenants and home owners from those of manual laborers.[8]

Late nineteenth-century Chicago was not a city of home owners and America was not a nation that touted home ownership. In northern cities in the years following the Civil War, as manufacturing replaced landed property as

3. Detail of Stereoview north from the top of the Water Tower, taken in the mid-1870s, by Copelin and Son. Chicago Historical Society.

a source of wealth and housing competed with corporate stock and government bonds for capital investments of aspiring entrepreneurs and striving professionals, home ownership rates hovered around 25 percent in Cincinnati, Detroit, Pittsburgh, Philadelphia, St. Louis, and Chicago. Urban residents, of course, needed shelter. But underlying the decision of whether to rent or own, to move into a multifamily apartment building or a single-family house, was the question of where and how to allocate household resources, whether putting significant portions of household income into residential property in the form of a down payment on a home would yield economic and social benefits for the household. But as growing numbers of European immigrants flowed into northern cities, property rights in urban housing acquired distinct social and economic meanings for the diverse and increasingly conflicted urban populace.[9]

In the 1870s and 1880s, Chicago's German, Irish, and Scandinavian workers, like those in other northern industrializing cities, claimed property rights in housing as a particular and significant goal. Lacking the resources to launch their own businesses and vulnerable to the whims of an erratic job market, the European immigrants who earned hourly wages in Chicago's booming manufacturing enterprises, its stone cutting and woodworking plants, its lumber mills, its building trades, its grain elevators, stockyards, and railroads, looked to home ownership to secure their economic and political status in the new urban world. In a low-wage economy plagued by cyclical depressions, many immigrants used their property rights to establish some financial security, taking in boarders to augment household income and using their dwellings as collateral for multiple loans. They treated home ownership as a mark of their newfound status in their new homeland, a symbol of escape from rigid Old World hierarchies and of independence and freedom in the New World.[10]

If not one of the city's handful of elite families who owned both elegant homes and large manufacturing enterprises, Chicago's home owners, probably less than 20 percent of the adult male population, tended to be skilled workers typically drawn from the ranks of those who had immigrated from the states consolidated in 1871 as the German nation. Germans were the city's largest immigrant group, making up about one-third of the total population, and German-born men had the highest rates of home ownership with an estimated 27 percent owning their dwellings. Irish and Scandinavian wage workers made up another 20 to 30 percent of the population and about one-fifth of each owned some property. Black Chicagoans, just a little more than 1 percent of the city's population in 1870, owned almost no property. That would change gradually; twenty years later, several hundred black men and women owned houses. But it was the city's European immigrants who launched the fire limits protest and pursued home ownership with particular zeal.[11]

For most immigrant home owners, property rights meant the purchase of one of the frame cottages that lined the muddy streets stretching west and north from the Chicago River. On the north side, the slightly more affluent German workers established tidy communities of brick two flats and two-story frame houses. West of the river, as the city recovered from the fire, one-and sometimes two-story frame houses were more common, with brick cottages here and there. The acquisition of property by men who typically earned less than needed to sustain a household required complex maneuvering through a labyrinth of house loans. Relying on family, friends, and what little savings they could accumulate, wage-laboring immigrants made down payments on their dwellings and acquired loans from many of the same sources. A small frame house might cost between $800 and $1,000, two or nearly three times the yearly income of an unskilled worker. "The ambition of the immigrant to own property in America is one of his most striking characteristics," wrote a student of Chicago's housing conditions in 1913. "For it, he will make almost unbelievable sacrifices both of his own comfort and of that of his wife and children." Though home owning required a significant struggle for a household living on income that barely covered daily expenses, the city's immigrant wage laborers, their names scattered across the pages of nineteenth-century property records, regularly saved and sacrificed to acquire their homes.[12]

The vocal commitment of foreign-born Chicagoans to home ownership stood in sharp contrast to the general indifference of their more affluent, and usually native-born, neighbors. Lower-earning middle-class workers, the small businessmen, clerks, and some professionals who separated themselves from the laboring classes by the decor and location of their homes, were less likely to own their dwellings than were the men who engaged in the physical labor of production. Men like twenty-three-year-old George F. Yates who worked in lower-paying white-collar occupations while striving for professional status, tended to rent dwellings. Yates was a clerk and medical student living in a boardinghouse when his parents moved from Ontario to Chicago in August 1884. He immediately searched for a "proper home" for himself, two unmarried brothers, and his parents. He rented a cottage and, listing all of the new amenities in his journal, purchased a new stove, bedstead, carpets, and dining room table. For Yates, deeply concerned about his spending habits, the decor of the home, the new furnishings, the dining room, and the cottage "secured" after "shav[ing]" $2 from the $18 rent meant that his family would be housed in respectable circumstances. He never considered purchasing a house. Home ownership was more common among the affluent salaried men who managed corporate enterprises and earned significant incomes in the professions. Just over one-third of these higher-earning middle-class households lived in owner-occupied houses. To many, property in housing was just one of many investment options, no better than and sometimes considered more risky than investments in business.[13]

Some among the middle classes moved to suburban communities along the North Shore, yet a move to a house in a semirural community did not necessarily mean a home purchase. Just as often, the city's striving entrepreneurs and professionals rented apartments on the North Side and the Near South Side, creating what the *Tribune* in 1883 called "flat fever."[14] Apartment hotels, or "French flats," particularly the new courtyard buildings fitted with separate entrances for clusters of two or three apartments, were considered the "modern" and respectable dwellings for white-collar workers and their families. In "family hotels," Chicagoans could "keep up appearances" by not living in a small cottage, at times rumored to be the sign of "falling fortunes" and of a "departure from the ranks of gentility." Home ownership rates among men who earned more than their wage-laboring neighbors remained around 35 percent through much of the late nineteenth century. Property rights in housing were not a priority, not a mark of status or of political authority, nor a source of wealth, for those who could more easily afford property in housing.[15]

While apartment living conveyed a particular social status, it also preserved household capital that with a house purchase would be tied up in a down payment for the land and house, often as much as half the total cost of a single-family house. Rent for an apartment might run from $15 to $25 per month, while the purchase of a house considered suitable for a respectable well-off family was priced at over $2,000. (While some very wealthy families borrowed money to pay for very expensive houses, most middle-class families aimed to save money to pay for a house outright.) Renting an apartment, or house, meant that well-to-do Chicagoans with income above daily necessities could invest some of their earnings in business partnerships or in the expanding numbers of corporate enterprises through purchasing stocks. As property increasingly referred to more than chattel or land, but also partial ownership of a business or a corporation in the form of a stock certificate, and as men increasingly sought to make their fortunes through the establishment of manufacturing enterprises, growing numbers of striving white-collar employees faced the choice of placing surplus earnings into housing or investing in business. Whether business investments, corporate stock, or housing yielded greater profits depended, of course, on the type of company, the location of the land, and the city's economy more broadly. Still, the distribution of home ownership in Chicago suggests that among the native-born middle managers, entrepreneurs, and professionals and even young men working as clerks in offices, home ownership often was a less attractive investment.[16]

Some native-born salaried workers did move into single-family houses, often on the city's West and North Sides, living in clusters of blocks of brick row houses within walking distance of the cottages of skilled and unskilled laborers. But while Chicago's native-born entrepreneurs, lawyers, and clerks placed great emphasis on the decor, design, and location of their homes, they apparently did not differentiate between those who held title to the property and those who leased their homes. Richard Sennett's study of Union Park, a middle-class enclave on the city's West Side, found owner-occupied dwellings and rental dwellings intermingled. Deeply conscious of their social position within the city's class and ethnic hierarchy, the residents of Union Park apparently did not distinguish between home owners and tenants.[17]

The city's complex land tenure system, which until the 1870s included a bewildering array of land leases, subleases, rental dwellings, and owner-occupied dwellings, probably contributed to a blurring of distinctions between owners and renters. Some of the city's 60,000 real estate owners were land speculators, wealthy men who had invested in large tracts of land, hoping to profit from subdividing and selling off unimproved lots. Others generated income by leasing lots to tenants who built frame cottages, which the tenants owned; the tenants sometimes moved when the land lease expired. Some real estate men held title to both land and dwelling, renting houses to individual households. Finally, there were those who owned and occupied both lot and dwelling.[18]

The land lease system collapsed in the wake of the fire, partly as a result of the debates over the fire limits ordinance. The proposed fire limits ordinance would have banned both construction of new wooden buildings in the burnt-out districts and the movement of existing wooden dwellings to locations within the city. Although the numbers are not certain, possibly the majority of the city's home owners in 1870 leased the land on which their dwellings sat. If the ordinance was approved, even those whose frame cottages had escaped the fire would find their status as home owners severely undermined. The ordinance, as P. W. Gates wrote in a letter published in the *Tribune*, would "mak[e] the landlord dictator," leaving the "owner of a frame cottage with near worthless property." Although this section of the ordinance was eliminated, working-class home owners apparently recognized the danger of the land lease system and within a few years after the fire moved to purchase or claim title to both land and house.[19]

Still, the effort to ban house moving reveals a significant concern of the city's wealthiest home owners and real estate speculators. Ostensibly designed to protect the city from fire, the proposed ordinance would have had the additional function of stabilizing property values in residential neighborhoods. Those who owned or leased brick houses, the *Tribune* noted, worried that someone leasing a neighboring lot might move a "shantie" onto the site, diminishing their property values and destroying the neighborhood's respectable reputation. With the proposed ordinance, Chicago's affluent home owners and real estate entrepreneurs sought to secure their investments in residential property and to extend proprietary claims beyond the boundaries of their own property to include surrounding lots. "This movement of old frame buildings from one locality to another is not only a nuisance in itself, but it is a check upon the permanent improvement," the *Tribune* editorialized, explaining the conception of property rights in housing affirmed by the city's real estate entrepreneurs and land speculators. "No man who erects a permanent building can tell the day when there may not be backed in on each side of his building some old rotten tenement." The "break up of the business of house-movers," would ensure that residential property owners reaped the profits from their investments by maintaining the value of surrounding properties.[20] But if the *Tribune*'s editorialists believed the fire limits ordinance served the interest of the city's property owners, those who gathered at the corner of Market and Illinois Streets in mid-January 1872 certainly did not agree.

———

In the petitions circulated in the weeks leading up to the protest and in the march itself, the protesters claimed that home ownership secured their rights as Americans and helped protect the city's poorer residents from the shifting ground of the industrial economy. One petition issued by the "Northsiders" and presented to the council in the days leading up the protest argued that the fire had "swept away, not only the great warehouses and costly mansions of our wealthy, but likewise the humble cottages of thousands of poor people." If the ordinance was passed, those "honest and industrious artisans, tradesmen, mechanics, and laborers" who had "invested their hard-earned savings in their homesteads" faced the loss of the "blessing of independent homes." The petition, signed by two hundred wage laborers, including plumbers, carpenters, painters, and stonemasons, claimed the ordinance would destroy the "independence" of laboring men by "compelling the small lot-owners to relinquish all hope of ever living under their own roof again." Banning wood frame construction and "crushing the poorer lot owners," the ordinance would "make the rich richer and the poor poorer." The fire limits ordinance, they contended, would further divide the industrial classes and posed a threat to the "working man's" ability to sustain himself in a city governed by "capitalists."[21]

To men who daily confronted the inequalities in the labor market, ownership of a family home was one mark of the "fairness" of wages and of the market relations of work. This question—the fairness of wages for free men—had become a central issue of public debate and a source of labor conflict in the years after the Civil War. Emancipation had eliminated the buying and selling of human beings, setting the market, the exchange of labor for wages, as the measure of a free society. But in industrializing northern cities where many wage laborers earned barely enough, if that, to survive, where workers and their advocates used the metaphor of the "wage slave" to describe their condition, many looked to "home life," to their ability to support their families and maintain a comfortable home, to distinguish the free man from the slave. The laboring man's "blessed independence," as the Northsiders' petition put it, rested on his ability to own a cottage and, more broadly, on what the city's labor leaders began in the 1870s to call "an American standard of life."[22]

Property rights in housing were not the only marks of a free man's status, but the city's labor leaders and the men protesting at City Hall contended that home ownership, probably the largest investment of a working man's wages, was a significant piece of the constellation of the rights that represented an "American standard of life." That "means what a workingman expects to enjoy in daily life as a result of regular work at full pay. He expects a comfortable home, sufficient nourishment, decent clothes, some useful reading matter and rational enjoyment at home and in society." Labor was a commodity, labor leaders contended, whose fair price was measured, in part, by the ability of laboring men "eventually to purchase and pay for a homestead." In a city that already had experienced labor conflict and would face bloody battles between workers and their employers in the following decades, the ability of wage laborers to acquire property in housing stood as one sign of the workers' autonomy, of their status as "free men" in the postemancipation industrial economy.[23]

The desire for "independence" through home ownership helped to forge a class-based unity that had eluded labor leaders in the years before the fire. Though during the protest some carried the flags of their homeland and Irish music rang through the streets, Irish, German, Scandinavian, and some native-born workers formed a unified movement around the demand for home ownership. "Harmony of all nations," proclaimed one banner. Since the collapse of the eight-hour movement and a failed strike in 1867, Chicago's English-speaking and German-speaking workers had organized separate citywide groups. Each had a public voice in a newspaper, the *Illinois Staats-Zeitung* for the Germans and the *Workingman's Advocate* for the English-speaking labor movement. English- and German-speaking advocates of organized labor had made several attempts to form cross-ethnic unions with little success. But the devastation caused by the fire in general and the threat to home ownership in particular bridged those differences. In the debates over rebuilding the city, ethnic differences faded as wage-laboring people across the city asserted their interest in home ownership.[24]

The unity did not last. The fire and the resulting reconstruction of the city further complicated any efforts to form a unified labor movement. The thousands of workers arriving in the city in the months following the fire brought their own views of labor organizing. Although some would come together under an umbrella movement with the formation of the Knights of Labor and leaders of the Trades and Labor Assembly worked to unite the city's ethnically diverse working classes, Chicago's labor movement would remain divided well into the twentieth century.

But for one evening at least, a couple thousand immigrant laborers sought to mobilize their social power to threaten a class-based conflict in the city and to lay claim to the city government's authority for their own benefit. "Liberty and equality for all is what we want," one protester commented, adding hopefully "and then fraternity will follow." The mass demonstration brought working-class men into direct conflict with municipal and state officials over control of and access to the city's streets. Public demonstrations were nothing new to nineteenth-century cities, or to Chicago in particular. German and Irish workers had taken to the streets in 1867 to protest temperance laws and building tradesmen had protested for higher wages. But in the weeks after the fire as rumors of looting circulated, the governor had called in state militia to patrol the city's streets. The rumors proved unfounded; there was almost no looting reported after the fire. But the troops remained in the city, with a nighttime curfew in effect for more than three weeks after the fire.[25] The march to protest the fire limits ordinance was the first mass demonstration in the city's streets since the fire, a move that revived public fears of urban disorder and marked an effort by German- and Irish-born wage laborers to reclaim the urban streets. With the demonstration, the marchers, almost uniformly men, claimed control of the city's public spaces to demand the right to ownership of domestic space, to assert that property rights in housing represented their independence in the public spheres of wage work and politics.

––––––––––

While on the evening of the march, the protesters presented themselves as wage laborers and "poor men," coverage of the "riot" in City Hall by the daily newspapers over the following weeks suggests that class was hardly the sole factor influencing the workers' and their opponents' views of home ownership. That many in the crowd were foreign born quickly became a central issue in the newspaper reports on the protest. During the week following the march, the city's papers provided extensive, and often contradictory, commentary on the event. In their differing accounts of the protest, the newspapers articulated distinctive and competing views of the meanings of home ownership and of American citizenship.

On the morning following the protest, the *Tribune's* headline blazed in large letters "Communism," followed in smaller type with "The Anti-Fire Ordinance Demonstration Last Evening." The protest, the *Tribune* argued, was an attack on the nation's democratic institutions. Calling the demonstrators a mob of "rogues" and "south side toughs," the paper reported that the "spectacle exhibited within the Council Chambers" was "one of the rare tastes of Communism." Announcing that the protest proved more dangerous to civic order than had the fire the previous fall, the *Tribune's* reporter added that he was reminded of "the invasion of legislative halls by the French canaille during the bloody periods of the French Revolution."[26] Two days later, the paper's editors wrote, "There has been an infraction of law which strikes at the integrity of our system of government for it seeks to substitute the will of a mob for the deliberations of the regularly-constituted authorities of the city."[27]

The city's leading English-language dailies highlighted the immigrant character of the crowd, claiming Irish and German "vagabonds and rowdies" did not deserve the rights afforded American citizens. On Tuesday the *Tribune* reported that many in the crowd were respectable "mechanics and artisans." But by Wednesday, the editors had forgotten their earlier assertion and repeatedly called the marchers "drunken saloon bummers." Warning that the unrestrained passions of the foreign-born threatened to undermine the city's responsible and stable government, the *Tribune* noted "the fire ordinance is not the only *casus belli* which is liable to bring down an army of Germans from the North or of Irish from the West before the present trying season is over."[28] The *Chicago Times* went even further. It argued that the men who "organize[d] a mob of rioters and march[ed] under the flag of a foreign empire to assault and disperse, by force of bludgeons and brickbats, the legislative authority of Chicago" stood outside the protections given American citizens. "If they do not like our American institutions and ways," the *Times* announced, "let them return from whence they came." Expressing growing fears of class conflict, "the labor problem," and local political chaos as the city's two-party system for a short time collapsed, the newspapers' reporters and editors aimed to paper over local social struggles with nativist attacks, language readily available, widely used, and effectively applied to blur emerging class distinctions by nineteenth-century Americans.[29]

Mayor Medill similarly emphasized the immigrant character of the protesters. In a message delivered to the Common Council Tuesday morning he called the protest "a great outrage," adding that the "disorderly and violent" assemblage had stormed the council chambers, "flaunting foreign flags, torches, banners and transparencies with intimidating devices." A day after the protest Medill urged the aldermen to "vindicate your right to legislate for the people of Chicago free of mob dictation." Medill added a striking attack on Alderman Thomas Carney, who in reply noted that there were "all nationalities" at a meeting in his grocery store.[30]

The mayor's speeches and the reports of the major dailies were, in a sense, accurate: foreign-born Chicagoans led the protest and would prove the most outspoken advocates of home ownership. Yet while the newspapers portrayed the protest as mob action, reminiscent of the anarchist uprisings of 1848 in Europe, immigrant laborers saw property rights in housing as an assertion of Americanism. For if the mayor and the English-language newspapers sought to make patriotism, not the fire limits ordinance, the central issue, Chicago's German workers were willing to engage in a debate on the meaning of citizenship. Wholly unwilling to accept an attack on their patriotism, the city's most vocal German and Irish immigrants struck back, offering their own version of American citizenship. Alderman Carney had roused the crowd gathered on the night of the riot by proclaiming America a "free country" and arguing that the ban on wood frame construction was designed to "deprive men of their liberty."[31]

German immigrants, moreover, pointed to their aspiration for home ownership to present themselves as more truly American than their nativist critics. Wilhelm Rapp, in a speech to the Chicagoer Arbeiterbund, urged his audience of German-born workers to demand an ordinance that would enable them to remain home owners. The eighteenth-century Anglo-American republican version of independence tied to property ownership became, in Rapp's hands, an ideal for all immigrants arriving in American cities. Home ownership was not, in his terms, an investment for speculators and "capitalists," but rather an emblem of the immigrants' American status. He argued that immigrants came to the United States seeking a form of economic autonomy unavailable to them in Europe. For those who settled in urban industrial centers, the claim to property rights in housing was the symbol of this dream. "The Germans have prevented the big money-bags from . . . bringing the worker into the same dependent position as in the big cities of Europe," Rapp stated. "You, my friends, are the recognized and honored champions of freedom and of right generally, and of the freedom and right of the worker and middle classes in particular."[32] American freedom was, in his hands, effectively tied to the immigrants' ability to purchase a house.

Debate over the ordinance, then, did not split simply along class lines. While the protesters had asserted the rights to home ownership in the name of the city's wage laborers, their defenders shifted the grounds of the conflict, highlighting the marchers' identity as immigrant laborers pitted against a privileged and often-insular native-born elite. By the 1870s, ethnicity was a central feature of the nation's political and cultural lexicon. Waves of immigration, beginning in the 1840s with the Irish, drew sharp attention to ethnic differences. Chicago had long served as a destination for German, Irish, and other northern Europeans. In 1850, half the residents of Cook County were born outside the United States; by 1872, more than half of Chicago's residents were foreign born.[33] In a city struggling to resolve conflicts over how to rebuild, the already obvious fissures between the native born and immigrants, their distinctive languages and religions, their separate neighborhoods and shops, seemed to many an acceptable explanation for the explosive debates over the fire limits ordinance. The native born found a ready-made language and well-worn target in attacks on immigrants, a language that obscured the still nascent but growing perception of class differences and conflicts in the city. The city's German population was well aware of the dangers of anti-immigrant attacks. Hesing, in a letter to the *Tribune*, reminded readers of anti-German violent outbursts in Chicago in the 1850s and warned against similar violence in response to the fire limits protest. The overt nativist language and the simmering threats to immigrants seeking to establish themselves in the city suggested that the English-language dailies and their supporters would tolerate little division in a city that aimed to present itself to potential investors as unified and determined to rebuild.[34]

Wage laborers were not alone in opposing the fire limits ordinance. The cause was supported and led by Irish and German politicians and entrepreneurs. Anton Hesing was a prime example. Owner of the second largest planing mill in Chicago and of the German-language newspaper, he had long championed the interests of German manufacturers, particularly brewers and distillers who were threatened by temperance laws in the 1860s.[35] Seeking to unite several segments of the divided city, Hesing invested home ownership with deeply symbolic meaning. Home ownership in Hesing's vivid language became an ideal designed to bring together immigrants across class lines and laboring people across ethnic lines. Home ownership, he argued, must remain within the reach of all the city's "good, honest and industrious citizens."[36] Countering the *Tribune's* warning against European mob rule, he sought to reclaim the meaning of American citizenship in the name of the working-class home owner. In a letter sent to the *Tribune* two days after the march, Hesing challenged the patriotism of the Fireproofers: "Those are not true Americans—no matter where born—who would consign our laboring classes to the condition of European 'proletaires' by depriving them of a fair chance to live under their own roofs." He asserted that the protesters, seeking nothing more than the "independence property ownership" provided, were "more American in sentiment" than those "prone to look down upon them as foreigners." It was ownership of residential property that signaled the immigrant's new status as an American.[37]

To Hesing, the battle over fire limits was central to the larger debate over how the city would respond to the forces of industrialization. Home ownership served as a particularly potent symbol to the city's skilled German workers: it marked their separation from the propertyless industrial workers in their homeland. The protest represented a fight against what the *Staats-Zeitung* called "the proletarianization" of Chicago's workers, a process that Hesing and many Prussian-born laborers had observed firsthand. Hesing claimed property rights in housing were critical to wage laborers' autonomy and warned that without widespread opportunities for home ownership, Chicago would deteriorate into a European city of "tenements and class hierarchies." Immigrant laborers in America, Hesing argued, had earned the right to ownership of residential property. German and Irish laborers had built, and were engaged in rebuilding, the city. The workers were thus the "creators of capital"; home ownership was their reward.[38]

To Hesing and his supporters, America's industrialization was distinctive: by combining wage labor with access to residential property rights, America's industrializing economy offered the promise of an empowered working class and a society free of class conflict. Rather than calling for workers to organize to improve working conditions in industrial plants, Hesing offered Chicago's workers, and its capitalists, an argument for the benefits of home ownership. If industrialization robbed immigrant wage workers of independence in the workplace, then home ownership would restore that sense of autonomy in Chicago's streets and residential neighborhoods and assure labor harmony in the city. He concluded a letter to the *Chicago Republican* by proclaiming, "To a large extent the rapid growth of Chicago is owed to the ease with which the industrious worker here can become an independent property owner . . . For luckily in our great west the population is still equivalent in wealth and our energetic workers are not poverty-stricken proletarians, who are dependent on the mercy of capital, rather they are the creators of capital."[39] Hesing set home ownership as the standard by which American identity and wage laborers' independence should be measured.

Hesing's plea emerged from a variety of competing claims on the allegiance of the city's wage-laboring men. Though still largely unorganized, a growing number of radicals, influenced by international socialist politics, were seeking support from Chicago's trade unions. By 1870, the German trades assembly was controlled by socialists, who strongly opposed the Franco-Prussian war of 1870–71 and sided with France as the home of the international working-class movement. Although rejected by the majority of their countrymen, these labor radicals posed a threat to Hesing's authority in German communities. Possibly of greater concern to Hesing were the thousands of laborers who streamed into the city in the wake of the fire, seeking jobs in the construction trades. Arguing that these workers, who came from the east coast, western farms, and Europe, had no strong bonds to the city, the *Staats-Zeitung* warned its readers against the emergence of a "rootless proletariat" in Chicago after the fire.[40] If the right to home ownership were revoked, the paper warned, both the working classes and the city at large would suffer.

In his plea for home ownership, Hesing offered an alternative to more radical politics, positioning himself as the defender of both the interests of long-time German workers and those of the city's struggling entrepreneurial classes. Hesing's effort would prove unsuccessful. Over the next fifteen years the ethnic ties that had linked German laboring people to the middle classes would be strained, if not broken, as radical labor leaders were drawn into violent confrontation with police, and employers and employees engaged in ongoing struggles over wages and working conditions. Ethnic, political, and generational rivalries continued to confound those who sought to organize laborers around workplace issues.

But in January 1872, the movement organized around property rights in housing proved largely successful. Whether it was because of the apparent unity of the city's working classes or the widespread publication of Hesing's arguments against a comprehensive ban on frame construction is unclear, the protest was effective. The Common Council met two days after the march to consider petitions for and against the comprehensive ordinance. Heated debates continued for several weeks, and the legislation soon became a "stupendous pile" of amendments. The aldermen finally passed an ordinance that gave the protesters most of what they had demanded. The new law not only sanctioned the construction of wood frame structures in many sections of the city, particularly much of the North Side, but it also permitted, with a few exceptions, the relocation, repair, and improvement of existing frame buildings.[41]

Several evenings after the march on the Common Council, another less boisterous gathering took place in O. Raggio's restaurant on the North Side, just west of Lincoln Park. There, a group representing the city's real estate interests gave voice to a version of property rights in housing that was very different from the ideal expressed by the fire limits protesters. In the crowd, which filled the restaurant "long before the hour of the meeting," were "property owners," a builder, a lawyer, a doctor, at least one land speculator, two real estate agents, and several of the city's "prominent men." Of the men mentioned in the *Tribune's* story the next day, nearly all worked in occupations that were connected to real estate sales, home construction, or home furnishing. Though not all of the men owned their houses, most had a business interest in the neighborhood's real estate market. Anton C. Hesing also appeared at the gathering and, as the *Tribune* reported, "discoursed freely to little knots gathered around the central stove." With the exception of Hesing and a handful of his supporters, the crowd at the restaurant favored including their section of the north division, the streets bordering Lincoln Park, within the fire limits.[42]

The half-dozen blocks just north of the river and west of Lincoln Park had been subdivided in the 1840s, with construction of residences and businesses booming through much of the 1850s. It was among the first residential districts rebuilt, in brick single-family and later row houses, after the fire. The park, paved streets, sewer and water lines, and the area's proximity to the central business district just across the river had combined to make this strip of the North Side one of the city's "first-class" residential districts. To the west were frame cottages and two-story brick dwellings, home to largely German-born skilled laborers and mechanics, many of the men who had participated in the fire limits protest. But in the blocks edging the park, streets were wider, property values were higher, and men tended to work in the professions or to own established businesses.[43]

The *Tribune* portrayed the event as a homey gathering of neighbors, men who happened to be "distinguished citizens" deeply concerned about their neighborhood and the city. As one speaker noted, "the object of the meeting was to consult in a friendly way upon the best interests of the city." In a show of civility and openness, even Hesing was allowed to address the crowd, although Hesing's remarks evoked the evening's only outburst. His speech was interrupted by a "gray-bearded inebriate" who asked "all sorts of foolish questions." Hesing's statements, the paper noted, were followed by a cogent rebuke from a builder who was erecting several brick houses in the area. The only other disruptions came from the crowd outside the restaurant, opponents of extending the fire limits, whose cries "mingled with shouts and curses in broken English."[44]

Despite the widely read newspaper debates about the patriotism of the antiordinance protesters, the men inside the restaurant hardly mentioned the issues that had drawn the attention of newspaper reporters. Instead, their concern was the impact of the fire limits ordinance on property values and on business transactions in the city at large. They opposed the ordinance, or sought an ordinance that made the fire limits coextensive with the city limits, the speakers said, because partial fire limits regulations would prove an obstacle to businesses seeking capital investments from eastern banks and insurance companies, and because insurers, uncertain about the city's future, would be unwilling to insure both landed property and business enterprises. Without assurances that the city would never again fall to devastating fire, eastern capital, needed to rebuild and expand Chicago's businesses, would never flow into the midwestern city. The *Tribune* too had editorialized about the dangers of reluctant insurers in a city still vulnerable to fires. But the analysis of the men speaking to the crowd at the restaurant was sharper, more specific, and more focused on their rights as property owners to profitable investments.

To the men gathered at the restaurant, property rights in housing represented a potential return on an investment, an opportunity for profits, which would be secured and rendered less risky by the fire limits ordinance. Theirs was a conception of property rights that diverged from the views of their foreign-born and wage-laboring neighbors to the west. After calling the meeting to order, Luther A. Beebe urged the inclusion of the property along the park within the fire limits "to protect it, and maintain its value and attractiveness as the finest residence property in the city." Beebe was president of L. A. Beebe and Company, a manufacturer of furnaces and dealer in hardware and house furnishings. After Beebe's introduction, speaker after speaker addressing the crowd that night argued that the fire limits ordinance was designed to boost and stabilize property values and to make residential real estate, or more specifically their property, a profitable and predictable investment. Beebe noted that since the city's taxpayers had spent a great deal of money to build the park, the area's property owners had an obligation to protect the value of their property. Franklin Hathaway, a real estate agent, also expressed a "deep concern about the prosperity" of the area, adding that an ordinance that permitted wooden buildings within a couple blocks of the park would "not only depreciate the property but ruin it forever for first class residences." Hathaway's real estate business would fall on hard times in the mid-1870s but revive by the end of the decade. In 1872, his aim, he said, was to "bring the greatest amount of valuable property into the fire limits."[45]

The fire limits ordinance's supporters' strategy was not simply to maintain the value of their property investments; they also intended to use the ordinance to draw investment capital and affluent home buyers to their neighborhood, a move that would further enhance property values. "If this section could be protected [by the ordinance]," Beebe said, "there were people enough in Chicago to cover it with first-class residences, and make it the most beautiful and attractive spot in the city." He and others had pushed for an ordinance that would set the fire limits coextensive with the city limits; if that was not possible, and most acknowledged it was not, they at least wanted the ordinance to ban wood frame dwellings in the area edging Lincoln Park. "Let this be done and there would be more houses in the north division and the property would have a vastly higher value in money than would be the case if this region were not protected," said David Goodwille, owner of a planing mill on the edge of the neighborhood.[46]

Warning of the threat of falling property values without protection of the ordinance, Goodwille, Beebe, Hathaway, and others sought to use the fire limits to distinguish their neighborhood from others in the city. They saw property ownership as an individualist strategy to advancement in the competitive industrial economy. In their hands, the ordinance would heighten the predictability of real estate investments by zoning out poorer home owners and tenants. By regulating the cost of building in the neighborhood and consequently the size and cost of dwellings and the "class" of neighborhood residents, the ordinance would secure each property owner's rights to extract profit from their real estate investments. Clearly exaggerating the fire limits coverage of other neighborhoods, Hathaway claimed, "Nine tenths of the south and west division were in the fire limits and the result of the fire ordinance would be to drive into the north division those who could not afford to build within the fire limits and thus ruin it for residence purposes for ever."[47]

The assertion by proponents of the coextensive fire limits ordinance that municipal governments were justified in regulating land uses was not new. City governments had used their authority to ban or isolate slaughterhouses and other noxious industries during the first half of the nineteenth century. Responding to those concerns, groups of butchers had in 1869 opened the slaughter and meatpacking plants that would become celebrated sites in Chicago outside the city limits in the town of Lake, although the town was annexed to the city in 1889. But governments had applied their authority to protect the public health when banning those "nuisance" industries. The fire limits legislation, though promoted as serving a "public interest" in protecting the city from another fire, would, as the men at O. Raggio's argued, also function to stabilize property values. The "public interest," then, would be equated with the interest of those who sought future profits on their investments in landed property. A nascent form of zoning legislation, the proposed ordinance would serve the interests of land speculators and real estate men by boosting and making predicable the value of the city's landed property. It marked an early effort to use municipal authority to regulate the market in real estate.[48]

Beyond boosting residential property values on the North Side, the speakers at the meeting aimed to use the fire limits ordinance to speed the processes of industrialization. Instead of highlighting the impact of industry on wage laborers, as had Hesing, the men gathered at O. Raggio's drew attention to the significance of investment capital on the city's growing manufacturing economy. Most important to all of the speakers at the meeting was the role of insurance companies in the city's revival. Hesing claimed it was cheaper to acquire insurance for a frame house on the North Side than to insure his brick newspaper offices. But the issue was deeper than that. Insurance companies, most based in east coast cities, were among the leading investors in the Chicago's reconstruction, both through construction loans to business owners and through direct investments in the city's growing corporate enterprises. Building owners wanted to insure their property against fire, but the city's business leaders had a broader purpose; they needed the insurance companies' investment capital and loans to expand commerce in Chicago. Permitting wood frame construction would, they argued, thwart the potential of the industrializing city. The Tribune's editorialists had drawn a similar conclusion. Allowing wooden buildings, the paper stated, "adds to the cost of all goods and merchandise sold in this city. It adds to the cost of insurance. It increases the rates of interest and seriously embarrasses the negotiations of loans." The editorialists added that passage of a fire limits ordinance "would be equal, in its financial effects, to the free loan of several millions of dollars . . . and would invite hither a large amount of capital for permanent investment, which will avoid us if we continue to be a city of shanties." As Goodwille concluded, "everybody thought brick to be the best. The insurance men, money lenders, property buyers and everybody else thought brick to be best."[49]

Not everyone. Hesing and his supporters standing outside the restaurant, along with the couple thousand men who had marched on the Common Council, continued to protest legislation that might prevent them from becoming home owners. Their views of the social value of property rights in housing, an expression of immigrant wage-laborers' autonomy in an industrializing economy, soon blended with the demands of organized labor, which from the late 1870s through the turn of the century treated home ownership as one of a cluster of rights illustrating the "fairness" of wage relations in an industrializing society. In articles published in the labor press, writers offered an incisive analysis of property relations in the city. Housing and working conditions, they argued, were interconnected: the elimination of property rights in labor—the rise of a permanent class of workers who were forced to "sell their labor to the capitalist" to survive—led to the deterioration of housing conditions in American cities. In a July 1881 call for a citywide strike, the Trades and Labor Assembly conflated the "evils" of employers with those of landlords, urging workers to strike "against the growing spoilations [sic] through rents, profits, commissions, pools, speculations and peculations of the miscalled middle classes." If industrialization rendered the worker at the "mercy" of the capitalist employer, then it also left urban workers vulnerable to the profit-seeking landlord, tenants in unsanitary and inadequate rental dwellings. Freeing workers from the rule of landlords, property in housing would, in the view of labor leaders, serve as an emblem of equitable wage relations on the factory floor.[50]

Industrialization and the resulting reorganization of work in American cities, rendered vividly in the 1870 census, which for the first time categorized workers according to the fields of labor rather than by skill—placing, for example, "factory hands" and "mill operatives" within the broad category of "manufactures and mining"—was expressed in the growing struggles for property rights in housing. As growing numbers of workers found wage labor a permanent condition, many saw property rights in housing as a primary means for workers to assert their autonomy in an industrial system.[51] Labor leaders employed the language of their foreign-born constituents, making home ownership a mark of the laboring man's independence and of the "comforts" of his home life. The values of immigrant wage laborers, filtered through the growing conflict between labor and capital, linked home ownership to a new, gradually emerging version of an American citizenship.

———————

The Great Fire of October 1871 had ignited among the wooden shanties on the west side, raced north and east, spurred by high winds and fueled by the jumble of wood frame cottages that housed the city's poor and wage-laboring residents. In just a few hours, the blaze had raged through the business district and jumped the north branch of the Chicago River, forcing many North Side laborers to seek refuge in the chilly Lake Michigan water and to watch as the flames devoured a wide swath of wooden houses, along with the brick homes of many of the men who met at O. Raggio's. A heavy rain finally doused the fire, leaving between one and two hundred people dead and nearly one-third of the city's 330,000 population homeless. In the weeks following the conflagration, as newspapers across the country spread word of the tragedy, donations, loans, and letters of moral support flowed into the city. The Common Council, with the help of private charities, set up shelters for the homeless and distributed food and clothing to the poor. In mid-January, even as hundreds remained in temporary shelters and many struggled to find the resources to rebuild their houses, nearly 2,000 men headed out on a wintry night to march through the "burnt district" to demand their rights to own their homes. The protest was the largest, most vocal and most unified expression of laboring people's commitment to home ownership in late nineteenth-century Chicago.[52]

The fire limits protesters proclaimed home ownership a particular aspiration of Chicago's wage-laboring classes, a mark of their independence and American status in the industrializing city. That their demands were met by vitriolic attacks from the city's leading English-language newspapers or largely overlooked by North Side businessmen demonstrated that the meaning of property rights in housing was hardly settled. By the early 1870s, a growing number of the city's land speculators and real estate salesmen viewed residential real estate as an investment, competing with capital investments in other forms of property, like corporate stock or business partnerships. Their support for the fire limits ordinance was part of a larger strategy to make investments in residential real estate relatively predictable and profitable. Theirs and the protesters' views of property rights in housing would resonate through late nineteenth-century struggles over control of the residential real estate market, over municipal regulation of residential property, over the distribution of city-financed infrastructure, and ultimately over the gradual racial segregation of the city's neighborhoods.

But in 1872, those struggles were only beginning. With the passage of a fire limits ordinance that excluded much of the city's West and North Sides, immigrant wage laborers would continue to build and buy houses, using home ownership to mark their status as Americans and, equally importantly, to augment household income in a low-wage industrial economy. In the 1870s and 1880s, as the city's economy lumbered through a severe depression and lurched from high employment rates to low, home ownership would prove a source of needed income, a bulwark against the vicissitudes of the industrial city.

CHAPTER TWO

Staking a Claim in the Industrializing City

In August 1879, Bernard Brophy, a bread peddler and Irish immigrant, borrowed about $1,000 from a fellow countryman and purchased a one-story frame house and the neighboring vacant lot on Newberry Avenue on Chicago's West Side. Twenty-nine years old, Brophy had lived in Chicago for at least a decade. His wife Margaret, the daughter of Irish immigrants, was born in Illinois and married at age fifteen. By 1879, the Brophys had four children under nine years of age, and Margaret would give birth to another daughter the following year. Bernard Brophy likely earned less than $400 per year, at least $150 less than the estimated $550 needed to sustain a household. Yet four years later, with five children under thirteen at home and having just paid off his debt of somewhere between $800 and $1,000 dollars on the family's four-room cottage at 23 Newberry, Bernard Brophy obtained another loan and bought the neighboring building, which he rented to a German family for a year and a half, then sold it. Brophy was not alone among his working-class Irish and German neighbors in playing his hand in Chicago's notoriously fickle real estate market. Nearly half the houses on his block were owner-occupied, a rate of home ownership well above the city average. Indeed, during a period of stagnant wages and in the wake of a sustained economic depression in the 1870s, Chicago's working classes regularly bought and sold residential properties. For immigrant wage laborers, even those who like Brophy lived on the edge of financial disaster, home ownership carried both symbolic and economic value.[1]

The pursuit of property in housing by immigrants struggling to sustain households in the rapidly industrializing economy defined Chicago's late nineteenth-century housing market, and established a score of smaller markets linking creditors and debtors (often the same people), bankers, grocers, builders, tradesmen, and households relying on the wages of workers employed by the city's industrialists. Like wage laborers in half a dozen other industrializing cities, Chicago's wage workers, including the low-wage unskilled, readily took on significant debt, sometimes forgoing household necessities or alternative investments, taking in boarders and putting children to work for wages to buy houses in an unpredictable labor market.[2] Wage-laboring immigrants effectively used property as collateral for loans and strategically used debt, often several loans on a single piece of property, to generate additional household income. In the early twentieth century, rising housing costs relative to wages would limit the ability of low-wage laborers like Brophy to acquire residential property and would, through the development of a segmented housing market, further stratify the working classes. Yet from the 1870s through the late 1890s, the aspiration for property rights in housing and residential lots linked the ideals and economic security of individual home owners to those of their neighbors while simultaneously fueling the industrializing processes in the larger city.

Labor leaders' published writings, petitions to the Common Council, and newspaper coverage of the fire limits protest, while articulating ideological imperatives behind the immigrants' pursuit of home ownership, reveal little of the economic incentives driving low-wage laborers to buy residential property. Their economic motives appear most clearly in property transactions themselves. In Cook County's handwritten tract books, which follow property transactions from the earliest subdivisions to the present, one page per lot, the ubiquitous late nineteenth-century practices of buying, selling, borrowing, and loaning, the circulation of capital among a handful of households within residential districts, can be traced with some precision. The Brophys and their neighbors recorded their conception of the financial value and social purpose of property rights in housing as they presented Cook County's recorder of deeds with property deeds, certificates of sales, trust deeds, warranty deeds, and a host of other legal mechanisms for conveying property and using property as collateral for loans. Despite the sterile legal template, the lists of grantor and grantees, dates and abbreviations for the legal instruments exercised, the documents are as articulate as a formal essay in revealing the Brophys' and their neighbors' skillful and strategic uses of residential property. Buying and selling houses and lots, as well as loaning money to friends and relatives seeking to purchase homes, Chicago's laborers used residential property to stake a claim in their new homeland and to strengthen their economic position in relation to employers and a generally inadequate wage labor market.[3]

The Brophys' and their neighbors' pursuit of property in housing was not unusual. It was, indeed, typical of Chicago's laboring people. The "Northsiders" who had gathered to protest the fire limits ordinance in 1872 acquired and used their homes much as the West Siders did. On a block of North Southport, for example, brick and frame two-story houses stood next to five vacant lots in 1880. Of the thirteen houses on the block, seven were owner-occupied with one owner, Fritz Rinehardt, a tannery worker, owning his house and the neighboring vacant lot. Home owners—six Prussians and the Swedish upholsterer Benjamin Ottenblad and his Norwegian wife, Matilda—included a shoemaker, a carpenter, a grocer, and a cooper. All of the men were married; wives kept house and looked after young children. (Of the block's six rental buildings, two were owned by men living within walking distance of the properties.) Tenants, some boarding in owner-occupied houses, included a teamster, two gardeners, an upholsterer, a carpenter, and two laborers. Most of the home owners had purchased their property just after the fire, borrowing money from friends and family, and most took out several loans on their properties in the decade or two they lived on the block. Capital circulated through the North Side community in the form of rents and loans for home purchases, just as it moved through similar credit networks in working-class neighborhoods throughout the city.[4]

Alone among the city's poor and wage-laboring families, African-Americans rarely owned their homes. In the 1880s, black Chicagoans, just over 1 percent of the city's population, rented dwellings on clusters of blocks on the West and South Sides. The district that would be known two decades later as the "Black Belt" housed some 2,500 people, mostly renters, and was in the 1880s just fifteen blocks long and three blocks wide. Immigrants from Ireland and Poland, a few Italians and African-Americans rented dwelling spaces in the frame cottages and two-story frame houses on surrounding blocks. In the corridor running from Harrison Street to just beyond 16th Street and moving further south as the end of the century approached, buildings were, in some cases, owned by nearby residents, but more often by property investors living in more affluent communities who held a smattering of lots and buildings throughout the neighborhood. The district's land and building owners, often just a transaction or two away from the original mid-century subdividers, used their property to generate regular income by renting dwelling spaces to recent migrants from the American south, single men and families who arrived in the city without the savings to invest in property ownership and, perhaps, without the networks of family and friends to help them purchase a house on arrival in the city. Many of those tenants, having saved or borrowed some cash, would over the following years seek to purchase a cottage further west, outside the increasingly run-down South Side district.[5]

Wage-laboring black Chicagoans, like their European-born neighbors, did pursue home ownership, often with less success, but also stressing the economic autonomy property rights might provide. Racial segregation, though an acknowledged custom, was informal and irregularly enforced in late nineteenth-century Chicago. Some black families rented cottages on the West Side, and a handful of black home owners purchased residential property on the West and Near North Sides of the city. By 1890, close to 250 out of the city's more than 14,000 black people owned their homes. Striving new arrivals from the American south, men like Wiley Cherry and his wife Margaret pursued business opportunities and home ownership, often outside of the Black Belt. The Cherrys, with their daughters Mattie and Lovie, arrived in Chicago in 1893; after renting for a short time, they purchased a house on Western Avenue surrounded by immigrant families, largely from Italy. Wiley Cherry opened a grocery store and later a masonry and plastering business, maintaining ownership of his home through the 1890s and earning enough to donate money for the construction of a new building for the Original Providence Baptist Church on Lake Street in the early twentieth century. Though Cherry's achievements were noteworthy, his ambitions for property ownership were typical of laboring and low-income black men across the city.[6]

Over the two decades following the fire, residential neighborhoods, often identified with immigrants from particular regions in Europe, were more clearly marked by the job types and income levels of residents, whether they engaged in physical labor for hourly wages or were white-collar workers who earned salaries in the offices of manufacturing plants. Working-class neighborhoods housed "representatives of the various nationalities" and even a mix of black and white families. The pursuit of home ownership by the families along North Southport and by men like Wally Cherry and Bernard Brophy suggests that while language, religion, culture, and race were obvious social divisions within Chicago, the aspiration for property rights in housing and the economic sacrifices to achieve it could be found in laboring households across the city. The experiences of the families living on Brophy's West Side block would have been familiar to those living on North Southport and to those in the frame cottages and brick two-flats lining the muddy streets west of the Chicago River.[7]

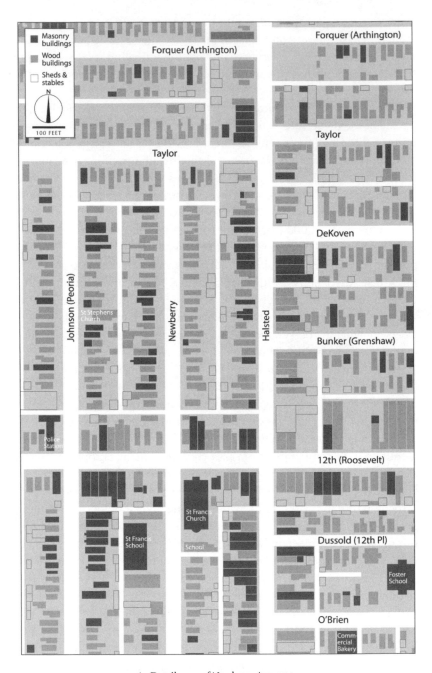

4. Detail map of Newberry Ave. area.

Untouched by the flames of the Great Fire, the Brophy's block had felt the fire's impact as scores of laboring families left homeless by the conflagration had moved into the West Side. Pushed out of the downtown by an expanding high-rent commercial district, which displaced those living in the old slums along the western edge of the business center, hundreds of working-class families had sought refuge on the increasingly crowded West Side. In 1876, the district was among the city's most densely populated, and the number of residents would continue to grow in the following years. By 1884, the Citizen's Association would list the Near West Side neighborhood among the city's most "squalid" and impoverished.[8]

A dusty unpaved street lined with wood plank sidewalks, Newberry Avenue was less than half a mile west of the planing mills and stonecutting plants in the industrial belt that stretched the length of the south branch of the Chicago River. A block west of Halsted Street, the West Side's major north-south thoroughfare, the Brophys' block ran north from Twelfth Street. It was less than two miles from Chicago's center, located amidst a web of dirt streets in which people dodged mounds of garbage, horse-drawn carts, and, sometimes, dead animals as they hurried to the industrial plants along the riverfront and the shops on Twelfth and Halsted Streets. Lined with "saloons, restaurants, clothing stores, all kinds of shops and cheap lodging-houses," Halsted Street was "the backbone of the congested district." Peddlers, scavengers, and children moved through the dirt roads that ran west from the river to the city limits.[9] Rail lines blanketed the eastern edges of the neighborhood, sending dust and noise throughout the district and creating a hazardous crossing for those who ventured into the city's center. The river, the rail tracks, and the roaring industries combined to mark a distinct boundary between the working-class, largely immigrant West Side and the clean lines of the rising skyscrapers in the city's fast-paced business district. The expansive views and cool breezes of the lakefront that the city's affluent enjoyed from their lakeside mansions were at least an hour away by trolley or, by the turn of the century, elevated train.[10]

In the twenty years after Brophy purchased his home, the neighborhood experienced many changes. In 1880, German- and Irish-inflected English were the languages of the West Side streets. By 1900, Italians, Poles, Russians, and Bohemians would move into the district's crowded apartments. Church steeples rose from elaborately adorned buildings, which often were so large they looked out of place amidst columns of narrow, low-rise residential buildings. As the Eastern Europeans moved in, Orthodox Jewish congregations sometimes replaced Catholics, and a Star of David took the place of the crucifix above the altar in an old house of worship.[11]

"The whole district was a region of flimsy wooden dwellings and dilapidated sheds, of poorly paved and unpaved streets, and filthy alleys," wrote one student of Chicago's housing conditions. The city's single-family cottages, the frame one-, one-and-a-half-, and two-story houses built within and beyond the fire limits from midcentury through the 1890s, came in a variety of floor plans, which were published in late-century builders' catalogues, real estate journals, and magazines. At its simplest, a cottage might include just a kitchen-living area and a bedroom, while more elaborate designs featured kitchen, parlor, living room, and two seven-by-eight-foot bedrooms on the first floor, or two bedrooms on the low-slung second floor. Most faced the street, with a few steps up, and sometimes a narrow wooden porch leading to the front door. Windows on the front of the cottage shed light into the front room, usually a living room or, in larger cottages, a parlor.[12]

Scattered throughout the West Side were some of the older mansions, once home to the city's elite, but by the 1880s subdivided into rooming houses or buildings with three- and four-room apartments. Several two-story brick buildings also appeared alongside the frame cottages, typically signs of the failed plans of prefire land speculators or builders. If they lived in one of these older subdivided brick dwellings, residents climbed the front stoop, entering a dark hallway with a wooden staircase leading to the second floor. In 1880, each floor typically contained one four-room apartment. Inside, the front room was well-lit from windows facing the street. Behind the front room, the apartment grew darker and dingier until the kitchen, usually overlooking a tiny, trash-strewn lot in the rear. Families moved into three- and four-room apartments, sharing precious space with recently arrived relatives and often renting beds to boarders.[13]

Reports from urban reform organizations and a handful of photographs from the 1890s suggest that most cottages, like apartments in larger buildings, were furnished with dark wooden tables, chairs, and beds and decorated with often faded patterned wallpaper. Photographs suggest that the mass of furnishings, some likely brought from the old world, left only narrow spaces for movement through the house's rooms. By the 1890s, reformers complained that the city's older frame cottages often were moved from the front to rear lots to make room for the construction of two- and three-story "tenement" buildings, allowing lot owners—sometimes immigrant wage workers who owned the lots, sometimes speculators living outside the community—to use residential property as income-producing commodity and to expand the owners' income by renting dwelling spaces to ever larger

5. Housing. Rows of frame dwellings.

numbers of people.[14] Maximization of profits from renting subdivided dwellings and massing cottages, shanties, and tenements on lots meant that interior and exterior spaces in wage-laboring districts were, by the 1890s, filled with furnishings, buildings, and people. As the city's population grew, as wages increased, along with rents and housing prices, as the two- and three-flats were subdivided into ever smaller and darker apartments, and as dwellings covered increasingly larger portions of lots, the Near West Side became a densely packed hive.

Some of the frame cottages that appeared in the years after the fire were constructed by the owners, with assistance from friends and neighbors, but more often local tradesmen—carpenters and bricklayers—were hired to build the neighborhood's houses. Carpenters, in particular, had been an active force in the city's housing markets since before the Civil War. They had organized several trades associations and were determined to control the city's house building businesses. Skilled carpenters who had lived in the city for more than a decade sometimes established small businesses, becoming a mix of entrepreneur and tradesmen, contracting out labor and building one to three houses each year. By the 1870s, carpenter-contractors largely controlled Chicago's house construction business; self-built housing, though still visible in the shanties and shacks along rear alleys, was in decline. With self-building viewed as an option of last resort, access to capital for construction costs, the ability of a potential home owner to pay for the construction or purchase of an existing house, was of primary importance to those aspiring to home ownership.[15]

Though Chicago's cottages might have appeared trim and comfortable, many of the houses owned by the city's wage laborers lacked indoor plumbing, a feature that proved central in determining the health of residents and the household labor required to maintain the home. In 1880, sewer lines had not yet reached much of the West Side, leaving residents to build wooden shacks over privies behind their homes. Each household within a two- or three-story building shared the privy with all other building residents. By the 1890s, when the population of the West Side hit several hundred thousand, as many as fifteen adults and children might share a single backyard privy. Although the Department of Public Works was busy digging sewers in the district throughout the 1880s, many dwellings remained unconnected through the turn of the century, and even those that were connected often lacked indoor plumbing facilities. With household waste often leaching into the area's water supplies, epidemic diseases periodically raged through the wage-laboring district. In 1902, when the blocks surrounding the Brophys' former home were hardest hit by a typhoid epidemic, Hull House investigators blamed "the wretched sanitary appliances through which alone the infection could have become so widely spread." The absence of indoor plumbing facilities, the lack of sewers and adequate water, though not visible in photographs, generated a serious public health threat and highlighted the dangers of even the "most comfortable little house."[16]

In the summer of 1880, when the census takers went door to door, filling out government forms in often barely legible handwriting, the Brophys' block on Newberry Avenue, like that of most surrounding blocks, housed a mix of nationalities. The Brophys' neighbors were Irish and German immigrants and native-born laborers, with the exception of the house painter, George Osterhaus and his wife, Christina, who were Dutch and rented a tiny frame cottage next door. Just north of the Brophys' house was a crowded frame three-flat, home to the Flanagan, Hopkins, and Cahill families. Owned by Christopher Flanagan, the building housed thirteen adults and children. Flanagan and his wife, Julia, had arrived in Chicago from Ireland more than twenty years earlier. Their eldest, Bernard, worked as a marble cutter in one of the stonecutting plants along the river. Their three daughters—twenty-year-old Mary, eighteen-year-old Nellie, and sixteen-year-old Julia—were seamstresses.

The Flanagans' tenants, the Hopkins and Cahill families, were younger. William Hopkins, a printer, and his wife, Mary, were in their midtwenties. Both born in Vermont, they had moved to Chicago in the years after the fire and were raising an infant son. Christina and James Cahill also were in their twenties. Christina was born in Illinois to Prussian immigrants; James, a railroad switchman, was from New York, where both of his parents had been born. They had an infant son and had taken in a boarder, John Kirch, a printer, who, like Christina Cahill, was born in Illinois to Prussian parents. Further down the block on either side were other Irish, German, and native-born families. While the wives raised children, kept house, and looked after boarders, husbands, sons, and daughters worked in a variety of skilled and unskilled occupations. There were teamsters, printers, shoemakers, black-smiths, plumbers, and peddlers.

Most colorful, perhaps, was the home of Cornelius Ryan, a large brick building at 9 Newberry Avenue. Born in Ireland and a Chicago resident of at least a decade, Ryan would spend most of the next twenty years moving in and out of occupations, all somehow related to liquor sales. Between 1875 and 1895, he owned and sold two saloons, and for a short time was a partner in a soda water business. By 1900, when he was fifty years old, Ryan fell on hard times, selling his saloon and taking a job as a bottler of mineral water, possibly working in the bottled water plant that opened in the 1890s just across the street. Throughout he managed to own his house, invest in some neighborhood real estate and keep his two children in school.

Nearly half of the twenty-four buildings on the Brophys' block were owner-occupied. In 1880, all the resident-owners were Irish, but by 1887, Emil Petri, a forty-four-year-old German immigrant and clerk in a dry goods store, bought the house at 27 Newberry from Michael Giffney, who had owned and occupied the house since 1880. Throughout the 1890s, Eastern Europeans, primarily Jews, from Russia, Poland, and Romania and a few Bohemian families, moved onto the block. In 1900, while the names and faces of the block's residents had changed, nearly half of the buildings remained owner-occupied.

On the Brophys' block, home owners tended to be slightly older than tenants. The home owners, such as the Flanagans, Brophys, Giffneys, and Petris, were in their thirties and forties when they purchased their homes. Some of the owning households, like the Flanagans, included unmarried children in their teens and twenties who were employed outside the home and likely contributed some of their income to the household. But the younger generation's income was not, apparently, necessary for the purchase of a home. The Brophys' eldest child, Rachel, was nine and still attending school when her parents bought the house at 23 Newberry.

No working-class household had the cash to pay for a house outright. Even the down payment for a house, which generally ran between 25 and 50 percent of the selling price, was likely a heavy burden to a working-class buyer. Down payments for cottages in working-class neighborhoods might be as much as a third or a half of a laborer's yearly income. There are no records of how working-class home owners came up with the down payments; most probably saved for several years or borrowed the cash from family or friends.

While workers' wages alone could never have generated enough capital to support the high level of home ownership common in working-class neighborhoods, their strategic use of debt to generate cash ensured that capital flowed into and among the neighborhood's households. All the property owners on Newberry Avenue, like laboring home owners across the city, took short-term loans, using the purchased property as collateral, to cover the cost of their houses. The loans came from a variety of individuals and businesses. One source of credit was neighbors and friends who used their savings or their own homes as collateral for second mortgages and loaned money to first-time buyers, creating an informal and internal credit market within many working-class neighborhoods and moving capital into and through the neighborhood's households. Credit networks further cemented personal bonds among neighbors and, more commonly, within ethnic groups as people tended to provide credit to other immigrants from their homeland. Cornelius Ryan made several loans to other Irish immigrants, possibly after renegotiating the loans on his own home or his saloon to generate additional money. Joseph Moritz was a grocer who lived behind his store on South Halsted Street in the 1880s and 1890s. He loaned money to several Eastern European families who bought homes in the surrounding neighborhood. Neighborhood credit markets, plagued by uncertain wage and employment levels but based on a seemingly solid faith in rising land values, helped to finance significant levels of home ownership among the working classes.[17]

Banks and increasingly insurance companies also provided some real estate loans, but even as working-class home ownership rates expanded rapidly in the two decades following the fire, few working-class home buyers sought loans from those large institutions.[18] In the 1870s and 1880s, Chicago's banking system grew substantially in numbers of banks and complexity of operations. By the mid-1880s, banks were becoming increasingly specialized with real estate loans handled only by state and private institutions and national banks providing commercial credit. As the their holdings grew, the banks took on an "air of metropolitan formality," which may have discouraged the city's laboring people from seeking the banks' services. Most banks were open from 10 a.m. to 3 p.m., making it difficult for a working person to apply for a bank loan. Bank buildings became opulent displays of the institutions' influence in the market. When the Union Trust Company moved to the corner of Dearborn and Madison Streets, it installed plate glass windows on the ground floor and lay stone sidewalks outside. "One of the banks, when leasing new offices, amazed the landlord by insisting that the basement below the banking floor should not be used as a saloon." Whatever their intent, the directors of the city's banks were creating distinctive environments for their businesses, buildings that would awe and perhaps intimidate working-class immigrants.[19]

If discouraged by banks and unable to find credit from friends and family, prospective buyers appealed to the city's growing population of lawyers and real estate entrepreneurs. Buyers paid off interest as high as 7 to 9 percent in monthly installments and portions of the loan at two-, four-, or six-year intervals.[20] These individual creditors tended to live in middle-class communities on the North Side or in the more elite North Shore suburbs. They had offices in the city's commercial center, and each held trust deeds to a dozen or more properties in a six- or eight-block area on the West or South Side. Some may have had personal connections with the neighborhoods in which they loaned money. The Irish lawyer, Thomas Keane, provided several home loans to Irish-born home owners on and around Newberry Avenue in the 1880s. Some bankers may have seen the real estate market as an opportunity to launch their own businesses. Charles F. Schumacher was a manager at the City Savings Bank in 1874 when he and his son, Charles Jr., opened a real estate and insurance company on the South Side. The Schumachers provided home loans for Irish, German, and Eastern European buyers throughout the 1880s. By the 1890s, as Eastern European Jews bought buildings in the neighborhood, creditors increasingly were of Eastern European origin. In this way, the rising entrepreneurs from the city's varied immigrant communities provided the loans that enabled their working-class countrymen to become home owners. Equally important, working-class home buyers, by taking on debt and paying interest on their loans, contributed to the wealth and status of their striving middle-class creditors.

A more formal system of home financing emerged in the 1880s with the rapid expansion of building and loan associations. Sometimes called savings and loans or cooperative building associations, the enterprises were community-based organizations through which members could save and borrow money. Although the city's first building and loan, the Chicago Building and loan Association, opened in 1849, there were just a handful of savings and loans, and only two launched by immigrants, in the city in the mid-1870s. Among the earliest was the Chicago Bohemian Building and Loan Association, No. 1, formed in 1874 with $250,000 in capital stock. Others soon followed and by 1883 the *Tribune* published an article about the savings and loans, remarking that there were "a score of building societies" in Chicago.[21]

Building and loan associations provided immigrant workers with a fairly reliable method to finance home ownership. Usually organized by workers from a single ethnic group, the associations functioned to formalize the older networks of neighborhood credit and, as Lizabeth Cohen notes, "reinforce[d] community solidarity." Workers joined with people from the same towns in Europe or the same neighborhoods in Chicago to create a pool of capital to provide loans to home buyers. Members purchased stock in the association by paying dues as low as twenty-five cents or as much as a couple dollars per week. When they had reached a certain level of savings, members could borrow from the association to purchase a home and repay their debt with small monthly installments. As Cohen notes, the associations' expenses were low: space in churches, community halls, or taverns was rented for monthly meetings. By 1889, there were an estimated 250 building and loan associations in Chicago. From about the mid-1880s until the 1920s, the building and loan associations were the leading source of credit for the city's working-class home buyers.[22]

Another source of credit appeared in the mid-1880s when builders began to provide financing for the houses they sold. Although just a few builders introduced this "easy payment plan" for low-cost housing, those who provided home loans were wildly popular among the working classes. Possibly the first builder to offer home loans was Samuel Eberly Gross, who introduced payment plans for his housing developments in the 1880s. Gross built and sold thousands of houses priced from $1,000 to $2,000 in the final decades of the century.[23]

Even as they took out substantial loans to buy their homes, the residents of Newberry Avenue could not count on steady employment or decent wages to help them pay their home loans. In the five years before he bought his house, Bernard Brophy had lost at least one job as a baker, an occupation that, at best, fit at the lower rung of those considered skilled jobs. He had taken up the even less stable and probably lower-paying occupation of peddling bread when he bought the house. Three of the other home owners on the block were teamsters, a job that might pay well, as much as $800 per year. But teamsters were commonly laid off during slack business months, usually receiving steady wages only seven to ten months a year.[24]

Brophy purchased his home (borrowing about $1,000 to pay for it) during a period of profound economic uncertainty, both personal and for the city at large. Chicago's major industries and commercial enterprises staggered through the 1870s, hobbled by a series of bank failures, an overbuilt and sluggish real estate market and drops in demand from eastern consumers. The economic depression began on the east coast and hit Chicago in the summer of 1873, when real estate sales began to slow and builders began laying off workers. In the fall, the stock market crashed, several New York banks suspended business, and scores of Chicago's banking and commercial businesses closed their doors. From 1873 through 1874, the number of workers employed in Chicago's manufacturing plants dropped from 60,000 to 52,000. Wages for unskilled labor fell from $2 to $1 or less a day. In 1873, and again during the panic of 1877, the Chicago newspapers reported that even skilled craftsmen were willing to work for board alone in order to eat. During the long depression of the 1870s, average earnings of unskilled labor fell from $25 per week in 1873 to $9 per week in 1879.[25]

Workers responded with strikes and mass demonstrations, often ending in violence. Without legal protection for labor organizing, striking workers faced unyielding opposition from their employers and from the local and federal government, which sent in troops to end work stoppages and arrest strike leaders. The most famous and violent was the railroad strike of 1877. It began on the east coast and hit Chicago on July 23, prompting massive street protests and leading to the deaths of at least thirteen people and scores of injuries at the hands of the city's police force and the Illinois state militia.[26] To many workers, the message was clear: they could not rely on local government to provide relief in times of hardship, nor to back them up in critical struggles with employers.

While 1877 marked the height of the decade's labor violence, it also was the year the real estate market hit bottom and then began, slowly, to rise again. Transactions increased over the next two years, as did rents and sales prices. By 1879, the city's industries also began to revive, hiring new workers and reopening dark plants. But even as industry recovered from the depression years, Chicago's workers faced an ongoing struggle to make ends meet. The long unemployed, coupled with the newly arrived who had continued to flood the city despite the lack of jobs, were willing to work for ever-lower wages. Between 1879 and 1881 food prices leaped an estimated 50 to 100 percent, while wages generally remained stationary and overall living costs increased another 15 to 40 percent the next year. Average wages began to rise again in the mid-1880s. But even in good times, the Illinois Bureau of Labor Statistics concluded, half of the "more intelligent, industrious and prosperous" were unable to stay solvent through their own efforts, and had "to depend upon the labor of women and children to eke out their miserable existence."[27]

These were the economic prospects in August 1879, when Bernard Brophy took a loan from a fellow Irishman and sunk the cash into a house on Newberry Avenue: stagnant wages, increasing competition for jobs, soaring inflation, slowly rising property prices, and leaping immigration. Despite the uncertainty of the city's economy, several of Brophy's neighbors also took on substantial debt to enter the residential real estate market. Cornelius Ryan, while holding on to his own home, bought and sold other residential properties and made loans to friends buying houses on nearby streets. Thomas Eccles, a carpenter who was unemployed in 1880, apparently also bought and sold a few houses on the West Side in the early 1880s. Three of the Newberry Avenue home owners lived in their homes for nearly twenty years, but others, like the Eccleses, the Giffneys, and the Fitzgeralds at the end of the block, sold their homes within ten years of purchasing them.[28]

Why, then, did Brophy, Ryan, and others living on Newberry Avenue, as well as on North Southport and throughout the city, take on the burden of substantial debt to buy residential property during a period of stagnant wages and financial insecurity? Home ownership and investments in residential real estate likely resulted from a variety of factors, including the immigrants' desire to establish themselves in a new city and a faith in the security of property ownership. For Brophy, his neighbors, and many others, however, ownership of residential property appears to have served a specific economic function. Even if they did not reap large profits from their investments, and it seems clear that neither Brophy nor Ryan became a wealthy man, they used the properties to raise capital for other expenses.

As the city's economy recovered from the panics of the 1870s, real estate values increased in the 1880s. With each increase in the assessed value of real estate, owners were able to obtain a second and sometimes a third loan on a single property. The loans, representing the incremental increase in the assessed value of the property and the portion of the loan already paid off, put cash in the hands of the property owners. Some owners used a second loan to pay off previous loans in full, while gaining cash income equal to the increased property value on the transaction. Others, however, maintained debts to two or three individuals or institutions for the same property. In other words, two or three creditors might hold trust deeds, and so hold some interest, in a single piece of residential property. The title holder then maintained substantial debt, but acquired cash in hand, with both the cash and the debt generated by a series of property transactions.[29]

These transactions could become fairly complicated as individual owners shifted debts among several properties. Brophy, for example, bought his home at 23 Newberry in 1879 with a loan from Walter McHowland. He paid off his debt to McHowland in December 1882. Less than six months later, on May 9, 1883, he purchased the building at 21 Newberry with a loan on that property. On the same day, Brophy took another loan on the 23 Newberry property. He may have used some of the 23 Newberry loan to cover the down payment on the 21 Newberry property. He then held title to two properties with the combined debts probably looming near $2,000. Three days later, on May 12, he paid off part of the debt on 23 Newberry, but did not pay that debt in full until January 1886. In the meantime, he had taken out two other loans on 23 Newberry. And in September 1883, five months after taking a loan to purchase 21 Newberry, he took out a second loan on the same property, possibly using a portion of that money to pay off the first debt two months later. In May 1884, Brophy obtained a third loan on 21 Newberry, which he paid off only on the sale of the property in September of that year. Not until November 1887, however, did Brophy finish paying off his loans on that property. During the year and a half he held title to 21 Newberry, Brophy obtained three loans on the property at approximately six-month intervals, holding debt on the property for more than four years. By 1887, when he paid off the last of his debts, his oldest daughter had left school to work as a typist. Rachel Brophy probably did not earn enough to pay off her father's loans, but when she went to work outside the home, the Brophy household income increased perhaps enough to ease a shortage of available cash to sustain the household.[30]

For the Brophys, the constant juggling of debt occurred during the few years between the birth of their fifth child and the entrance of their oldest into the wage-labor market, a period during which the household's income was likely most tautly stretched. Brophy might have considered the second property, 21 Newberry Avenue, an investment, but he held title to it for less than two years. Instead of holding the property for future returns, he used it to generate debt and cash in hand. The acquiring of debt to purchase residential property was risky since there was no guarantee that Brophy could hold on to his job and earn enough to repay his creditors. But the risk possibly was outweighed by Brophy's ability to obtain a series of loans on the two properties, with each loan representing an incremental increase in property values and each transaction putting needed cash in the hands of a family struggling to cover daily household expenses.

Investments in the real estate market along with the consequent loans on the properties functioned to subsidize working-class families living on inadequate wages. While Brophy's income as a bread peddler, probably no more than $400 per year, might not have covered the expenses of a growing household, his property transactions generated additional income during a critical period of his family's growth. As wages remained below levels needed for a household head to support his family, workers could turn to the residential real estate market to buttress inadequate wages and expand the availability of cash both for their households and their neighborhoods. By using transactions in residential property to generate additional income, working-class families helped to subsidize and sustain a low-wage economy, leaving massive profits in the hands of business owners and bankers, while forcing working-class tenants to work ever longer hours and struggle that much harder to get by.

The purchase of housing by low-wage laborers enabled workers and their communities to gain some economic autonomy while simultaneously fulfilling the needs of industrial capitalism. Since labor was a leading cost of doing business in the industrial city, business owners aimed to keep wages as low as possible, often below levels needed by workers to sustain households. Low wages enabled capitalists to distribute ever-growing profits to investors, further fueling investor interest in stock purchases and enhancing the value of nonlanded forms of property, like stocks and bonds. Growing business profits combined with growing investments from stock purchasers enabled business owners to reinvest some profits in new manufacturing plants and new technologies of production. The pursuit of home ownership, with its income-generating potential, by laboring households coincided with the capitalist interest in maintaining low wages and further spurred the industrializing processes within the city's larger economy.[31]

Yet in supplementing wages and in generating income outside of the employer-employee relationship, property rights in housing blurred and sometimes confused contemporary struggles over the meaning and value of the wage in a free labor society. While labor leaders and their supporters among urban reformers argued that the "fair" value of a workers wages could be demonstrated by the workers' ability to maintain a "comfortable home," the use of property rights in housing to supplement inadequate wages undermined organized labor's use of the home as a symbol, and real example, of the inadequacy of the industrial wage system. Chicago's civic reform organizations regularly pointed to the "tidy cottage" and "regular payments" made by even the lowest wage workers to show that workers could, if they were "thrift-minded," sustain themselves on their incomes. Charity organizations too treated home ownership as a sign that struggling families, particularly those saddled with an ill or injured adult, "deserved what little help" the group could offer. Home ownership did provide some economic security to wage-laboring households, but living conditions in owner-occupied homes, particularly those that lacked indoor plumbing, often were no better than in low-cost rented rooms. Even as civic reformers and philanthropists touted it as a sign of workers' well-being, home ownership did not generate income enough to erase the burdens of low wages and dangerous working conditions, or to provide workers with middle-class levels of income.[32]

The strategy of generating income through property transactions was risky. For workers plagued by illness and unemployment, there was little certainty that debts on property could be repaid. The risk, of course, was that missed loan payments would result in creditors claiming title to the property and the borrower losing both the property and all his previous payments. Workers regularly took this risk, sometimes with disastrous results. In 1884, the Chicago Relief and Aid Society reported several cases of families seeking assistance to make loan payments on residential property. In one case, the wife of a Swedish painter who had been in and out of work appealed to the society for assistance, "concerned that [the family] will lose what has already been paid" on a house. The effort to purchase a home, even with the seemingly reckless gamble on an unstable household income to repay the debt, seemed to garner sympathy from local charities. Despite noting that the husband was "partially deranged and has been in the asylum," the society's interviewer reported that "the family is industrious and economical[, as is] proved by the fact that payments have been made for the purchase of the little cottage occupied as a residence."[33] The family received the assistance needed to hold off creditors and retain their home, at least in the short run.

For those, like Brophy, who had witnessed the depression and its consequent drop in real estate transactions, the risk of taking on a debt to purchase residential property might not have appeared such a gamble. To a careful observer, the lessons of the depression and its impact on small-time residential property owners were not clear cut. The weeks following the stock market crash of 1873 were characterized by a series of bank panics as depositors crowded to savings banks seeking to withdraw their savings. Several of the city's banks closed their doors, and depositors lost their savings. Although few working-class people put their money in the city's large commercial and state banks, they could see that banks were not secure places to leave their money. As Homer Hoyt, the most rigorous analyst of Chicago's land values noted, "the failure of practically all the savings banks in Chicago by 1877 had caused the laborers to avoid them as places for deposit their savings."[34]

While bank failures seemed to frighten those with small savings away, a close observer of the real estate market, particularly during the later depression years, might conclude that residential property was a fairly secure place to deposit savings. The depression ultimately hit speculators and creditors harder than owners of single residential lots or houses. The real estate market had gone from boom to bust in less than five years, bankrupting many land speculators and leaving creditors cautious of large land investments. Although demand had, in Hoyt's words, "sent values kiting upwards," in the spring after the fire, by the summer of 1873 the rush to replace the city's commercial center with more and bigger properties spread over a larger area had left scores of business locations unfilled, and construction slowed.[35] Prospective home buyers, particularly the skilled workers who builders and speculators had expected would pick up the new homes and newly developed suburban lots, lacked both the savings and the faith in the security of land purchases for home buying. Speculative lot purchasers found it difficult to dispose of their investments just as they were required to make second payments on loans for those purchases. Even those who could come up with the cash to make the loan payments were unwilling or unable to risk further property investments. Decreasing purchases sent land prices tumbling and as prices fell, the desire to invest dropped. "Nothing so quickly stops an upturn as the belief that a commodity can be bought next month or next year at the same price," Hoyt comments.[36] The *Real Estate and Building Journal* noted in June 1876, "Never has there been so little land for sale in this city and county as now."[37] A year later, land prices hit bottom, pushed downward by the failure of the largest savings banks in the city, the Columbian and the Bee Hive, and by labor violence, which frightened investors and left the wealthy hoarding their capital.

The lack of potential purchasers, particularly for individual houses in neighborhoods filled with often transient workers, helped to rescue some working-class home owners from the loss of their investment. Smaller, residential property owners were hard hit by joblessness and a shortage of capital for new loans. Those who could not meet loan payments found that the market for second loans had dried up. Though neighbors and friends might be willing to permit a jobless family to remain in their home and postpone loan payments, institutional creditors sought to get something back on their loans and foreclosed on the properties. Many debtors, however, were able to hold on to their homes simply because no one else would bid on the property when the holder of the mortgage put it up for sale. The resident "bid on the property at his own price, sometimes as low as one-fourth of the amount of the mortgage, and secured a deficiency judgment for the balance."[38] The use of property debt to generate cash functioned only when the assessed value of residential property was increasing. But those who bet on rising property values in the late 1870s might have realized that even when the market sours, small-time residential property owners might salvage their investment.

Wage laborers might also have noted that small business owners were more likely to face financial ruin than were skilled laborers who owned residential property. As consumer spending slowed, business loans to purchase retail commodities were among the earliest to disappear. Small business owners were caught between consumers seeking to buy on credit and unable to pay their debts, bankers unwilling to provide needed loans, and landlords jettisoning tenants who could not make rent payments. The shortage of cash meant that shopkeepers with businesses in rented stores—most small business people in the city—faced the desperate choice of simply selling off their stock at bargain prices and taking the loss or being thrown in the street by impatient creditors. By the winter of 1875, the *Tribune* was warning small business people against "land-sharks" who offered to trade mortgaged lots for the remaining stock in a retail business. Desperate retailers, the *Tribune* cautioned, might be tempted to accept the offer. If the trade were made, the paper suggested that the retailer would find he held worthless titles and the swindler would sell off the stock in the store, disappearing without paying rent on the shop. The *Tribune* claimed that such "villanies" [sic] create "greater havoc, caused more actual suffering and, do more damage to the morals of the community than any other."[39] Residential property owners might find themselves in similarly sticky situations except that the state banking laws required that mortgage holders wait at least one year before foreclosing on residential property. While a small business owner might lose his business within months of insolvency, a home owner could hold out for a year. The lesson for skilled workers was that putting money into home ownership might prove a more secure long-term investment than an investment in a small business.[40]

If ownership of residential property proved a short-term strategy to generate additional income for some, it also was a long-term investment, a hedge against future uncertainties, and, at best, a strategy for leaving something of value to the next generation. The Brophys lived at 23 Newberry Avenue until 1898, when they sold the house and moved further west to Sawyer Street. Both the Ryans and Flanagans owned their homes for twenty years or more. By 1900, Bernard Flanagan, the oldest of Christopher and

Julia's children, was married and raising his own six children in the building he inherited from his father. His parents, by then in their seventies, still lived in the building. And another couple, recent Irish immigrants, rented an apartment in the building. Over the years, the building generated income both in the form of rent payments and new loans, income that ultimately helped to sustain two generations of Flanagans.

Daniel and Eliza Horan were not so fortunate. Irish immigrants in their forties, the Horans were tenants at 17 Newberry, raising five children in a four-room frame cottage in 1884, when they decided to purchase the house. By then, the two eldest Horan children, James and Ellen, had left school. James, like his father, worked as a teamster; Ellen was a seamstress. But within a year after the Horans took out a loan and bought the building, Daniel died. Eliza stayed in the building until 1895, keeping house for her children and living on the income from occasional boarders and her children's wages. When her son James moved, Eliza apparently could not sustain herself, or did not need a house, and so sold the building, paying off her husband's debt only at the time of the sale.

Cornelius Ryan's commitment to home ownership was so deep that despite setbacks in his career as a liquor salesman and saloon keeper, he maintained his home. Ryan did, however, take out several loans on his property, perhaps using the money to subsidize his business enterprises. Whether he used the cash to stave off business creditors is unclear, but it is clear he was willing to forgo his businesses before selling his home. Home ownership did not enrich immigrant wage laborers like the Brophys, Ryans, and Horans, but it did provide some, if not all, with a financial cushion to soften the weight of inadequate wages, job losses, and an erratic economy.

The pursuit of home ownership and the desire to improve housing conditions within propertied districts linked individuals to their neighbors, sometimes creating common interests across differences of nationality, language, and religion. Out of these communities of creditors and debtors, of local capital markets, grew neighborhood groups determined to protect their property rights and values as they faced growing labor conflict in factories, packinghouses, and railyards, and as they confronted the gradual emergence of a citywide real estate market. In the decades after the turn of the century, however, as growing numbers of African-Americans moved from the rural south, seeking industrial jobs and dwellings in Chicago, property rights claims that bound neighbors together and linked property values to economic stability of the community would prove a decisive force in the increasingly rigid racial segregation of the city's residential districts.

While European immigrants and sometimes their children acquired residential property and fought to maintain access to home ownership throughout the city in the 1870s and 1880s, African-Americans, less than 2 percent of the city's population in 1890, found their opportunities for home ownership already constricted. Fewer people and thus fewer property owners meant that less capital circulated within African-American communities, meaning there was less capital available for new arrivals seeking to purchase property with loans from family and friends. A greater obstacle, however, was the higher rents charged to African-American tenants. Most black Chicagoans paid a higher portion of their earnings in rent than their white neighbors, leaving little surplus beyond daily expenses to add to savings toward a home purchase. Informal segregation combined with lower wages to prevent many black Chicagoans from using the strategies of European immigrants in achieving their goal of home ownership.[41]

Property rights, increasingly linking the interests of European immigrants, became a mark of status distinguishing white from black Chicagoans. An emblem of their autonomy in the workplace and of their "American" identity, home ownership helped European-born laborers to survive in the low-wage economy while leaving American-born black workers struggling ever more to pay rent and sustain families on low wages. In the 1880s, when the Brophys lived on Newberry Avenue, home owners and tenants, a handful of black Chicagoans and much larger numbers of European descent, shared blocks and sometimes dwellings along the grid of dusty streets lined with brick and frame houses on the West Side. Two decades later, the social geography of the city would be divided by a tense, if ever-shifting color line.[42]

———

Home ownership was just one of several strategies used by working-class families to augment household income. Wives and children could enter the wage labor market. By their early teens, the children of working-class families often left school to work for wages in the city's industrial plants, but employers often were unwilling to hire married women. In the stockyards, packinghouse owners employed few married women, preferring single women and teenage boys for those low-wage occupations. Married women did supplement the household earnings by taking in washing and hiring space in the home out to boarders; as the 1880s wore on, married women increasingly earned meager wages through piecework in the home.[43]

But child labor, women's wage labor, and taking in boarders proved highly controversial. Labor leaders seeking a "family" wage for working-class men viewed the entry of children and women into wage labor as undermining their cause. Middle-class reformers similarly opposed wage labor by children and married women on the grounds that both subverted the family structure and posed serious health threats to both the workers and the city at large. At the turn of the century urban reformers were discouraging wage-laboring households from taking in boarders, arguing that unrelated male boarders threatened the morality, privacy, and well-being of the household. By 1900, the reformers' campaigns, which were designed to improve the economic and "moral" standing of working-class families, began to function to close off long-standing practices used by working-class households to subsidize the inadequate wages of household heads.

As Chicago's growing pool of business managers, entrepreneurs, and other white-collar workers began to purchase single-family homes in ever greater numbers in the 1890s, the size and price of housing began to rise. Increased costs for labor and materials, most significantly the costs of supplying indoor plumbing and central heating mechanisms, pushed up the prices of single-family houses. Even as wages, salaries, and the prices of consumer goods rose in the final decades of the nineteenth century, prices for houses increased even more rapidly. By 1900, on North Southport, owner-occupied houses had fallen to three of nineteen. Most of the residents of 1880 had moved, though many of the new tenants were German immigrants or the children of German immigrants. Several Polish families had moved onto the block; one owned his home. In 1910, thirty-one years after Bernard Brophy purchased his house, the vast majority of households on the Brophy's block were tenants. Immigrants—typically Jewish, from Russia and Bohemia, along with a few Italians—husbands, wives, and children in their teens and younger lived in the frame and brick cottages that formerly housed the home-owning Brophys and their neighbors. The occupations of the heads of the households—a factory worker, two cigar makers, a broom maker, six laborers, a couple of peddlers, a junk dealer, several dry goods clerks and a musician—put them toward the lower rungs of the immigrant working classes. Some of the teenage sons and daughters worked for wages outside the home, and some families took in boarders to augment their household income. Two Italian laborers owned their homes, but the census taker in 1910 found that the rest of the families rented their dwellings. Skilled workers continued to pursue home ownership, but by the early twentieth century, the low-skilled and impoverished found it increasingly difficult to buy homes and to use home ownership as a means to stake a claim in the industrial city.[44] Unable to purchase a single-family house, an expanding number of unskilled and impoverished Chicagoans were forced to rent space in multifamily dwellings called tenements.

In the decades following the Great Fire, the apparent paradox of low-wage workers investing significant amounts of money in residential property—property that, on the surface at least, seemed to have no productive capacities—established a score of smaller real estate markets in immigrant neighborhoods around the city. For many European immigrants to Chicago, the pursuit of home ownership was part of a larger communal effort to acquire economic security in a seemingly unpredictable and often chaotic industrializing city. Joining together to circulate capital for housing loans, they created markets in residential real estate in communities where wages alone would have proved insufficient to sustain such high levels of home ownership. Taking in boarders, engaging in waged labor within the home, and, most importantly, using their property as collateral for loans, the city's immigrant laboring classes used property rights in housing to generate additional household income. Even with low wages, they achieved levels of home ownership that rivaled, or surpassed, those of men earning significantly greater incomes. The laboring classes' conception of residential property as serving the interests of the entire community forged strong ties among neighbors, contributed to the formation of a residential real estate markets in low-wage districts, and helped fuel the industrializing processes in the late nineteenth-century city.

Though Chicago included few, if any, tenements at the time of the fire, by the mid-1870s a small but growing number of poor families were moving into subdivided single- and two-family houses. The emergence of this new dwelling type prompted heated responses from both wage-laboring and well-to-do Chicagoans, who associated tenements with disease, immigration, and poverty, forces that many believed threatened civic order. Tenement housing proved an issue on which skilled laborers and business leaders could reach some agreement. In the late 1870s, a growing number of journalists and business and labor leaders called on the municipal government to regulate tenement housing, a move that enhanced the authority of the city's new Board of Health, the first municipal agency charged with regulating housing conditions in the industrializing city. The resulting municipal regulations of multifamily, low-cost dwellings were the first housing laws to separate the rights of home owners from tenants, the opening wedge that would further stratify the working classes and enhance the social power of those who, through stable jobs and adequate income, maintained their access to property rights in housing.

CHAPTER THREE

Health, Morality, and Housing

Within a few years after the Great Fire leveled nearly a third of Chicago's residential buildings, another scourge appeared, posing a perhaps more insidious threat to the well-being of the city. Even as wage laborers sought to purchase lots and one and two-family dwellings, the city's newspapers, business and labor leaders, and a number of municipal officials insisted that Chicago faced a serious housing problem. The rows of two- and three-story frame dwellings that a few years earlier had been seen as a sign of the city's resurgence after the devastating fire were by the mid-1870s viewed as a harbinger of its potential downfall. Tenements—low-rent multifamily dwellings—it was argued, threatened the health of the city's populace, the stability of its businesses, and the morals of its laboring classes. In September 1874, the *Chicago Daily Tribune* issued a stern warning to its readers: "It has been a common boast among citizens of Chicago that the peculiar human residence known as a 'tenement-house' did not flourish in their midst." Those "sanguine and egotistical" citizens, the article added, would be astonished to learn that "we are cursed with a tenement system, which although not so general, is infinitely more offensive than that of New York."[1] The tenement "threat," described and condemned in increasingly lurid newspaper accounts, mobilized a group of reformers who, while debating the causes of the problem, agreed on at least one point: tenements and their residents required municipal regulation. The city's first housing ordinances, passed in 1880, effectively codified a distinction between the rights of tenants and those of home owners. Municipal regulations and public rhetoric designated tenants as vulnerable, dependent, and a danger to public health, while home owners, largely exempt from regulation, retained distinctive rights to the uses of and control over their property. Under new city laws, home owners preserved their claims to autonomy.

The *Tribune's* report was among the first of what would become a stream of stories detailing new dangers associated with urban living. In the labor and business press, and in reports issued by municipal officials and leaders of civic reform organizations, the tenement loomed as an emblem of a wide array of social problems in the industrializing city. Defined as any dwelling housing three or more households living independently, the tenement quickly became associated with the city's unskilled laborers, immigrants, and impoverished families. Lacking indoor plumbing and often housing several families in a few tiny rooms, tenements did endanger the health of residents. Diphtheria, typhoid, cholera, smallpox, and yellow fever regularly appeared in working-class neighborhoods.[2] Many of the city's journalists, however, framed the "tenement threat" in language that resonated beyond the immediate menace of contagious disease, warning against a host of social dangers associated with the industrializing city and drawing readers' attention to the potential benefits of single-family home ownership.

More than a decade before lawmakers approved legislation designed to regulate factory conditions or set maximum working hours, city and state officials moved to regulate the uses, forms, and functions of urban residential property.[3] Asserting a public health interest in regulating tenement dwellings, municipal officials distinguished housing from other commodities, like clothing or labor power itself, and established a government presence in housing markets.[4] The fire limits legislation, the first effort by Chicago authorities to regulate urban housing, had generated significant controversy and divided the city along class and ethnic lines. But beginning in the mid-1870s and lasting through the turn of the century, despite increasingly hostile conflicts between labor and capital, there was widespread agreement that the public had an interest in regulating the housing of some Chicago residents. This shift in views of the relationship between the law, markets, and housing had long-term consequences on property relations in the city.

In an 1874 article, a *Tribune* reporter described himself as an "explorer," taking readers on a tour of three buildings, the "like of which can not be imagined outside the realms of the damned." The image of the urban explorer, a literary trope repeated in articles published in late nineteenth-century urban newspapers in British and American cities, established the reporters' authority as an objective observer, a student of dark, dangerous, and apparently foreign sections of the city. Functioning as guides to exotic landscapes, "urban explorers" offered readers a mix of the spectacular and the grotesque as they toured impoverished districts, typically drawing a map of the city that distinguished the respectable from alien communities.[5] But in Chicago, where multifamily and single-family dwellings were intermingled, the *Tribune*'s reporter roamed through neighborhoods and streets well-known to his readers; his aim was to highlight specific buildings and expose the "alien" spaces inside. Tenements, he stated, stand "in our midst," housing dark and threatening environments largely invisible to Chicago residents. Commenting that the facade of one tenement "present[ed] no very bad appearance to the careless observer," the reporter added, "Within however all this is changed." Tenement dwellings, the reporter implied, threatened the health and morality of Chicago citizens of all classes precisely because tenements stood, largely unrecognized, on well-traveled streets. "These places are not confined to one section of the city," the reporter asserted, "but are scattered through its whole system, even as leprosy is dispersed through the human frame." Hidden pockets of contagion, emblems of terrifying, deadly, and inexplicable disease, the tenements could at any moment launch an invisible attack on the city as a whole.[6]

Certainly epidemic disease did spread quickly through mud-soaked basement dwellings and two- and three-story buildings housing as many as twenty adults and children, including attic apartments with few windows. Journalists' depictions did draw attention to the dangerous and debilitating conditions of much of the city's housing. "I found in a basement, the kitchen so dark as I entered that I could see no one to own the voice that saluted me," wrote an advocate of tenement reform. "An alley ran by the side of the small window, but an immense wall shut out all the light." The resident of the two-room basement dwelling, a sixty-three-year-old widow "was full of genuine aches and pains, in head, limbs and lungs. . . . I stepped into the dark, dingy bedroom, and wondered to myself how it was possible for anyone in sickness ever to get well when confined in such a place." Tenement dwellings might cause and exacerbate sickness, writers agreed. The issue then was in diagnosing the source of the "tenement problem."[7]

The *Tribune*'s reports focused on tenement residents' national origins and their "inherited" behavior. Reporters linked dwelling types to various "races" of humanity, translating the social difficulties associated with poverty into "biological flaws" and highlighting the "better sort," the residents of single-family dwellings. By blurring the effects of poverty on housing conditions with the national origins of the tenements' residents, the article presented readers with an elaborate chart of racial hierarchies and a corresponding geography of property relations in the city. Wandering into a row of "dilapidated wooden houses" the reporter found, "Italians—men, women, and children—of the lowest order. Their chief vocation is rag-picking, and the entire charnel-house smells of tainted raiment, steeped in swill beer and stale alcohol." Invoking the deepest fears of nineteenth-century racists, the reporter implied that the tenement's residents transgressed a "natural law" by mixing races. The "Italians," he commented, were the "lowest types of human society—almost black—a cross between Polish Jews and the very worst class of plantation darkies. It is impossible to suppose that these beings have in their veins the blood of the conquerors of the ancient world." Asserting that tenement residents posed a "chronic threat" to the health and riches of the city's propertied classes, the reporter offered a "biological" explanation for deteriorated dwellings and their residents' apparent "degradation," transferring the social inequalities of property relations to the immutable realm of biology.[8]

A depiction of tenement living conditions as determined by the residents' race highlighted the contrast between the tenant and the "healthy house-holder," while at the same time justifying government regulation of the seemingly inevitable actions of tenement dwellers, of those who lacked the "character and independence" to purchase their homes and were "unfit" to maintain sanitary dwellings. The distinction between tenant and home owner obscured the role played by the city's landlords in controlling the quality of housing for lease. Landlords of low-cost rental dwellings typically refused to invest capital in sanitary improvements, like well-fortified privy vaults, sewer services, or indoor plumbing, which would have gone a long way toward preventing the spread of contagious diseases. Once a lease was signed, the law held tenants responsible for maintaining their dwellings, protecting the property owner from accountability for the public health threat of tenement living conditions and further enhancing the profits a landlord could extract from his investment in multifamily dwellings.[9]

Certainly, concern with sanitation was part of a genuine effort to improve the health of the city's residents. But images of disease and contagion buttressed by the emerging field of biology also served "the institutionalization of fear." An analysis that linked disease to race or national origin of tenants permitted propertied Chicagoans to avoid investing capital in improving tenement dwellings and provided them with (pseudo)scientific justifications for regulating the immigrant poor.[10] The *Tribune* reporter launched his article by claiming that the tenement "has been the nucleus of contagion and the recruiting-sergeant of death." Even in tenements where the Board of Health had "done all that lay in its power to render the den less offensive," municipal regulations were not stringent enough to compel tenants to improve their behavior. He concluded that the public interest in preserving the city's health demanded conceiving of tenants' rights in housing as unlike

6. Interior of a tenement home. Chicago Historical Society.

those of home owners and, of equal importance, unlike other commodities, an arena open to government regulation.[11]

The city's labor leaders welcomed the *Tribune*'s call for municipal regulation of tenement housing. But advocates for organized labor framed the problem of tenement housing, and a rationale for municipal regulation, in terms very different from those of the *Tribune*'s reporter. The *Progressive Age*, the city's leading English-language labor paper and the official newspaper of the Trades and Labor Assembly, campaigned for legislation to require health department inspections of tenement housing. When the law was passed in 1880, labor leaders claimed responsibility for the legislation. Priced at $1.50 for a year's subscription, the paper was widely read among English-speaking laborers. Though probably not read by recent immigrants, and at times critical of immigrants who, the paper argued, were willing to work for low wages and undercut the wages of native-born laborers, the *Progressive Age* represented the views of the sometimes competing leaders of the Trades and Labor Assembly.

By the late 1870s, housing conditions, and particularly tenements, were attracting increasing attention from the paper. In the hands of *Progressive Age* writers, disease was a real and frightening danger to urban workers, but the "tenement problem" also provided another point of contention between labor and capital. Unlike the *Tribune* and *Chicago Times* reporters, the *Progressive Age* writers equated landlords with employers, arguing that just as capitalists sought to wring the most profit from workers, landlords aimed to draw large profits from the shelter needs of vulnerable working-class households. As industrial labor relations limited the power of wage laborers, so too had the industrial housing market left working-class tenants "at the mercy" of landlords." Tenants, the paper commented, "are in their [the landlords'] power, and they exercise it without stint or mercy."[12]

Framing the tenement problem in terms of class conflict, labor leaders cast tenement residents as a dependent class and urged the passage of legislation to protect them. "The health and comfort of this vast population, entirely at the mercy, as they are, of employer and landlord, so far as sanitary matters are concerned, fix and control the death rate, and cry aloud for protection," a reporter noted.[13] *Progressive Age* writers argued that the "capitalist class" sought to exploit low-income tenants by raising rents and providing few, if any, "sanitary improvements" in the buildings. "[T]here are thousands of families in this city renting houses who do not know where or how to seek relief from the imposition of landlords, who build pest houses by contract to the lowest bidder," wrote a Socialist Party leader in a letter to *The Plumber and Sanitary Engineer*, a locally published monthly journal. Distinguishing between the amenities available in single-family and multifamily rental dwellings, the *Progressive Age* noted that landlords garnered greater profits from poorly maintained tenements than from "first class residence property," which were single-family houses. "[T]hat latter," the paper continued, "being rented out in entire buildings to one family, of course puts them beyond the reach of poor people, whose limited means compel them to occupy apartments where the monthly charge is small, regardless of the inadequate accommodation and the unwholesome surroundings."[14]

The paper was not portraying all wage laborers as dependent. Indeed, it regularly published advertisements for building and loan associations, which urged working-class men to join the association and purchase a single-family house. These advertisements, along with articles detailing the benefits of home ownership, functioned to contrast tenement rentals to single-family home ownership. The paper's readers might not be able to afford to purchase residential property, but they would likely be informed that tenement residents, unlike home owners, were vulnerable and dependent.

Though at least some tenements were owned by skilled workers who had no connections to the city's native-born elite, the newspaper critiqued the concept of landed property as an investment, asserting that "[p]rominent capitalists buy up every desirable piece of property in the market with the sole object of forcing the price still higher by raising the rents to create this fictitious valuation."[15] When treated as an investment, as supporters of the city's fire limits legislation had demanded, residential property was thus invested with "false" value, a move that undermined the ability of laboring men to purchase their homes. The paper clearly simplified what was a complex housing market, including multifamily dwellings owned by wage laborers who often could not afford to maintain their properties, provide sewer and water hookups, and accumulate some profits with the rents they charged. Though many of the skilled workers who supported the labor movement were home owners and some owned multifamily dwellings, the paper assumed an undifferentiated working class, one that sought home ownership as a means to assert autonomy and generate additional household income. The *Progressive Age* writers overlooked the differing resources of skilled and unskilled wage laborers and their varied uses of property rights in housing.[16]

Tenement housing was dangerous precisely because it threatened the health of tenement residents. Landlords' strategies for generating profits combined with inadequate municipal funding for "sanitary purposes," the paper argued, was "responsible for the terrible scourge of small pox as well as the exceptional mortality from other forms of disease." The paper's writers rejected the *Tribune*'s concern about contagion to the city's propertied classes by noting that wealthier families living in single-family houses already were protected from the spread of disease. "Wards where every available foot of ground is occupied by tenements into which the people are crowded and packed to the point of suffocation have less sanitary provision, less than one-third the extent of sewerage per acre, and less attention from scavengers (day or night) than other wards where single families occupy large houses set in the middle of lots." Unequal distribution of municipal services, limited as they were, left tenement dwellers at greater risk for disease.[17]

Seeking protection for vulnerable tenants, labor leaders urged the passage of laws requiring the board of health to inspect tenement housing. The legislation, they argued, would mediate between the housing market and the shelter needs of the city's impoverished classes. "Landlords are not philanthropists," the paper proclaimed, "and it is useless to expect them to fulfill the letter of the law unless the law is supported by a stronger power than moral sentiment." Since landlords, like employers, would maneuver to gain the greatest profits from their property, the city needed laws governing the construction and maintenance of residential properties. "The Health Commissioner shall cause to be visited at least once a month every place of employment and habitation," a group of labor leaders affirmed in January 1881, just weeks before the Common Council addressed the issue. Labor leaders sought to place at least some of the financial burdens of maintaining rental dwellings on the property owners, calling for inspectors to ensure that landlords abided by the law. To secure the health of tenement residents and to protect them from the "greed" of landlords, they called on the council to deploy the police power of the municipal government to monitor the households of the urban poor.[18]

Though identifying different sources of the tenement problem, these distinct strands of argument were drawn together by the urban sanitation movement, which in the 1870s was seeking a stronger position in the city's government bureaucracy. A mix of physicians, lay reformers, builders, engineers, and public officials, the sanitarians, as the health reformers were called, led efforts to improve urban living conditions in the 1870s and 1880s.[19] Though industrial waste was polluting Chicago's water and airways, tenement housing would serve health reformers as a wedge issue, providing the new field of public health with a stamp of legal authority. Drawing on the language and concerns of the city's business and labor leaders, Chicago's health officials maneuvered between scientific, social and moral explanations for the tenement problem to establish the legitimacy of their field and legal authority for their interventions in the homes of the urban poor.

————————

The history of Chicago's Department of Health and its expanding focus on tenement housing offers a particularly vivid illustration of the ways ideas about property rights in housing were transformed in the late nineteenth century. In the 1880s, Chicago's health department commissioner Oscar Coleman De Wolf was among the most vocal of the sanitarians to articulate a public interest in regulating the interior space of the working-class home. He sought to regulate both industry and housing, but rising opposition from the city's employers gave his efforts to monitor multifamily rental dwellings success that largely eluded his campaigns for supervision of industrial production. Though the state's 1881 tenement and factory ordinance, designed to replace the city's 1880 law and promoted and implemented by De Wolf, gave the Health Department the authority to review plans for new construction, it left legal responsibility for maintaining existing dwellings with the tenants, permitting landlords to evade responsibility for their properties.[20] The health department's inspections of tenement housing established a legal and bureaucratic distinction between the property rights of home owners and business owners and those of tenants.

The growth of Chicago's health department also provides a striking example of the tangled development of municipal governance in the post–Civil War years. The Board of Health, and later the Department of Health, often acted ahead of the city and state legislative bodies, issuing regulations and sending sanitary inspectors into the homes of Chicagoans before the elected officials voted on those policies. By 1876, when the Illinois Supreme Court ruled that the Board of Health as an appointed body had no authority to regulate business, the board had already issued and enforced a string of regulations concerning business and housing. When butchers and packinghouse owners balked at the health department's attempts to ban the sale of adulterated foods, the department reinforced its authority by stressing its inspections of tenement housing. Health department officials effectively used tenement housing as an area through which they could expand the department's authority and gain legitimacy for the new field of public health.[21]

Chicago organized a board of health in 1862, when in the midst of a particularly widespread smallpox outbreak the Illinois general assembly enacted legislation providing that the mayor and six other persons be ap-

7. Oscar De Wolf. Chicago Historical Society.

pointed by the judges of the superior court to constitute a board of health. Three members were to be physicians. Following the lead of the legislature, the Common Council passed an ordinance calling for the hiring of a city physician, who would be appointed by the mayor. The initial resolution provided that the physician be paid $1,000 per year, but when the ordinance was passed, the council did not finance the position. Lacking a salary and a staff, the position was never filled. The 1862 ordinance detailed the responsibilities of the health board, providing health officials a decade later with a document on which to rest their claims to legal authority. The physician was to supervise "the sanitary condition of the city and to report to the mayor all nuisances, the prevalence of any epidemic, contagious or infectious diseases, which in his opinion, may require the action of the police authorities." Under the ordinance, the physician's duties were broad and vague.[22]

With the establishment of the city's first permanent Board of Health on March 9, 1867, the Common Council asserted a public interest in the health of the citizenry. A physician was hired, with a salary, to serve as the city's sanitary superintendent and oversee the work of a wide variety of city employees. In the tradition of antebellum health reformers, the physician, John Henry

Rauch, launched a vigorous public campaign to cleanse the city's streets, establishing a scavenger service to remove garbage from the streets and hiring
sanitary inspectors to patrol the streets and alleys and report those who suffered from contagious disease. In the days and weeks following the fire of
1871, Rauch organized health services and worked to provide clean water,
food, and housing for the 112,000 people left homeless. A former lieutenant
colonel and surgeon in the union army, Rauch helped found the American
Public Health Association, becoming the organization's president in 1876.
He was appointed to chair the Illinois State Board of Health in 1877.[23]

In the years immediately following the Civil War, there was little consen-
sus over the role and function of the Board of Health. Health officials promoted the extension of the city's sewer and water lines and urged more extensive sanitary inspections of residential neighborhoods and industrial
sites, but these and other efforts prompted opposition. The city comptroller,
arguing that Rauch had exceeded his legal authority in hiring sanitary inspectors, refused to pay the sanitary inspectors, raising the prospect of a
struggle over which city agencies were authorized to hire and pay municipal
workers or to distribute patronage jobs. When the board sued the city, the
case was decided in its favor, but only after several years of battles among city
officials over expenditures for health-related activities.[24]

By 1874, the board, under the leadership of Dr. Brockholst L. McVicker,
again sought to expand its authority by highlighting the dangers emanating
from tenement dwellings and warning the Common Council that regulation
of tenement housing "deserves the most serious consideration." Like the
health reformers in New York City two decades earlier, the board called for
"stringent regulations" to oversee the "cleanliness and ventilation" of tenement buildings. Defining health as a public interest unrestrained by property
lines, McVicker argued the health "not only of the inmates of such buildings,
but the entire population" was at stake. "A combination of growing "manu-
factories and the high price of real estate" in the city would, McVicker's report to the council stated, over the next few years "throw large communities
together in buildings, where rooms can be obtained at a cheap rate." Tenements' inmates, McVicker contended, required immediate regulation.[25]

When a smallpox epidemic appeared in several of the city's poorer neighborhoods just a few months after the *Tribune* story was published, the board
again took steps to strengthen its position. It authorized its sanitary inspectors to remove those suffering from smallpox to the city hospital, involuntarily if necessary. McVicker's program, which was recommended by Rauch,
was designed to gain support from the city's business interests. Rather than
enact a "shot-gun" quarantine of large sections of the city, he sought to iso-

late sick individuals "thus effecting an immense saving to commerce" (and not quarantining those who did not need to be quarantined).[26] The board's policy generated some opposition. The commissioner, in his report to the council in 1876 strained to articulate the larger public interest in supporting his program. "In some cases," he wrote, "it may seem hard to isolate and remove a parent or child, but for public safety it should be done and no exceptions made."[27]

In July 1876 the mayor, under pressure from McVicker's opponents, disbanded the board and replaced it with a Department of Health. Instead of a six-member board that supervised the city physician, the new department would be run by a single commissioner, a physician appointed by the mayor. That fall, Mayor Monroe Heath called Oscar Coleman De Wolf to a meeting in his office. There, he apparently announced, "My board of health of six members is a set of thieves. I have secured the authority to abolish the board, and to appoint in their place a single commissioner. Will you be the man?" De Wolf accepted.[28]

———

Oscar Coleman De Wolf had arrived in Chicago in 1874 and set up a small and struggling medical practice. Medicine, public service, and a reformer's zeal were in his blood and in his training. He was born in 1835 and raised in Chester Center in the Berkshire hills of Massachusetts, where his father, Thaddeus K. De Wolf, practiced medicine for sixty-two years and participated in a local temperance movement. Thaddeus De Wolf's temperance activities apparently angered some of his neighbors. During Oscar's childhood, Thaddeus De Wolf received several threats on his life and the family's house was reportedly set on fire. "My father was a man with a host of strong friends and a host of strong enemies," Oscar later commented to a reporter. Oscar De Wolf studied with his father, then attended a two-year course at the Berkshire Medical College in Pittsfield before heading to New York in 1858 for further study. Two years later, he went to France, where he studied medicine for nearly five years. When the Civil War began, he returned to the United States and was appointed assistant surgeon of the First Massachusetts Cavalry in 1861. A year later he became the surgeon for the Second Massachusetts Cavalry and served throughout the war.[29]

De Wolf's training in New York City and in France may have brought him in contact with many of the ideas that would influence the emerging field of public health. But his service during the Civil War likely crystallized those ideas into a more practical form. The war, the nation's largest and most devastating medical event in the nineteenth century, sparked unprecedented involvement in medical matters by government. Many physicians who watched as thousands of recruits died from diseases associated with poor sanitation in army camps left the service with a new appreciation for sanitation and hygiene. Their experiences during the war seemed to demonstrate that disease could strike even the best of men; disease was not a moral but a sanitary problem. The work of the United States Sanitary Commission demonstrated that government could play a significant role in preserving the health of recruits.[30]

De Wolf was forty-two when he was appointed health department commissioner by Mayor Heath. His nearly thirteen years as commissioner of the Department of Health marked the centerpiece of his medical career. As he used his position to expand the authority and the bureaucracy of the health department, he established a national reputation as a leader in the growing public health movement. In 1882, the British Association for the Advancement of Science made De Wolf an honorary member. A year later, he received the diploma of the Society of Hygiene of France. On his death in 1910, the *Journal of the American Medical Association* remarked that De Wolf "had achieved national prominence in sanitary matters."[31]

De Wolf used his position to create a professionalized bureaucracy to supervise the city's health. Under De Wolf's leadership, the Department of Health was transformed from a small semiofficial entity into a firmly established agency within the city's government. "When he took charge of the office it could hardly be called a department of health," the *Chicago Inter-Ocean* reported in 1889. "The department has since developed into the most active and efficient health service in the United States." Under De Wolf's command, the department's staff increased from one physician, an assistant commissioner, two secretaries, two meat inspectors, and thirteen untrained sanitary inspectors to nearly fifty inspectors and physicians in 1889. In 1877, the department's budget stood at $36,640, excluding amounts designated for scavenger service and dead animal removal, representing a little less than nine cents per capita for general health work.[32] By 1885, the department received a total appropriation of $240,460, including $171,383 for scavenger work and removing dead animals. Since the city's population had grown rapidly, hitting 664,000 in 1885, the department's per capita expenditure for health-related work increased to just over ten cents per person.[33]

De Wolf's aim was not merely to establish the newly specialized field of public health, but also to create areas of specialization within the field. Possibly using New York's Health Department as his model, he divided his staff among various specialty areas. There were medical inspectors, sanitary policemen, meat inspectors, and tenement and factory inspectors as well as a physician managing a smallpox hospital. Each unit of inspectors was supervised by a manager, who worked directly under De Wolf and was required to produce a yearly report of his unit's activities.

De Wolf's methods for preventing the spread of contagious disease represented a transitional period in medical science and in the field of public health. In the 1880s, a new field of medicine, bacteriology, emerged from the discovery of the cholera vibrio by German physician Robert Koch. Similar independent experiments by Louis Pasteur in Paris had demonstrated decisively that disease was caused by microorganisms, not by dirt. Several Chicago researchers were among the first in the United States to publicize the new germ theory of disease, and courses on germ theory were introduced into the Chicago medical school curricula in the mid-1880s.[34] De Wolf, apparently ambivalent about rejecting the older views, gradually introduced germ theory to public health work. In 1888, he declared that diphtheria was "not a filth disease, but an infectious disease, like smallpox."[35] By then he already had published a paper on Asiatic cholera, mentioning Pasteur and asserting that bacteria caused disease. "It is not probable that the cholera poison is wafted about in the atmosphere except in a very limited extent," De Wolf wrote in the 1885 essay. While he promoted sanitary measures, such as the expansion of the city's sewer system and regular cleaning of privy vaults, his agency helped shift focus of public health practice from a primary concern with the cleanliness of the urban environment to the diagnosis and prevention of specific diseases.[36]

In Chicago, as in cities across the country, the gradual incorporation of bacteriology into public health measures initially prompted renewed efforts to identify disease and prevent its spread. De Wolf established new and more rigorous requirements for reporting all varieties of disease. His yearly reports to the City Council, beginning in 1880, included an array of statistics covering all causes of death and all outbreaks of disease, carefully listed by the sufferer's age, nationality, and residential district. To demonstrate the need for full inspections of tenements, De Wolf in 1879 appointed a voluntary corps of thirty physicians to survey all tenement dwellings in the city. With that report in hand, he appeared before the Common Council and urged the members to pass a tenement housing ordinance.[37]

The city's first housing ordinance, passed by the Common Council in 1880, further fueled the growing debate over how best to balance the public interest in a healthy environment against the responsibilities of owners of multifamily dwellings. Asserting a public interest in the cleanliness of the city's factories and housing, the law granted the health department the right to inspect and regulate sanitary conditions in places of employment and in tenement dwellings. It required property owners to remove all stench-causing refuse and to provide tenement residents with containers for garbage. Builders and landlords objected to the regulations, complaining of the additional costs and challenging the city's right to regulate the sanitation of private property. Claiming that a man "should have complete jurisdiction" over his private property, one landlord urged the council to repeal the ordinance. "The law of the survival of the fittest," another argued, should "appl[y] in all these cases of disease," making "the rigid inspection of tenement houses" an unnecessary invasion of a property owners' rights. Debates over the extent of property rights and over the legal responsibilities of property owners would repeatedly emerge in struggles over housing and factory laws.[38]

With landlords refusing to comply with the municipal ordinance, the General Assembly, under pressure from labor and housing reformers, passed the state's first tenement and factory ordinance on May 30, 1881. The legislation, reflecting De Wolf's concerns and fulfilling the demands made by the *Tribune* and the *Progressive Age*, provided Chicago's health officials with legal authority similar to that of New York's. The law put the sanitation and construction of all tenements, workshops, and lodging houses under the supervision of the Department of Health. Under the law, all plans for new construction required the department's approval. The commissioner was required to review specifications for "the ventilation of rooms, light and air shafts, windows, ventilation of water closets, drainage and plumbing."[39] Tenement dwellings were placed in a legal category that included factories and workshops and excluded single-family houses. Tenements, defined as those buildings housing three or more independent households, were open to inspection and regulation in ways that owner-occupied or rented single-family dwellings were not, and though property owners were responsible for scavenger services, tenants would be cited for violations in existing buildings. As De Wolf expanded the reach of the Health Department and its inspectors, property rights in the family home increasingly were conceived as rights that adhered only to owner-occupied and single-family dwellings.[40]

The establishment of building regulations disturbed many who were accustomed to assume rights over private property were permanent and complete. Initially, builders opposed the measure and routinely sought to evade the department's inspectors. De Wolf noted that many builders, resisting the health department's regulations, seemed "to think that the law should leave them to construct buildings entirely of their own ideas." As New York's tenement reformer, Robert W. DeForest, would note two decades later, legislation designed to regulate construction on private property seemed to run counter to the most fundamental ideals of American liberty. "Most of us have been brought up to believe that, as owners of real estate, we could build on it what we pleased, build as high as we pleased, and sink our buildings as low as we pleased," he wrote. "Our ideas of what constitutes property rights and what constitutes liberty are largely conventional."[41] By the middle of the decade, however, builders were submitting design plans and gaining department approval for most new residential construction. In 1883 and 1884, 2,444 permits were issued for construction of dwelling places. Of these, 1,142 were for so-called "flat" buildings (two- or three-story buildings fitted for only one family on each story), 484 for tenement houses containing three or more families each (including one, not yet under construction, to contain thirty-four families), and 116 brick cottages to accommodate one family each. The remaining 702 houses included "all classes of one and two family buildings from the mansion of the millionaire to the hostler's living apartments in the upper story of a barn."[42] As emerging building codes suggested, property rights claims were not absolute. Tenants living in multi-family dwellings would—after builders who submitted plans for construction—be the first to confront this reconception of property rights.

While generating conflicts over control of landed property, the ordinance also incited challenges from builders, architects, and plumbers who rejected the codes as unfair government interference with the practice of their trades. At stake were not the rights of the building owners, but the professionals' and tradesmen's claims to ownership of the body of knowledge associated with the construction trades. The conflict was smoothed over in the spring of 1887 when De Wolf participated in a conference jointly sponsored by the Illinois Association of Architects, the Chicago Master Plumbers Association, and the Health Department. The conference attendants agreed to an amendment to the state tenement and workshop law of 1881. Instead of assigning ordinary sanitary inspectors to survey new construction, the conferees proposed that the Health Department hire "a fixed ration of thoroughly practical plumbers as tenement and factory inspectors." De Wolf fully approved the proposal, saying it would "entirely satisfy an increasing opposition on the part of architects and plumbers to having these inspections made by men of no previous education or experience in their profession or guild." The amended law, he added, would "certainly remove much of the friction and inconvenience of the present law," resolving the tensions among the trades and professions involved with home construction.[43]

Though both wealthy and working-class Chicagoans seemed to welcome the tenement legislation, even the Health Department's seemingly minor efforts to regulate the property rights of the city's more affluent residents proved controversial. Many who recognized an abstract public interest in preventing the spread of contagious disease balked when they realized the regulations might impinge on the home owner's claim to control the household. Just days after his appointment as commissioner, De Wolf announced a policy that drew the attention of newspapers in New York and Boston and attracted much local opposition. The program called for sanitary inspectors to place a red card on the door frames of houses in which scarlet fever was found. Opposition came from business leaders and some physicians, who argued that the red cards threatened the security of the family home. In a speech at the fifth annual meeting of the American Public Health Association, which was held in Chicago in 1877, Dr. Henry M. Lyman deplored the waste of cards and tacks, claiming the people revolted against the "yellow card nuisance."[44] The policy, which affected owner-occupied and rental dwellings, remained but was rarely implemented in later years.

Few complaints were heard, however, when De Wolf urged regular inspections of the rented homes of the city's laboring and impoverished population. During his first year in office, De Wolf expanded the squad of sanitary inspectors and pushed the Common Council for new appropriations to employ them year round. Only close inspection of tenement districts, he argued, could prevent the spread of contagious disease. "Incessant, systematic and searching inspection from house to house and street by street, from January to January, can alone prevent the growth of sanitary evils, which when matured and in full force, are beyond the control of men."[45]

The "incessant, systematic and searching inspection" for disease was performed by former policemen who personified the department's authority in the streets and dwellings of the city's laboring classes. Sanitary inspections, De Wolf noted in a speech before the state medical society, represented the "police authority" in tenement "districts." The Health Department granted sanitary inspectors the same "powers" as "regular police," with one exception. "This," according to the board's yearly report, "is the power to enter any house without a search warrant between the hours of sunrise and sunset." Moreover, the sanitary police were authorized to involuntarily remove those suffering from smallpox to the city's smallpox hospital.[46] The inspectors faced little resistance. Health Department reports from the 1880s generally include comments about the two or three households per year that refused entrance to the sanitary inspectors. In most cases, the inspectors called regular police, the homes were forcibly inspected, and sick residents were forcibly removed to the city's hospital. Not until 1922 did a legal challenge to the inspectors' authority reach the state appellate court, which ruled that the state's health officers had the legal authority to inspect dwellings and quarantine the carrier of contagious disease, in this case boardinghouse owner Jennie

Barmore, a carrier of the typhoid bacillus.[47] Sanitary inspections likely incited some ethnic hostility among the city's recent immigrants. The inspectors were predominantly Irish, charged with entering and inspecting the homes of recently arrived Polish, Greek, Italian, and Eastern European families. The city's labor leaders, along with much of their constituency, however, affirmed the need for housing inspections and urged all Chicagoans to allow the health department's inspectors to enter their homes.[48]

Ethnic conflicts between the inspectors and tenement dwellers, however, prompted De Wolf to seek administrative control of the sanitary inspectors, an issue that became a point of conflict, possibly the only conflict, between De Wolf and Mayor Carter Harrison. The mayor, whose immense charisma and masterly control over the distribution of patronage jobs yielded five terms in office, personally hired all sanitary inspectors. Harrison though born in Kentucky and a Democrat, pulled together a diverse coalition to win in a city that regularly voted Republican in national elections. He was, as Richard Schneirov notes, "a broker between most of the city's organized interest groups," including middle-class reformers, business moderates, German socialists, and Irish immigrants. To reward supporters and stifle opposition, Harrison placed several Socialist leaders in the Department of Health. But the mayor's power was rooted in the city's Irish communities. In the 1880s, the Irish were not the largest of the city's immigrant groups, but they were among the most vocal and most politically active, a powerful force in the Democratic Party since the 1850s. By 1865, one-third of Chicago's police were Irish and in the 1880s, under Harrison's patronage, the Irish gained an even greater proportion of the coveted jobs. Sanitary inspectors, hired from the police force, were predominantly Irish. Despite De Wolf's repeated complaints that the system was tainted by politics, Harrison refused to relinquish control of even a slice of the city's patronage jobs to the health commissioner.[49]

The Health Department's inspection procedures illustrate the distinction drawn between the property rights of tenement dwellers and those enjoyed by people living in single-family dwellings. While health inspectors regularly entered tenement dwellings without warrants or court orders, they also made "special examinations" of dwellings occupied by a single family, but only at the request of physicians, occupants, or owners. "This class of work [inspection of single-family homes] was not at first intended to form a part of the 'regular' work of the inspectors," De Wolf announced in 1882; nevertheless, "the public generally are recognizing the true value and benefit to health of perfect house sanitation," which such inspections and the suggestion of "proper remedies for all defects found" contributed to. In most cases, these inspections were made "as a last resort" by the occupant seeking relief from odors or poor construction. Unlike owner-occupied or single-family homes—and unlike businesses owned by corporate and individual entities—multifamily rental dwellings could be entered by policemen without particular cause.[50]

No single area of the city was targeted for inspections, but the single-family homes of the city's elite were excluded. The department's report for 1885 noted that inspections covered every area of the city, "except those classed as strictly 'residence' streets of the most expensive and thoroughly improved character." Neighborhoods with large numbers of multifamily rented dwellings, often the subdivided homes of poorer or working-class families, were more likely to be inspected than streets lined with single-family dwellings. "The method adopted," the report commented, "was to apply the entire working force of inspectors to the most insanitary localities first, following this with the next most urgent localities, and so on to the end of the work."[51] This approach, which reinforced distinctions between elite districts and those housing the laboring classes, further enhanced the status of those who could afford to rent or buy single-family houses in districts beyond the reach of the department's inspectors.

Presenting his achievements and sense of mission in his yearly reports to the Common Council, De Wolf revealed his somewhat inconsistent analysis of the link between tenement dwellings and public health. De Wolf initially attributed the most intractable tenement conditions to the immigrant families. Like the *Tribune*'s reporter, De Wolf contended that the national origin of the occupants determined the sanitary conditions of tenement dwellings. Native-born Americans lived in "well-furnished" flats; Germans tended to occupy tenements that were "comfortably built, but having less of the so-called modern conveniences." That native-born and German workers tended to congregate in higher-skilled and better-paying jobs, thus enabling them to afford more comfortable housing, did not apparently occur to De Wolf. Instead, De Wolf blamed the inferior quality of the tenements occupied by Italian, Polish, and Bohemian immigrants on a mix of custom and biology. "There are a great many old buildings in this city which are unfit for habitation by civilized people," he wrote. "yet they are inhabited, and generally by Italians, Poles, Bohemians, and others, who, in their trans-Atlantic homes have been accustomed to live in crowded quarters, in close proximity to their domestic animals, which in this city are not allowed to be kept within the premises used for human habitation." De Wolf added that it was difficult to enforce tenement housing ordinances "against such habitual and hereditary insanitary modes of living." Since these immigrants rarely understood health departments' regulations, they required "constant watching" by sanitary inspectors."[52]

But De Wolf did not believe that the residents' nationality was the sole source of the tenement problem, and the consequent spread of disease in the city. Property rights and the ability of wage earners to acquire "sanitary" housing also entered his analysis of the public health threat. Pointing to the 1880 census, De Wolf wrote "that the whole number of occupants of tenement houses is about equal to the foreign population, not because of their nationality, but because it is wage workers of all nationalities who are compelled to occupy tenement houses." De Wolf's views proved an exaggeration; more than one-third of the city's wage laborers, most of whom were immigrants, owned some real estate in 1880. Yet De Wolf contended that property rights in housing, the difference between the home owner and the tenant, were a primary feature separating the healthy from the diseased, the sanitary from the unsanitary home.[53]

This had been labor's position for nearly a decade. By the early 1880s, Chicago had become the headquarters of the nation's socialist and anarchist movements and a center of strength for the more moderate Knights of Labor. As De Wolf's inspectors roamed the tenement districts, unions associated with the Trades and Labor Assembly held regular meetings on the city's South and West Sides. More significantly, some of the city's labor activists worked with the sanitary reform movement, seeking to use health regulations to improve living and working conditions for the city's working classes. Carter Harrison, aiming to reconcile his often conflicting coalition of supporters, had placed at least one outspoken socialist on the Health Department staff. Factory inspector Joseph Gruenhut was a leader of the SDP and a columnist in the *Progressive Age*. Gruenhut regularly attacked both employers and landlords for their treatment of the "laboring classes." He had been an early advocate of the tenement and factory ordinance, issuing a report, approved by the Trades and Labor Assembly, which called for monthly inspections of "every place of employment and habitation to enforce the laws, ordinances, and regulations for the safety and health of the occupants." Gruenhut's proclamations, rejecting more radical demands for worker control over business, ultimately left him alienated from the Socialist Party, but he remained a steady advocate for sanitary reform. De Wolf, clearly aware of the rumblings of the city's labor movement, hardly commented on labors' battles.[54]

Yet the increasingly aggressive language and tactics of organized labor did not escape the attention of sanitary reformers. As collective organizing threatened to undermine the growth and stability of the businesses on which Chicago's industrializing economy was based, the reformers looked to the Health Department for solutions. The Citizens Association of Chicago, the oldest permanent civic reform organization in the nation, organized in 1874, began to argue for the construction of "model tenements," a solution first proposed in London and later promoted in New York in the 1840s. Working with volunteers from the association, the Health Department in 1884 conducted a nine- month survey of all tenement dwellings. The "unpleasant fact," De Wolf wrote, was "that practically no provisions are being made to house the toiling multitude of wage-workers in our city." The association's committee on tenement housing, reporting its findings, was more explicit. Remarking on the recent conflict between labor and capital, the association argued that the construction of model tenements would "be a long stride in the direction of a general movement to bring capital and labor into closer economic union." Those willing to construct rental housing for wage workers would not be expected to forgo a profit. Pointing to the success of the community built by George Pullman just south of the city, the reformers argued that the construction of "blocks of tenement houses on the most approved plans for the wage working poor" could prove "highly profitable." No one came forward to test this thesis. But in ignoring the relationship between wages and the ability to buy or rent "sanitary homes," the sanitarians moved to separate housing from other issues of conflict between wage laborers and their employers.[55]

If constant surveillance of tenement dwellings did not eliminate contagious disease, the Health Department's inspection program did establish the municipal government's legal claim to intervene in the households of the laboring poor. The widespread destruction caused by the fire of 1871 had helped to affirm a larger social interest in regulating the construction of urban dwellings. In casting tenement housing as an equally compelling danger, sanitarians argued that the public interest in the health of the urban populace as a whole justified government surveillance of the interior space of the tenement households. Legally sanctioned inspections of tenement dwellings conflicted with the head of household's customary rights to supervise the family home and undermined the rhetorical separation of public from domestic space. When home owners resisted the placarding of their homes and builders resisted building codes, De Wolf either backed down or negotiated with his opponents. No one in the late nineteenth century, however, challenged the legitimacy of tenement inspections in the courts. In the absence of any legal challenge, De Wolf established the principal that the public welfare was best and most efficiently protected by regulating the living conditions in the rented dwellings of working-class households. Property rights in a home, it seemed, adhered only to owner-occupied single-family dwellings.

────────────

During the same years that tenement housing alarmed municipal officials, fears of adulterated foods provoked new public outrage. The same industries that drew thousands of workers who lived in tenement dwellings also processed foods that were sold in Chicago and throughout the northeast. The most famous were packaged beef and pork produced from the thousands of animals slaughtered, butchered, and packaged each day in the Union Stock Yard. Just as he fought to reform tenement housing, De Wolf sought to inspect the meat sold by the city's packinghouses. The contrast between the two public health campaigns—the easy achievements of tenement inspections and the decades-long legal battles with slaughterhouse owners—reveal much about power relations and politics when it came to property rights in the industrializing city.

De Wolf's crusade against the packinghouses gained widespread publicity in the fall of 1879, when Boston reformer George Angell arrived in Chicago to investigate the prevalence of contaminated food in the city. Within days of his arrival, the *Chicago Daily Tribune* published a series of articles calling on the Common Council to pass an ordinance banning the sale of contaminated meat and urging Chicagoans to respond to the danger of "poisoned" food. The generally staid and staunchly probusiness *Tribune* urged the city's citizens to form a "protective health association" to expose "every merchant guilty of adulteration." An association was formed and immediately sent a petition to Congress, which was published in the *Tribune*, demanding legislation to protect the nation from adulterated food.[56] It would be another twenty-five years before Congress moved to inspect the nation's food supplies.

By 1879 Chicago's health officers had made several largely unsuccessful efforts to regulate the slaughterhouses and restrict the distribution of contaminated food. (Though most of the slaughterhouses were outside the city limits, the packers dumped waste in the Chicago River and sold meat in the city, which the department attempted to regulate.) The city's food processors proved powerful opponents. In a letter addressed to George Angell and published in the *Tribune*, De Wolf commented, "While I fully appreciate the necessity of additional laws, I must add that it is in my judgment absolutely impossible for the public officers in this country to contend successfully with great financial interests unless sustained by active organizations of good and patriotic citizens."[57] Despite the efforts of the Association for the Suppression of Food Adulteration, the "patriotic citizens" did not garner the political influence to tackle the corporations marketing processed meats.

As De Wolf recognized, the city's "financial interests" could and did deploy substantial resources to protect the interests and property rights of corporations. While the *Tribune* devoted several weeks in the fall of 1879 to whipping up public outrage over adulterated food, the owners of the city's slaughterhouses already had spent the previous eight years battling Chicago's health officials in the courts.[58] Almost since the Union Stock Yard opened in the village of Lake just south of the city border on Christmas day 1865, residents of neighboring communities had complained about the "noxious odors" emanating from the plants. Drawing on the eighteenth-century legal concept of "common nuisances," long applied in northeastern cities to bar industries like tanning, bone-boiling, or butchering within residential districts, the city's health officers sought to eliminate the stench by regulating the businesses.[59] In Chicago, however, the doctrine proved highly controversial. When the Department of Health issued a dozen citations for "noxious odors" in 1877, after nearly eight years of legal battles over regulating the slaughterhouses, jurors in the city's police courts refused to convict the packinghouse owners, instead "censoring the health officer for interfering with legitimate business."[60] Undeterred, De Wolf continued to argue for inspections of meat sold in the city and for the regulations of noxious odors emanating from the stockyards. George Angell provided De Wolf with his first broad public support.

Spurred by the *Tribune* coverage of the health reformers' investigations of adulterated foods, the Common Council in the fall of 1879 engaged in heated debates over how best to control the sales of contaminated meats. In previous years, when health officers discovered tainted meat in the city's markets, they soaked the meat in kerosene and left it with the butcher, assuming the kerosene rendered the meat unmarketable. De Wolf urged legislation to authorize health inspectors to confiscate and destroy all tainted meat products. He gained support from the mayor, whose personal experience with tainted meat outweighed the substantial influence of the industries' representatives. The mayor and several members of his family had become seriously ill after eating sausages "sprinkled with kerosene." Although his cook denied purchasing contaminated sausage, an investigation "found that all the diseased meat subjected to a bath of kerosene by the Health Officer was sent to sausage factories."[61] Despite the mayor's vigorous support, aldermen aligned with the meat packers successfully held up the legislation for several weeks. The *Tribune* editorialized that "Dr. De Wolf, our Health Commissioner, has for eighteen months fought this diabolical trade with an energy and determination that have won for him universal honor and praise." Even the mayor received the *Tribune*'s acclaim. "The Mayor, to the credit of his head and of his heart," the newspaper commented, "insisted that the consumers of meat should have some protection from the death-dealing dishonesty of the dealers in rotten meat."[62]

While De Wolf cast the controversy in terms of protecting the public health, the meat packers defended their rights to control their property. Arguing that city officials could not legally take their property, the packers sought payment for all confiscated meats. In attempting to negotiate compromise legislation with the mayor and health commissioner, they urged that confiscated meat be sold at public auction with the receipts going to the meat's original owners. De Wolf rejected this suggestion. His stance generated additional support from the *Tribune*, which claimed that diseased meat did not "constitute property."[63]

Ultimately, arguments for a public interest prevailed over the meat packers' assertions of property rights in tainted meat. Under sustained pressure from the city's newspapers and health reformers, the council finally granted the Health Department the authority to confiscate and destroy diseased meat. By the late 1880s, health inspectors were stationed at the gates of the packinghouses and authorized to examine all livestock entering and all packaged foods leaving the premises. Each of the department's yearly reports listed total amounts of meat confiscated by the inspectors. Although the law came down on the side of the Health Department and the controversy over adulterated foods subsided, enforcement of the regulations was limited. Health reformers repeatedly criticized the meat inspectors and renewed calls on the commissioner to better enforce the meat inspections. Significantly, the campaign to regulate packaged meat resulted in a new mayor—DeWitt C. Cregier, a Democratic rival of Harrison—firing De Wolf in 1889. The Health Department had successfully asserted its right to regulate private property, both tenement housing and packaged meat, but corporate entities, better financed and with substantial political muscle, had put up a strong fight and would continue to resist health regulations through the turn of the century.[64]

In the late nineteenth century, as lawmakers and judges contended with legislation designed to regulate corporate property, municipal agencies like Chicago's health department moved, almost unnoticed, to redefine property rights in the homes of the city's poorest residents. Ultimately, industrial production would come under municipal and later federal regulation, but not until a new generation of reformers had sufficiently expanded the definition of the public interest to include the regulation of corporate property. Some tenement dwellers probably welcomed the sanitary inspectors, hoping that the inspections would force their landlords to improve living conditions in the tenements. Even those cited for violations of the sanitary codes had little choice but to let the department's inspectors into their homes. Impoverished and lacking the language and the finances to maneuver the American legal system, tenement residents proved weak opponents to health and housing reformers determined to control their dwelling spaces. It is not surprising that the meat-packing industrialists put up a more effective fight in the courts and on the floor of the Common Council.

While De Wolf's decade-and-a-half-long battle with the meat packers ultimately resulted in his removal from office in 1889, De Wolf had helped to redefine the scope of property rights in housing by establishing the principle that tenement and factory inspections served a public interest in protecting the public health. Faced with opposition from single-family home owners and corporate entities, De Wolf proved most successful when he focused on the multifamily rental dwellings of the urban poor. His reports further solidified categories of ethnic and racial identity by linking housing conditions to the "blood" or "heredity" of the dwellings' occupants while at the same time divorcing housing from other areas of conflict between labor and capital. Most significantly, his sanitary housing inspections established a legal distinction between the property rights of tenants and those of home owners.

The factory and tenement legislation, the most far-reaching housing laws passed in the twenty-five years following the Civil War, did assist impoverished and working-class households to improve living conditions somewhat. The law and its implementation in Chicago neighborhoods also functioned to draw attention to the potential benefits of property rights in housing; home owners could call on the Health Department for assistance without facing regular and unannounced inspections. With its regular inspections of the homes of tenement residents, the Health Department helped to crystallize the legal definitions and social benefits of property rights in housing. By 1900, when urban reformers looked to single-family dwellings as the solution to the problem of tenement housing, the Health Department had developed legal and bureaucratic structures to justify their claims. At the turn of the century, however, many of those concerned about tenement conditions would find that efforts to legislate solutions to the city's housing problem would prove inadequate. Even in the 1880s, as sanitary reformers and municipal officials began to rely on major and expensive infrastructure improvements, particularly sewer and water lines, to ensure the health of the urban populace, the Health Department was less able to, and often less concerned with, ameliorating the dangers of tenement living.

CHAPTER FOUR

Cleanliness and Capital Investments

In the summer of 1900, the City Homes Association, a newly established reform organization, hired five skilled plumbers to conduct a house-by-house canvass of plumbing facilities in a four-by-twelve-block area on Chicago's West Side, then survey the plumbing in dwellings in two nearby neighborhoods. The three districts studied were not, in the view of the association's investigators, the "worst" in the city, but were "representative . . . of the city where the problems of the old and the menace of the new housing evils are both manifest."[1] The plumbers' findings, part of a larger investigation published in 1901 under the title *Tenement Conditions in Chicago*, offered a vivid portrait of tenement dwellings, describing in detail the crowded, dark, and dirty rooms in which thousands of Chicagoans lived. The investigators expressed outrage over many aspects of tenement life. None proved more surprising than the lack of adequate plumbing facilities.

Nearly fifty years after Chicago began installing sewer and water pipes along city streets and two decades after the Department of Health began inspecting tenements, thousands of home owners and tenants continued to use back alley privies, and to bathe and clean only when they had the time and stamina to lug buckets of water from city hydrants or backyard pumps. Urban residents acquired indoor plumbing and the health it provided only if they could afford to rent or buy a home connected to the city's sewer and water lines and fitted with porcelain sinks and toilets, and bathing rooms designed to conform to "modern" standards of cleanliness. Many Chicagoans could not afford such amenities. The plumbers found that more than 80 percent of the sinks examined were in "dangerously defective condition." Equally troubling were the more than 10,000 people, or about 40 percent of the population in the dwellings studied, who used outdoor privies. "The most shocking conditions prevail in the districts infected with this remnant

8. Map of Chicago, 1900.

of the broad spaces of village days," the report asserted. "It is unworthy of Chicago to permit the evil to continue, and the Board of Health without favoritism should execute the law which provides for these privies to be abolished."[2] Indoor plumbing, representing a mix of public financing for sewer and water line construction and a capital investment for the property owner in sinks, tubs, toilets, and hookup fees, improved the health of the household while increasing the cost of housing. It proved a significant inducement to home ownership for those who could purchase health with the purchase of a house, while for others it meant a new and painful choice, the balancing of the need for shelter against household health.

Citing "favoritism" by Health Department officials, the report obscured a complex politics of housing and health, the nearly half-century of struggles among builders, land speculators, sanitary reformers, tenants and landlords, home owners with adequate incomes, and those fighting to maintain their access to property rights in housing over where and when to invest public resources in urban infrastructure. Municipal funding for the laying of sewer pipes down urban streets and the construction of pumping stations and water lines were central to broader conflicts over how residential real estate acquired value. Indoor plumbing added value to a dwelling while the new infrastructure might add greater value to land owned by speculators and designated for subdivision, raising the prices for lots and new single-family houses. By the late nineteenth century, the politics of sewer and water line construction already had generated a new language of property rights claims that transformed both Chicago's housing markets and its social geography.

Public debates over where and when the city government would put new sewer lines strengthened bonds among neighbors, sharpened the lines separating one neighborhood from another, and ultimately enhanced the property values and health of some neighborhoods at the expense of others. In the mid-1880s, expanding contests over the deployment of municipal funds made residential neighborhoods a central arena in power struggles among the city's competing industrial classes. By 1900, indoor plumbing had become a privately financed amenity, determining the value of the home and surrounding neighborhood and marking a clear distinction between the dwellings of the poor and those of the rest of the urban populace. If sewer and water lines created, in the words of historian Joel Tarr, "a networked city," the new services also functioned to redefine the home, locating it as part of a community of public service consumers linked by underground pipes. Yet, as the City Homes Association's study revealed, those who lacked the resources to connect their homes to this new urban community were left

9. Seventeenth Ward alley, ca. 1908. Chicago Commons Slide Collection, Chicago Historical Society.

increasingly isolated and near invisible to the municipal officials charged with providing and regulating sewer and water services.[3]

The technology for constructing sewer and water systems, like the dirt, smells, and disease generated by growing numbers of people living in close proximity, was available long before American municipalities began laying pipe and building pumping stations. Among the host of new services publicly debated and rapidly expanded during the final decades of the nineteenth century, clean water and indoor plumbing—even more than electricity, telephones, and streetcar lines—had a profound impact on housing designs, household labor, and, most significantly, public health. Indoor plumbing set new standards for the design and function of the family home and for the work required to maintain the household.[4]

Philadelphia was the first American city to build a municipal water works, in 1802. New York, Boston, and Detroit also built pumping stations and laid water pipes in the first half of the century. None, however, served all residents of those expanding metropolitan areas. Although the technology to construct water carriage systems, or sewers, was available by the 1840s, most American municipalities did not begin to construct sewers to remove household wastes until after the Civil War. Chicago was an exception, launching construction on the largest and most technologically innovative public works project, an underground sewer system, in the mid-1850s. By 1900, the city had built what many engineers and sanitation experts considered the most advanced drainage, sewage, and water systems in the country.[5]

In Chicago, as in other cities until about 1850, individual home owners and tenants generally were responsible for their household's waste and water needs.[6] Most Chicagoans got water from a backyard pump attached to a well dug ten to twelve feet into the sand and clay bottom soil. Others made regular trips to the river or lakefront to collect water, and some purchased water from street peddlers, who took a horse-drawn cart to the lake, filled a keg with water, and then went door to door selling water for between five and ten cents per barrel. Though a private company, the Chicago Hydraulic Company, won a charter from the state legislature in 1836 to provide Chicago with water, its services were limited and inadequate.[7] Most Chicagoans continued to consider the availability of clean water a private matter, regulated by market forces and individual incentive.

The elimination of household waste was similarly considered a responsibility of individual households. Garbage typically was dumped directly into the street or a rear lot. Scavenger services, private companies hired by the day for $2.25 to $3.50, carried dead animals off the streets and picked up household garbage. Even after 1887, when the Department of Health signed long-term contracts with scavenger companies, the work was intermittent and inefficient. Visitors to the city in the 1850s often commented on the piles of garbage and the horrible odors emanating from alleys and rarely cleaned streets. Human excrement was emptied into privy vaults, sunk into the same soil as, and often right next to, water wells. The vaults were seldom tight, often leaking into the nearby water supply. Regular outbreaks of dysentery, typhoid, and cholera are ample evidence that the city's water supply often was tainted by waste.[8] In the early 1850s, a series of severe epidemics, especially an 1849 cholera outbreak, generated public pressure to improve the city's water quality.

Public funding of the sewer and water systems initially benefited property owners throughout the city by making those services available to nearly all Chicagoans. But as the city grew after the fire, municipal funding, which continued to pay for the laying of sewer and water pipes, was not adequate to quickly connect all dwellings to the sewer and water systems. The resulting uneven distribution of those services and ultimately the costs of connecting a building to the publicly funded systems, borne by the property owner, enhanced the property values of some while stabilizing or diminishing property values of others. By the turn of the century, many homes remained unconnected and sewers, the underground pipes that linked private dwellings to public services, separated the health and housing of more affluent neighborhoods and suburbs from those of impoverished home owners and tenants. Prompted by concerns about public health in general, the construction of sewer and water systems ultimately redefined the public as those who had access to the systems and redefined property rights in terms of those who had the authority to demand or reject—and many poorer home owners fought the installation of sewer and water lines on their blocks—those public services. The Department of Health distinguished between the rights of tenement residents and those of single-family dwellers; sewer and water services sharpened those distinctions and, probably more importantly, made home ownership the basis for new rights-based claims on municipal funds.

––––––––––

When the Common Council, long a fairly small and ineffective entity, began financing a city-owned water system, it transformed the relationship between property owners and the municipal government. In nineteenth-century Chicago and most other antebellum cities, services like street paving, and garbage removal were allocated through tax assessments of "interested" property owners. The municipal government served as a kind of umpire, allocating services "in proportion to the value of the 'interested property.'" Most streets were paved only when a group of property owners petitioned the council, agreed to an assessment of their property and then paid the assessment to cover the cost of paving the street. The construction of sidewalks followed a similar pattern. The result was that wealthier neighborhoods had both sidewalks and paved streets and poorer communities had neither. But the initial construction costs for sewer and water systems were so great, and demands for these services so widespread, that the assessment system proved inadequate.[9]

Reversing the older financing mechanisms, city officials paid for the bulk of the construction costs from the city's general funds, then charged individual households hookup and user fees. In the mid-1850s, the Board of Water Commissioners financed the largest construction costs—the central pumping station, lake intake tunnel, and main pipes—with bonds (and the council levied a "water tax" for its debt service), yet it required individual property owners to pay for the network of pipes that brought water into Chicago homes. The board levied special assessments for the pipes laid in particular streets and assessed user charges to connect buildings and annual water rents set according to building size and expected water usage.[10] User charge revenues proved lucrative. Between 1854 and 1872, more than four million dollars in water fees was paid to the board. By 1878, the board ended its fiscal year with a surplus, and the commissioners retired some of the bonds that had financed the original construction. Though the board spent more money on extending the system than on retiring debts through the turn of the century, it began to function as a profit-making company by the early 1860s.[11]

The water board's financing mechanisms, which determined who would or would not receive water services, guided property values and shaped the city's real estate markets. With profit as an incentive and land speculators an influential political force in the city, the board proved highly selective when deciding where and when to lay pipe. The water board initially laid pipes in the most heavily populated area in and around the city's commercial center. By 1861, nearly the entire district was supplied, despite the huge growth in its population from 66,000 in 1854 to 120,000 in 1861.[12] But as the city's population grew, residential construction moved beyond the limits of the original water district. By 1864, the water commission refused to extend pipes into residential areas that would not generate sufficient income in fees, commenting in its annual report, "To avoid entailing a heavy, unproductive debt on the Water Works, the Board is compelled to limit the laying of the pipes to such places as are in most urgent need of the water and where, also, the buildings needing water are most numerous and will yield the greatest amount of water tax."[13] But the board determined that laying pipes across some unimproved sections could prove profitable. Spurred by owners of large tracts of land on the North and West Sides, the board laid pipes through the prairie, commenting that the "laying of pipes is speedily followed by the erection of new buildings and such streets soon become self-supporting."[14] Property values on undeveloped prairie increased and the houses that sprang up along those recently built streets began to attract Chicagoans seeking housing fitted with indoor plumbing. The board had created value in property outside the built-up sections of the city, making those newly developed areas more attractive to builders, home buyers, and well-to-do renters.[15]

In 1874, the Board of Public Works, which was established in 1861 to supervise water and sewer services, blamed the fire limits ordinance for the disparity in water services throughout the city. By permitting the construction of "wooden tenements" outside the fire limits but within the city borders, the ordinance encouraged residential construction "far away from the center of population." It was, in the board's view, too expensive to extend water pipes to the distant settlements. The solution was to make the fire limits co-extensive with the city boundaries, a suggestion implemented by the council, forcing all new construction to be of masonry materials and denying builders and buyers the option of choosing less costly wood frame housing. "[W]hen the cost of building is made uniform," the board commented, "people will be likely to build as near to the business center as possible, as the convenience of transit will more than justify the trifling additional cost of real estate."[16] The board's view of the problem seems slightly exaggerated since most of the frame construction after the fire was located on the edges of the fire limits, just beyond the city's commercial center. Still, the board implicitly acknowledged the relationship between real estate values and water services. Chicagoans similarly saw a link between property values and sewer lines.

In the lakefront city, the problems of disposing of waste and supplying clean water were connected. Chicago, however, tried to solve them separately. Responding to public outrage over the 1854 cholera epidemic, the Common Council in 1855 established a Board of Sewerage Commissioners. William Ogden, owner of hundreds of undeveloped acres edging the city and one of the three-member board, was instrumental in bringing in Ellis Sylvester Chesbrough, designer of Boston's water distribution system, to develop plans to save Chicago from another health crisis. Chesbrough, a self-trained canal and railroad engineer with little formal education and no previous experience in building sewers, carried through the construction of the first comprehensive sewage system in the country and became a leading voice in the city's sanitary reform movement for the next two decades.[17] Though troubled almost from inception, this massive public works project made Chesbrough a kind of civic hero. He seemed to many to have an incorruptible sense of civic duty, working tirelessly, though often mistakenly, to improve the city's water and sanitation systems.

Like many American urban reformers both before and after him, Chesbrough looked to Europe for guidance, then developed what he and his supporters contended was a "purely American" solution to urban problems. Chesbrough toured European cities, studying water carriage systems. He was particularly impressed by the ideas of the British sanitarian Edwin Chadwick, who in the 1840s had advocated the adoption of a system of earthenware pipe sewers to replace London's cesspools and privy vaults. Believing that odors from decaying organic matter caused the spread of many fatal diseases, Chadwick maintained that this "arterial-venous system" could dispose of human wastes and free the city from disease. Chadwick's system was never implemented as he planned, but his ideas influenced American sanitarians like Chesbrough.[18]

Chesbrough returned to Chicago with plans for a "combined" system that would carry both household waste and storm water in a single line of pipe. Since the city lay just a few feet above the lake and river, the new brick sewers could not be laid underground. Instead, Chesbrough laid the pipes down the center of streets and connected them by ducts to buildings, then covered the pipes with mounds of dirt. As construction moved away from the river, the sewer pipes were elevated to an angle sufficient to allow them to drain by gravity into the river. The river was dredged to handle the loads of sewage, and the dredged soil was used as fill to raise the street grades enough to cover the sewage pipes. Roadbeds were then guttered and paved with either stone or cedar block. With the new street and sewer construction underway, the Common Council voted to raise the grade of the city as much as ten feet in places. But the new brick sewer lines, which emptied waste into the Chicago River, which flowed into Lake Michigan, hardly solved the city's drainage and water problems. Rather, as the city grew, as spring flooding and expanded sewer usage drove waste water from the river into the lake and into the water system, the problems became more acute. Officials then approved another Chesbrough plan.[19]

With approval from the state legislature and funding from a three million dollar bond issue, Chesbrough deepened the bed of the shipping canal and reversed the flow of the Chicago River. Instead of dumping the city's waste into the lake, the river would flow away from the lake, sending waste through the canal and toward the Mississippi River. The project was completed in July 1871, much to the dismay of downstream communities, farming towns, and rural villages, which complained of the smell and pollution of their drinking water. Fortunately for the downstream residents, the river became a stagnant pool when Ogden and his partner, John Wentworth, used the public works project to enhance their real estate holdings by digging a drainage canal from the Des Plaines to the Chicago River to drain their holdings of swamp land west of the city. The canal, which the *Tribune* aptly named "Odgen's ditch," served Ogden's purposes, but diverted almost all the water from the narrow Des Plaines River into the south branch of the Chicago River, forcing the river to backwash into the lake. A year after the river was reversed, its current slowed and eventually stopped, leaving the city center bordered by a stagnant pool of waste water and its residents still subject to regular outbreaks of disease.[20]

Industrial waste, particularly the remnants of cattle and hogs dumped by the packinghouses, was largely responsible for the filth flowing into the Chicago River. Though Health Department officials in the 1870s and 1880s urged the Common Council to restrict industrial waste, the council refused. Elected officials, however, did attempt to respond to public demands for clean water and the elimination of odors on the river, using the city's general funds to reverse the flow of the river, rather than restricting dumping or assessing the packers for the costs of project. Government revenues then served to redistribute wealth upward, using property tax dollars to protect industry from regulation that might cut into corporate profits. The socialization of the costs of constructing water and sewage systems made those services available to property owners who could afford the fees and the cost of installing indoor plumbing and protected industry from the financial burdens of assessments, but left those who could not afford water and sewer hookup fees without indoor plumbing.[21]

Up through the 1870s, public funding for sewer construction benefited working-class home owners and tenants, augmenting their property values and enhancing their households' health. Unlike the water board, the sewerage board was never conceived as a quasi-private company expected to profit from its investments. In 1855, when sewer lines were first laid, the sewerage board mapped a service district, using primarily bond revenues and the city's general funds to lay pipes throughout the central residential and commercial area. While the water system relied on water usage fees to expand, sewer construction was financed by the city's general funds. Home owners who could afford the hookup fees reaped the benefits; by the 1880s, sewers were more common in many working-class neighborhoods than were paved streets. Wealthy areas had both; most poorer neighborhoods had neither. Public financing may have put sewers into neighborhoods with high rates of working-class home ownership, communities that otherwise would not have been able to afford them.[22] Chicago's working-class home owners, apparently, welcomed the new waste disposal methods as long as the cost did not force them to choose between paying for their homes and acquiring sewerage systems.

In the final decades of the century, however, government funding for sewer construction proved inadequate, with serious consequences for working-class home owners and tenants. The sewerage system expanded more slowly than the water system. In 1861, the city had 95 miles of water pipe but only 54 miles of sewers; by April 1874, more than 351 miles of water pipe had been laid and nearly 198 miles of sewer pipe. The difference likely resulted from different financing mechanisms. While the water board could charge regular fees for water usage, the sewerage board charged a one-time hookup fee, but garnered no further income for its services. In 1874 alone, water rents yielded nearly $750,000. Lacking a steady income from consumers, the sewerage board regularly pleaded with the Common Council for funding increases, pleas that often went unanswered. The sewerage board went bankrupt in 1861 and was put under the auspices of the new Department of Public Works. Although older built-up sections of the city, including many working-class neighborhoods, had gotten sewer lines, other areas, including the Brophys' West Side neighborhood, were largely left outside the sewer network through the 1880s.[23]

Financing of sewer construction remained a source of debate, an issue that divided propertied Chicagoans, through the final decades of the nineteenth century. Once their homes were connected to the new sewer system, property owners balked at paying property taxes when the revenues went to laying sewer pipes in other districts. Many also complained about the city's practice of issuing bonds to finance sewer construction, arguing that the city could hardly afford to take on additional debt.[24] In the 1880s, Chicagoans already connected to the water system complained about the quality of the water flowing into their homes, pressuring the public works department to build new pumping stations and extend existing pipes further into the lake. The Citizens Association led the campaign for new pumping stations, demands that Mayor Carter Harrison, angry about public criticism of his government, resisted for several months. But the reform organization, led by some of the city's most prominent residents, whose homes already were connected to the intricate network of water and sewer pipes, achieved its goal. Arguing that Chicago's commercial growth was slowed by inadequate and low-quality water services, the association pushed the mayor to finance and speed the construction of new pumping works. The Public Works Department then divided its limited city funding between capital improvements and extending pipes to unserviced districts.[25] Although the agency gained some additional financing for sewer pipes in the 1880s, sewer construction fell far behind the needs of the expanding housing market.

Even when the city paid to lay the pipes, poorer households, whether tenants or home owners, often lacked the financial resources to pay a one-time hookup fee, which the sewer board, like the water board, charged to connect buildings to the system. Some landlords rejected sewer connections since it would have required them to install plumbing fixtures in rented dwellings. Others refused to pay for repairs when plumbing fixtures, or the sewer and water pipes attached to buildings, fell into disrepair. "The filthy and rotten tenements, the dingy courts and tumble-down sheds," one West Side resident said, were as common as "the foul stables and dilapidated outhouses, the broken sewer pipes, and the piles of garbage." In 1893, a U.S. Commissioner of Labor study found that 73 percent of Chicagoans had access only to an outside privy. A year later, the Common Council, recognizing that landlords often refused to connect their buildings to existing sewers, outlawed the privy vault on premises "abutting upon or adjoining any street, alley, court or public place," in which was located a public sewer. The move placed new financial burdens on both landlords and poorer home owners.[26]

For tenants and landlords, fees for water connections raised new questions about who was responsible for the well-being of the household and the value of the property, the property owner or the household residing in the dwelling. In some cases, owners and tenants engaged in long-running feuds over who should pay the hookup costs; landlords left hundreds of buildings unconnected throughout the final decades of the nineteenth century. Even when tenants won the battle, they lost the war as landlords, forced to pay the fees and to install plumbing fixtures, passed the cost to their tenants by increasing rents. Some landlords simply compelled tenants to pay all assessed fees on the rented homes. Walter L. Newberry, who owned scores of residential properties around the city and rented to skilled craftsmen and middle-class families, added new clauses to lease agreements, requiring tenants to pay property taxes, water taxes, and sewer connection fees. If the buildings were located on streets lacking sewers, Newberry's leases stated that tenants must keep "outhouses, and washbasins in sanitary condition in accordance" with city ordinances. Newberry further protected himself with a clause stating that a Department of Health citation "shall be, among other things, conclusive evidence [among] the parties hereto of the breach of this covenant." With rents running as high as twenty-five dollars per month, Newberry's properties were priced beyond the means of unskilled laborers.[27]

By the time the City Homes Association sent its plumbers through the West Side district in 1900, many tenants and home owners like those along Newberry Avenue, aware that the introduction of indoor plumbing facilities would render their homes unaffordable, protested against the very services the reformers sought to provide. "Cleanliness," the tenement housing report commented, "is almost a luxury in Chicago and a high price is paid for it. A family with too much work to do—and most working people have too much already—can hardly be clean."[28]

Indoor plumbing had become, in the words of historian Ann Durkin Keating, a "personal amenity."[29] The need for a large initial capital investment to construct sewer and water systems had functioned to puncture the decades-old property assessment mechanisms for financing urban services. Yet once the city's wealthier property owners had access to running water and waste disposal, the city's political and economic elite were willing to pay for private services for their own homes and neighborhoods rather than support another bond issue or new taxes to service the city as a whole. By the 1880s, expenditures for plumbing fixtures, fees for hookups, and assessments for sewer pipes and water taxes represented capital investments paid for by private property owners, making water and waste disposal facilities in the home privately financed amenities. While in the 1850s Chicago's boosters had successfully merged their business interests with public health dangers to draw on city and state funds to build sewer and water systems, thirty years later the city's more affluent residents no longer conceived of their health concerns as linked to those of the city's poorer communities. Financing for sewer and water services was increasingly privatized and outcries over threats to the public health were no longer capable of mobilizing large government investments in services. Household sanitation was again left to the resources of the private household. Home ownership, which might signal a laboring man's autonomy in the industrial city, would not necessarily assure him the good health to retain his status.

––––––––

If the city's affluent residents no longer saw their health as connected to the city's poorer residents, it may be because the city's poorest residents lived in neighborhoods increasingly isolated from the rest of the city. The construction of sewer and water lines had a decisive impact on real estate markets. In the 1850s, those whose homes were located within the city's original water and sewer districts quickly made the connections and by the 1870s property values there were the highest in the city. City residents living outside the original service area faced difficult decisions. Some moved to a neighborhood fitted with sewer and water lines, sometimes moving houses as well as belongings to an area where hookups could be made. Poor and working-class Chicagoans, unable to afford the hookup fees and indoor plumbing, remained in low-cost, unserviced areas. By 1873, maps of the sewer system and maps of property values show a near direct correspondence between higher property values and high concentrations of sewer lines. Sewer lines grew increasingly rare as property values declined. Sharply divided by income levels, rich and poor Chicagoans also were increasingly divided geographically.[30]

Changes in property values resulting from the advent of indoor plumbing separated some Chicagoans from others, while also creating new bonds of common daily experiences and political concerns among others, sometimes crossing ethic boundaries, sometimes linking the interests of the regularly employed skilled laborers with those of the city's salaried workers. Just north of the Chicago River, sewers bridged differences between the German and Scandinavian mechanics who had protested the fire limits ordinance and the striving entrepreneurs who had met at O. Raggio's. The blocks of brick and frame houses owned by German and Scandinavian laborers as well as the streets edging Lincoln Park enjoyed heavy concentrations of sewer lines and rising property values. Sections of the West Side, where real estate was most expensive and where skilled workers owned homes, also had sewer services. But large sections of the jam-packed immigrant communities, the rows of frame cottages and two- and three-family houses owned by wage laborers, remained unconnected through much of the 1880s. Tenants and home owners on the Brophys' block, as on blocks to the west and south, continued to share back alley privies and to lug water from city pumps. Sewers, water lines, and the sinks, toilets, and bathing rooms appearing in some neighborhoods were further dividing urban residents according to income, skill, housing design, and ultimately health.[31]

In the 1880s, Chicago's wealthier families began to separate their enclaves, the blocks and neighborhoods where property values were highest, from other residential areas by forming neighborhood associations to pay for underfunded municipal services. Rather than urge the Common Council to better finance and improve street cleaning and scavenger work, wealthier home owners simply turned to privately financed remedies, an option not available to the city's poorer residents. In 1884, the *Tribune* reported that many wealthy home owners formed associations to pay private companies to sweep their sidewalks, clean nearby streets, and collect garbage. Police services in wealthier neighborhoods were similarly financed. "There is not an aristocratic section of the city that is not compelled to maintain a private police force, and yet thousands of dollars are yearly expended for police protection," the *Tribune* noted. Citing corruption and "imperfect management" for causing the problem, the disgusted *Tribune* reporter added, "the city is positively suffering for sewers."[32] Whether sewers or street cleaning, sanitation costs increasingly separated residential districts, a shift that did not go unnoticed by those who sought to profit from investments in landed property.

In the 1880s and 1890s, Chicago's builders and politicians and the city's wealthiest families effectively directed municipal funds to areas designated for new enclaves of expensive residences, using infrastructure improvements to enhance property values and to clearly identify housing, or whole communities, that were designed specifically for more affluent home owners. "Groups of promoters and politicians," Homer Hoyt wrote, "combined to secure such public improvements as sewers, water pipes, and wooden block

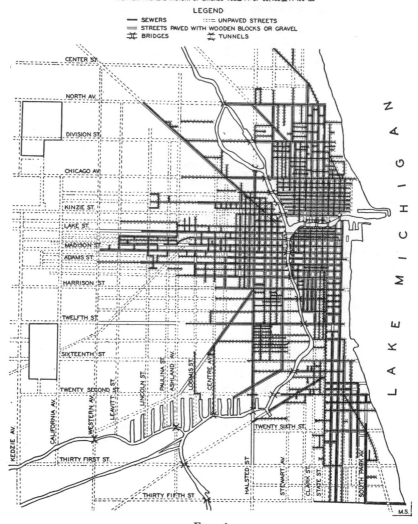

10. Map: Sewers, paved streets, and bridges. Homer Hoyt, *One Hundred Years of Land Values in Chicago: The Relationship of the Growth of Chicago to the Rise of Its Land Values, 1830-1933* (Chicago: University of Chicago Press, 1933) 92.

MAP OF CHICAGO
–SHOWING–
LAND VALUES – 1873
AVERAGE VALUES FOR EACH SQUARE MILE IN DOLLARS PER ACRE
SOURCE: ACTUAL SALES

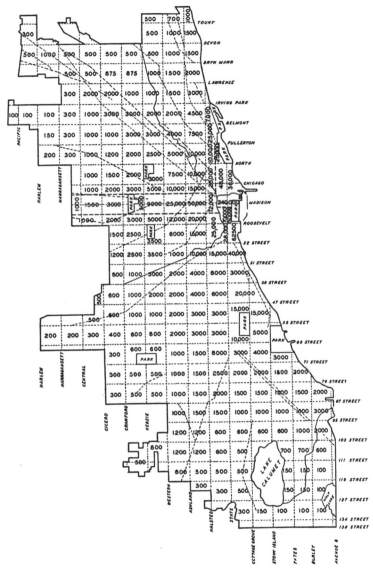

FIG. 21

11. Land values by square-mile sections, Homer Hoyt, *One Hundred Years of Land Values in Chicago: The Relationship of the Growth of Chicago to the Rise of Its Land Values, 1830-1933* (Chicago: University of Chicago Press, 1933) 114.

pavements on the streets they had selected for development as fashionable sections." Builders and land speculators, with the acquiescence of public officials, used sewer and water lines to attract more affluent buyers to new, "thoroughly modern sanitary" houses. As sewers and water lines made indoor plumbing available, elite along with middle-class households clustered in newly developed residential communities, some buying houses in suburbs beyond the city limits, increasingly distant from neighborhoods housing recent immigrants and low-skilled laborers.[33]

Rather than moving, skilled workers began demanding that the city put sewer lines in their neighborhoods, giving rise to a new politics of housing. While more affluent Chicagoans formed neighborhood associations to privately finance services, working-class home owners organized to demand public funding for those services, asserting that as property owners and tax payers, their households had "rights" to city-financed services. In 1873, property owners on the West Side issued a petition claiming "the west division paid all the taxes and received none of the benefits." The mayor responded by presenting a *Tribune* reporter with a detailed description of all services and funds allocated to the West Side neighborhoods and asserting that the West Side received more than its share of services. West Side workers met again on May, 22, 1873, at the Workingman's Hall on Twelfth Street, a site often used for labor protests, to demand that the city appropriate funds for "the construction of sewers as a sanitary measure; also a full and reliable system of scavenger labor; the distribution of pure water." The group also noted that "we very much doubt the propriety, at the present time, of purchasing land for new parks" and created a "Sanitary and Improvement Committee" to represent the neighborhood. Not for another decade would much of the area receive sewers. By then, West Side residents had "from one to three times a year" been "subjected to the greatest inconvenience, and often [have] sustained actual damage to property by the inundation of nearly every foot of ground." Skilled North Side workers, also faced with yearly flooding, organized neighborhood improvement associations to demand sewers and better scavenger services.[34]

Wage laborers, asserting their rights to municipally financed services based on ownership of their homes and their payment of property taxes, worked a remarkable shift in the use of republican rhetoric. Not content with merely voting for representatives in city government, working-class home owners sought government services in return for their property tax dollars. "We will hold our representatives in the City Council to a strict accountability for their actions in this regard," the West Side petitioners wrote. They would "withhold their taxes" until they had "some guarantee that their interests and rights would not be wholly neglected." Until the Civil War, republican theory, which informed American politics and law, linked claims to political rights to proprietary claims to productive property, land, or skills and tools. But in industrialized urban centers in the late nineteenth century, those who did not own the mechanisms of industrial production, the factories and workshops scattered around the city, looked to proprietary claims over their dwellings to legitimize rights-based claims to public services. Industrial laborers, of course, formed organizations based on their relationships to their employers. They also organized within the boundaries of their neighborhoods and around their proprietary interests in their homes to claim rights as citizens and make claims on the municipal government.[35]

Neighborhood improvement associations, cementing political bonds among neighbors, helped to set the boundaries of increasingly cohesive and distinct neighborhoods. The groups, which in essence formalized and expanded the networks of capital circulation among working-class home owners, shifted the balance of political organization and power from City Hall to the city's neighborhoods. Organizing block by block, skilled workers petitioned their aldermen, who then introduced ordinances before the council for sewer lines on their streets. "Almost every Alderman has made some request for a sewer in his ward," the *Tribune* reported in 1877. "As the time approaches for the passage of the appropriation bill, the Aldermen have been particularly active in piling up 'imperative demands' for sewers." By organizing residents within distinct geographic boundaries, skilled workers helped to create the organized constituencies for the powerful ward organizations that by the final decades of the century distributed jobs and services in return for votes and money. Where skilled workers organized neighborhood improvement associations, sewers generally were provided and property values increased.[36]

The political maneuvering of skilled workers to gain sewers for their blocks functioned to further divide the working classes both geographically and by standard of living. By the early twentieth century, several blocks of the Back of the Yards neighborhood, the sprawling South Side community surrounding the packinghouses, were distinguished from the rest of the neighborhood by the residents' higher skill levels and enhanced housing amenities. Winchester and Robey Streets, the neighborhood's most expensive, were lined with brick houses owned by skilled laborers, typically of German descent. Most were immigrant families who had lived in the city for more than a decade and had managed to save money to pay off their loans and to pay for sewer and water services. Unlike the children of unskilled workers on nearby blocks, their children were likely to move into skilled and white-

collar occupations. Skilled workers, generally home owners, successfully deployed their political influence to improve their housing conditions, creating enclaves of serviced districts within working-class communities and leaving the less skilled and more recent immigrants to the houses and tenements
that were unconnected to sewer lines.[37] In some sections of the city, workers
who were less skilled or had lower-wage jobs organized to fight the introduction of sewers, refusing to pay the cost of connecting their homes to the
system. Their determination to keep taxes and property assessments to a
minimum, their commitment to property rights in housing even when they
could not afford indoor plumbing, heightened the contrast between serviced and unserviced areas.[38]

Instead of purchasing health by buying a house, the unskilled relied on
the health and vigor of the household's wage laborers to purchase houses. By
the late 1880s and through the turn of the century, unskilled packinghouse
workers, mostly recent immigrants from central and southern Europe, were
buying houses on "easy payment" plans. "These payments," wrote Mary Mc-
Dowell, founder of the University of Chicago Settlement House, "depended
upon the health of the family and the continuous work of the father, who
was able to make less than 21 cents an hour when he had work." Unable to
afford sewer hookups and indoor plumbing, unskilled workers in the Southwest Side neighborhood were more likely to suffer from contagious disease
than their wealthier neighbors living in sewered areas. Illness or injury,
which was a common occurrence in the packing industry, could force the
family to forgo payments, leaving them homeless or seeking rental space in
the neighborhood's increasingly crowded tenements. While most families
paid for death insurance to cover the cost of a "decent" funeral, "sickness
was the great risk that was not insured." For those forced to pay doctors' bills
and unable to make up for lost wages, "sickness meant expense that often
stopped payments on the mortgaged home that was being purchased on installments." Rather than acquiring health through property rights, unskilled
workers living in unsewered areas often found they had to choose between
home ownership and health.[39]

Poorer home owners often gained support from an unlikely source: the
larger land owners who owned multiple rental properties in working-class
neighborhoods. Landlords, sometimes neighborhood residents and sometimes more affluent investors, sought to draw profit from their properties by
minimizing capital investments, such as sewer fees and indoor plumbing. As
property values in unsewered areas remained lower than in serviced districts,
areas lacking sewer lines or in which large numbers of property owners refused to connect their buildings to existing sewer pipes attracted growing

numbers of recent immigrants, black migrants from the rural south, and un-skilled workers who could not afford houses or apartments along the slightly more expensive blocks of skilled working-class communities. "A house with plumbing was very expensive; so wherever it was possible to avoid plumb-ing it was avoided," recalled Hilda Satt Polacheck, a Polish Jewish immi-grant. For recent immigrants, the unskilled, and the irregularly employed, in-door plumbing so increased the cost of housing that it was an amenity, even a luxury, that could not be acquired.[40]

At the turn of the century, landlords, employing a variety of strategies to hold down capital investments, vividly demonstrated the Health Depart-ment's legal distinctions between the rights of tenants and those living in single-family houses. In areas where land speculators bought up rows of multifamily dwellings, seeing property rights in housing as an investment, which should generate profits, living conditions rapidly deteriorated. Most heavily burdened by this property system were African-Americans, particu-larly the most impoverished and most recent arrivals from the south, who by 1900 faced both growing housing costs and increasingly rigid racial segrega-tion of the housing market. The expanding Black Belt, home to well over half of the city's 30,000 African-American population in 1906, received few sew-ers and few other sanitation services in the late nineteenth and early twenti-eth centuries. Since white land speculators owned most of the buildings occupied by African-Americans, black tenants and civic activists could not deploy property rights claims to demand infrastructure improvements. Nor could black tenants rely on the Health Department, which, if called, typi-cally cited renters for building ordinance violations but rarely enforced housing regulations in the neighborhood. Fannie Barrier Williams, a South Side resident and settlement house volunteer, commented in 1905 that though black Chicagoans did "not occupy all the worst streets and live in all the unsanitary houses in Chicago, what is known as the 'Black Belt' is alto-gether forbidding and demoralizing." Property in housing, conceived as an investment as profitable as corporate stock, allowed the neighborhood's property owners to maximize profits by rejecting capital investments in their properties, refusing to install indoor plumbing in rental dwellings.[41]

Though rents in the Black Belt tended to be higher than in other working-class neighborhoods, African-Americans did not receive cleaner or more san-itary dwellings for their money. Instead, most found that landlords, guiding the racial segregation of the city's housing market, raised rents and provided few if any services to their tenants. When Alzada P. Comstock, a Mount Holyoke sociologist, surveyed the neighborhood in 1912, she reported that most buildings were constructed before the 1902 tenement ordinance was passed and that a majority of apartments lacked indoor toilets. The ordinance, which required indoor plumbing in all new construction, was hardly enforced along the streets lined with multifamily frame dwellings. In a housing market increasingly divided by the race and economic resources of residents, and in a rental market in which wages hardly kept pace with rising rents, landlords refusing to pay for sewer hookups and indoor plumbing facilities could continue to profit from their investments in residential property.[42]

While landlords amassed ever-larger profits by rejecting plumbing facilities, builders used sewer and water services to market single-family homes in outlying areas. Rail lines often opened new land to development; sewer and water lines were as important an element in the growth of communities beyond the built-up area of the city.[43] Builders and developers used the requirement that the city respond to their petitions for street paving at the home owners' cost to secure water and sewerage services at the city's expense. When the Common Council approved the street paving petitions with the paving costs borne by property owners, the Department of Public Works was compelled to lay water and sewer pipe to save the cost of tearing up the streets in the future. With this complex system of financing road paving and sewer construction, undeveloped tracts of land edging the city often gained sewer services before the homes in some of the older built-up neighborhoods had indoor plumbing.[44]

Along with the plumbing fixtures that supplied it, health had become an amenity to be purchased through the city's expanding single-family housing market. While some tenants and working-class home owners rejected indoor plumbing because of the cost, builders seeking to develop a new market of middle-class buyers advertised the healthful environments of their single-family homes. "The question of pure water is one of the most important in the selection of a home," an 1890 brochure for the new North Shore suburb of Kenilworth proclaimed. Needing a strong marketing tool to draw the middle-classes out of their apartments and into new houses further away from the city center, builders like Joseph Sears, who was advertising lots and cottages in Kenilworth, stressed the suburban community's "improvements," such as "water, gas, sewers" and "healthy land." Health, it seemed, could be acquired with the purchase of a home.[45]

The selective distribution of sewer and water services, as the City Homes Association recognized, came at a cost to the city's poor and unskilled laborers. The ability of builders and wealthier home owners to leverage modest capital to generate government resources to enhance their property values and their health left the city's poorer residents living in unsewered and disease-plagued districts. Graphs of the city's disparate mortality rates and property values by ward, ever more stark as the century wore on, generally correspond to maps of the wage and skill levels in residential communities. Neighborhoods with high mortality rates and lower property values tended to have fewer per capita feet of sewer lines than communities with low mortality rates. Health commissioner John Rauch noted in 1873, "Little did these parties think or care that the enhanced value of the property incident to drainage was at the expense of the lives of some of their fellow beings, to whom life is as near and dear as to themselves." Five years later, the recently appointed health commissioner, Oscar Coleman De Wolf, presented the Common Council with a report linking the lack of sewers to the growth of disease. Arguing that there were "nearly 100 percent more deaths from filth diseases" in wards of the city not yet provided with sewers, De Wolf pleaded for more city financing for sewer construction.[46]

The health commissioner's pleas for new sewers in poorer neighborhoods were outweighed by official refusal to fund them and by changes in the housing market that left unsewered buildings and blocks increasingly isolated from more affluent neighborhoods. While the tenement problem attracted concern from some city residents and reformers, it did not inspire those with their hands on the city treasury, nor those with political influence, to invest large amounts of money in new sewer and water facilities to serve those neighborhoods. Fewer sewers and higher mortality rates tended, not surprisingly, to force down property values, creating whole neighborhoods that were seemingly designed for the city's poorest families.[47]

The lack of sanitation services in the impoverished immigrant neighborhood surrounding the University of Chicago Settlement near the packinghouses offers a stark portrait of the municipal government's retreat from providing sewer and garbage services to impoverished communities in the 1890s. In 1894, the year stockyard workers launched a bloody and failed strike for an eight-hour day, Mary McDowell, who had spent four years at Hull House, the city's first social settlement, moved into a four-room apartment on the second floor rear of a wooden tenement building on Gross Avenue at the heart of the home to thousands of unskilled packinghouse workers. Intending to offer educational and charitable services, as well as to "Americanize" immigrant packinghouse workers, McDowell soon found herself involved in more mundane pursuits. Back of the Yards had become a dumping ground for the city's garbage; the neighborhood had few sewers, and most streets, with the exception of Forty-seventh Street and Ashland

Avenue, were dirt. In some sections, one in three children died within their first year. Living conditions in the neighborhood stood in sharp contrast to Hyde Park, a middle-class community a few miles to the east, where nearly all the streets were paved and all homes serviced with sewer and water lines.[48]

McDowell helped organize unskilled workers in Back of the Yards to demand the Common Council remove city dumps from their neighborhood, increase garbage collection, and construct drainage and sewer pipes along the neighborhood's streets. Among McDowell's proudest moments was a protest before the council's finance committee in the spring of 1900. Hundreds of workers "gave up a day's wages" to attend the hearing and demand that a private company, the Chicago Reduction Company, stop dumping garbage in their neighborhood. Arguing that the city largely ignored the sprawling community of unskilled stockyard workers, McDowell charged that the neighborhood had become "a district segregated for unpleasant things," including odors, smoke, garbage, and an open cesspool. The protesters were successful in pushing the council to relocate the city's dumps, but the neighborhood did not gain complete sewage, drainage, or garbage removal services until the 1920s. In an essay entitled "City Waste," written in 1927, McDowell described the protest, adding that the "dirt and filth" pouring from the neighborhood's densely packed homes was a leading cause of the community's spiraling mortality rates, a problem, she added, that city officials chose to ignore.[49]

McDowell was right. By the mid-1890s, requests for funding for sewer services and elaborate graphs mapping mortality rates to the city's sewer system had largely disappeared from Department of Health reports. While in 1885 sewers along with accompanying graphs and maps of sewer lines had constituted nearly a third of health commissioner De Wolf's yearly report, by 1894 the department's chief inspector for the bureau of sanitary inspection, Andrew Young, took just 6 pages in the 268-page report to discuss sewage, drainage, light, and air in the city's homes. A typhoid fever epidemic raging through the city's West Side in the summer of 1902 graphically demonstrated the Health Department's approach to enforcing existing housing codes. The West Side ward contained just one-thirty-sixth of the city's population, but registered one-sixth of the total typhoid deaths. When Hull House residents conducted a housing survey to identify the causes of the epidemic, Jane Addams remembered, "It was discovered that the wretched sanitary appliances through which alone the infection could have become so widely spread would not have been permitted to remain, unless the city inspector had either been criminally careless or open to the arguments of favored landlords." Hull House launched a campaign to identify negligent landlords and corrupt building inspectors. Protests resulted in a "[l]ong and stirring trial before the civil service board" and the firing of eleven Health Department employees. The resulting publicity, Addams commented, did little to improve sanitary conditions in West Side tenements, but it further strained Hull House volunteers as the settlement house's work, including uncovering "graft in connection with the plumbers unions," generated new hostility from neighborhood property owners.[50]

As the elite and middle classes retreated to private homes in well-serviced neighborhoods, city officials explicitly placed new emphasis on individual initiatives to improve urban sanitation. Rather than requesting extensions to the system, Commissioner Young used his yearly reports to exhort all Chicagoans to take on the responsibility of ensuring that their homes were sanitary. "If every individual in a city appreciated the fact that he is to some extent responsible for the condition of the public health, and in order to keep his conscience clear would keep his own back yard, cellar, alley and street in good condition, the reports of the Commissioner of Health would show the result of the multiplied effort in the annual death rate," he proclaimed. "Everyone can do a little, if only to make one room more bright, more cleanly, more wholesome." While McDowell repeatedly asserted that low wages and irregular employment were directly linked to the inadequate shelter and poor health of many urban workers, Young glossed over possible causes for the city's death rate. He instead asserted, "Health is wealth. Sickness in a community breeds demoralization, vice and crime, and adds to the burdens borne by the citizen and the community at large."[51]

Despite growing acceptance of the germ theory of disease, Young offered a complex, and slightly convoluted, explanation of the causality of disease, reviving the old formula of linking immorality with poor health. "The fact is clear to us that crime is begotten by sin, and sin begotten by disease, disease begotten by filth and filth begotten by ignorance and neglect of the individual or the inefficiency of the agencies employed by the municipality to correct such conditions." Yet in his view, the municipality and its health department were hardly inefficient. "So beneficial have been their [the health inspectors'] operation that to-day the bath and toilet rooms of our hotels and residences are the altars of cleanliness, luxurious in their appointments, tasteful in every detail and construction. The bath and toilet room has justly taken its place as the first room in the home."[52] No doubt, the housing reformers five years later were surprised to learn that the "bath and toilet" rooms in the homes of large numbers of impoverished Chicagoans were either nonexistent or in dangerously defective condition.

————

As sewage and water systems transformed the urban environment, separating the neighborhoods of skilled from those of unskilled workers, laborers of European descent from African-Americans, and elite enclaves from impoverished urban communities, waste and water services also dramatically altered the home's interior and the labor required to maintain it. Managed and produced by wives, daughters, and servants, the home, which the rhetoric of industrial society, women's literature, and household advice guides removed from market relations, was increasingly viewed as producing the health of the family and surrounding community. "I want to strongly enforce that it is the women on whom full sanitary light requires to fall," one sanitary reformer commented. "Health in the home is health everywhere."[53] Sewer and water services, the buried mechanisms for producing health, transformed working conditions for women in the home and further strained the ideology that made invisible the waged and unwaged labor they performed.

Running water and pipes for waste removal revolutionized cooking, cleaning, and bathing. Once the city put water pipes on the street and the property owner paid the fees to connect the pipes to the building, it was possible to install indoor plumbing with water closets replacing backyard privies and kitchen sinks with faucets replacing washtubs filled at city hydrants. With running water, women no longer had to haul buckets of water from the hydrants or the lake. Efficient waste removal, including sinks and bathtubs connected to drainage pipes, and toilets, eliminated the constant and hated chores of carrying filthy water and waste out of the home. Whether these facilities actually cut back on the labor performed by wives and daughters is debated.[54] What's clear is that the labor changed.

In Chicago, water pumpage grew from approximately eight billion gallons in 1870 to over eighty-six billion in 1893, and the per capita consumption more than doubled from 72.8 gallons per day to 146.8.[55] More water meant more bathing and more washing, setting new standards for personal hygiene and household cleanliness. It also meant more commodities to be washed and more frequent cleaning. Eliminating the weekly drudgery of carrying buckets of water in and out of the house, running water permitted women to fill laundry tubs directly from the sink and drain dirty water through the pipes. Sewer hookups, running water, and water closets inside the home eliminated the chore of collecting slops, but added the work of cleaning toilets. (Cleaning outhouses and cesspools had previously been contracted to commercial enterprises, or a collective task of several families, or left undone.) The water closet privatized some household labor while sinks with running water expanded the number of commodities to be washed and the frequency of the cleaning, placing new burdens on individual women and setting new criteria for assessing a woman's household skills.[56]

Higher standards for household cleanliness created more work for domestic servants, inspired new calls for the efficient management of the home, and restructured the relationship between an employer and her servants. With indoor plumbing, the estimated 15 to 30 percent of Chicago households with live-in servants (another 20 percent hired domestic workers who lived elsewhere) were increasingly and explicitly enmeshed in the industrial city. Undermining the rhetoric that defined the home as a pastoral refuge from industrial labor relations, indoor plumbing contributed to a redefinition of the home. Lucy Maynard Salmon, whose book, *Domestic Service*, became a well-known guide for middle-class women, enhanced the social value of work performed within the home by equating household labor with factory work. With household health as a goal and efficiency as the means of achieving health, the employer was advised to delegate the various household tasks and "subdivide the labor" performed by each household worker. New household technology, Salmon argued, would ease the transition to the scientifically managed home. "It is idle to complain of poor servants and of poor mistresses so long as domestic service is divorced from general labor questions and employers everywhere are ignorant of the economic laws, principles, and conditions underlying the household." In the efficiently managed home, the employer would replace the "familial bonds of the colonial period" with a clearly defined relationship between the wage laborer and the employer. The home would come to embody the market relations of the industrial city.[57]

In the final decades of the century, manufacturers introduced new lines of household machinery associated with running water, appliances that added to the cost of housing and further distinguished the homes of the more affluent city dwellers from those of the laboring and impoverished classes. The washing machines marketed by Sears and Montgomery Ward fitted with hand-cranked agitators and priced between two and six dollars once again transformed household labor. Metal mixers circulated dirty clothes through soapy water, eliminating washboards and hand scrubbing. Sears also offered sinks, washbasins, and urinals designed to connect to water and waste pipes.[58] But those who could afford it did not bother with washing machines. Instead, they sent their clothes to commercial laundry services that

12. Girls carrying laundry tub. Chicago Commons Collection, Chicago Historical Society.

sprang up around the city. With the commercialization of one of the most labor-intensive chores in the household, laundries proved highly popular, until after the turn of the century when manufacturers began mass-producing electric washing machines and laundry was again returned to the private home. But during the final decades of the nineteenth century, what had once been unwaged labor performed in the private home became wage labor for working-class women. And if the laboring women who worked in commercial laundries could not afford the household machinery, or the garments and the time required to cleanse them, the middle classes could display their wealth and social influence by adorning themselves in newly cleaned clothes. Just as the aspiration for home ownership revealed much about an urban dweller's social position, the city's residents increasingly elaborated their status in Chicago's social order through the design of their houses, the type and extent of household labor required to maintain them, and the products— the clean clothes, well-scrubbed bodies, and healthy workers—issued by that labor.[59]

For households that could not afford the capital investment in sewers, water fees, and plumbing fixtures, household sanitation remained labor intensive, made even more burdensome by new standards for cleanliness. Even at the end of the century, poor women continued to haul water from urban street hydrants and dump household wastewater into the streets and alleys near their homes. Even bathing was hard work. "I still recall the huge kettles of water being heated on the stove and the wash tub being dragged into the kitchen for our weekly baths," wrote Hilda Satt Polacheck. "But we did get scrubbed once a week. There were, however, many people in the neighborhood who did not have the stamina for carrying kettles of hot water."[60] By the turn of the century, the homes of those "who did not have the stamina" for lugging buckets of water and waste in and out of the house or for scrubbing filthy privies were emblems of an increasingly isolated but ever-larger mass of the urban poor. In the daily labor of household cleaning and in the elaborate rituals of regular bathing and putting on clean clothes each morning, in the capital investment in indoor plumbing, the middle classes and skilled workers sharpened the lines separating them from the city's poor and lower-working classes.

The urban sanitation movement reached its peak in the 1870s and 1880s, as engineers and health reformers filled women's magazines and architectural and building journals with detailed instructions on household cleanliness. In 1872, a group of physicians, engineers, professors, architects, and others formed the American Public Health Association, creating a forum for discussions of and research into a variety of subjects under the umbrella of sanitary science. In articles published around the country, association members' interests ranged from municipal waste removal to epidemic diseases, from quarantine to sanitation standards for factories to adulterated foods. Mostly, however, the sanitarians, as this burgeoning group of professionals came to be known, were concerned with life and health in the expanding American cities. Inspired by new knowledge about disease causation, a devotion to science, and a determination to ameliorate the dangerous effects of industrialization, the sanitarians described the city as an interconnected whole, an organic entity whose growth and health were governed by scientific principles.[61]

Sewerage and clean water services, the networks of pipes connecting homes throughout the city, were among their most prominent projects, concrete achievements in public health work and, almost as importantly, a useful metaphor for the sanitarians' aims. In the "modern" era, one municipal engineer stated, cities had "been transformed from loose aggregates" of scattered houses "into well-organized systems" of "intimately connected" elements. The streets and sidewalks transporting people, the underground pipes carrying water, waste and gas—all functioned as "component parts" of a "wonderful" machine. In sanitation, the sanitarians argued, "there is a perfect solidarity among all the inhabitants of any given town or city." In their enthusiasm for the interconnectedness of all urban residents, all infrastructure, all forms of property and housing, the sanitarians effectively, and conveniently, neglected those who for lack of capital—whether tenants or home owners—were unable to install indoor plumbing in their homes.[62]

Under the guidance of the sanitarians and domestic advice givers, the home became a showplace for the latest plumbing technology. Advice columns in *Good Housekeeping* urged women to remove ornate cabinetwork around kitchen sinks and bedroom washbasins. As Harriette Plunkett wrote in 1885, "There is a growing fashion of arranging all fixtures in what is called the 'open' manner." Readers of Plunkett's exhaustive guide on household sanitation, *Women, Plumbers, and Doctors,* were told that openness and simplicity of design were the keys to proper household sanitation. "The bathtubs stand up on feet, the lavatory-slabs are supported by metallic brackets, and the whole arrangement leaves no dark corners to become filthy," she wrote.[63] By the century's final decade, manufacturers could mass-produce porcelain sinks, tubs, and toilets, and American builders and home buyers could choose plumbing fixtures from standardized lines of products. Those who could afford indoor plumbing, then, could purchase or build homes fitted according to a standard design that further distinguished the homes of the poor from the rest of the urban populace and changed very little in future years.[64]

The sanitarians further enhanced the legitimacy of their advice with the emergence of a new and deadly threat to household health. Sewer gas, produced in the vast network of pipes scattered through the walls of the house and beneath urban streets, proved a national menace. Stories circulated through magazines and newspapers described the lethal vapor that threatened the homes of rich and poor, urban and rural Americans. Seeping up through poorly ventilated and corroded pipes, the sickly odor passed through the traps designed to prevent a backwash in sink and toilet drains, permeating the homes of even the most careful housewife. "Ten years ago," Plunkett commented, "nobody comprehended the fatal risk he ran in not excluding sewer-air from his house." Stories abounded of whole families sickened and killed by this household evil. In articles published throughout the country, sanitarians debated the causes and solutions to this threat, urging builders and home buyers to seek out expert advice on how best to install indoor plumbing.[65]

Expert advice could be found in women's magazines, which became a central forum for the sanitarians' debates and exhortations, advertising plumbing fixtures as an essential element of an efficient, scientifically managed home. "Domestic science" became the basis of a national home economics movement that emphasized science, efficiency, and rationality in the home. The emerging field of home economics urged a uniformity in home design, standardized cleaning practices, and "modern" plumbing fixtures, new weapons to fight the new but ever-present dangers of germs, sewer gases, and disease. "Personal cleanliness takes on a new meaning and all the daily operations of the house and school and city are elevated into the region of scientific work, done according to well-known laws," wrote Ellen H. Richards, an instructor in the new field of sanitary chemistry at the Massachusetts Institute of Technology. Richards, considered the founder of the field of home economics, urged wives and mothers to gain "specific" training in the science of household hygiene. Indoor plumbing had remade the home into a site for the scientific management of labor and the production of the household's most valuable commodity, health. Home ownership combined with the resources to install indoor plumbing and the use of property rights to make claims on public finances had become the basis for the new properly managed family home.[66]

By the final decade of the nineteenth century, the urban house had been transformed from an isolated unit to a part of service system connecting it with other homes and with publicly financed and regulated services. Comfort and health at home depended not only on the cleaning skills of its occupants but also on the financial resources of the household and the availability of service connections in the street outside the home. The leaders of the sanitary reform movement had imagined an organic entity whose individual parts were connected by networks of underground pipes, where the boundaries marking the private home were traversed by a municipally owned system of water and waste removal, where the individual's moral responsibility for the health of his household was replaced by a civic responsibility for the well-being of the community at large. This dream, articulated in scores of articles and pamphlets, had instead achieved a city sharply divided, a community of interdependent consumers and another of impoverished households excluded from the new urban water and waste systems.[67]

During the decades when the sanitarians were most influential around the country, their articles were read by middle-class men and women in Chicago, by builders who sought to use their language to sell houses, and by manufacturers who sought to use public concern about health to sell new household technology. Even as the sanitarians' ideas spread, the city government was retreating from its midcentury commitment to provide all Chicagoans with clean water and efficient waste disposal. As those services were privatized and increasingly treated as amenities, middle-class and skilled working-class Chicagoans looked to home ownership to ensure the health of their households, and they generated a new rights-based language to lay claim to municipally financed services. While asserting proprietary claims to the well-being of their neighborhoods, home owners also turned inward, looking to fit their own homes with the latest technology and ignoring the growing environmental crises just blocks away. In a sense, the sanitarians' proposals and articles functioned to render invisible those homes not connected to the services, those left out of the new water and waste consumer network, those who would increasingly be relegated to unsanitary dwellings and impoverished neighborhoods. As well-to-do Chicagoans began purchasing health with home ownership and moving from the city center to new "healthy," single-family houses on the edge of the city, the urban poor were increasingly isolated and neglected by the public officials charged with maintaining the city's housing stock.

Selling Health, Independence, and Home Ownership

In 1873, as Chicago sank into economic depression, the Riverside Improvement Company went bankrupt. Launched by a group of New York investors five years earlier, the company had set out to build a model suburb. Riverside was designed by the nation's most famous landscape architects, Frederick Law Olmsted and Calvert Vaux, the men responsible for New York's Central Park. The 1,600-acre suburb, located just nine miles west of Chicago, was projected to include scores of single-family houses scattered along the banks of the Des Plaines River. Advertisements for Riverside highlighted its healthy supply of clean water, landscaped lawns and shade trees, and the train depot with a regular commuter line running into downtown Chicago. But the reconstruction of Chicago after the fire absorbed much eastern investment capital, and the economic depression halted housing sales. Although the community eventually was completed, Riverside was "an impressive failure."[1]

Twenty years later, when another severe economic depression hit the Chicago region, a south suburban community fared much better. The builder, Samuel Eberly Gross, had begun selling houses in Grossdale in 1889. Like the Riverside developers, he publicized the community's healthy environment, picturesque lawns, and commuter train depot. The economic slump slowed sales, but Grossdale quickly recovered and Gross continued to prosper. Although the two suburban communities and the circumstances surrounding their development differed in many respects, the success of Grossdale rested in large part on the ability of late nineteenth-century builders to transform the process of building and marketing single-family homes. In the 1890s, as the city's industries were increasingly held by large corporations, as growing numbers of native-born white men held salaried jobs as accountants, lawyers, and managers in corporate office buildings, house builders effectively marketed home ownership to the city's professional and salaried classes. No longer simply a financial boon to struggling working-class households, home ownership gradually emerged in the 1890s as a symbol of middle-class autonomy, gender order, and status.

In the twenty years between Riverside's bankruptcy and Grossdale's success, a younger generation of businessman-builders developed elaborate strategies to promote sales of single-family homes beyond the built-up sections of the city. Labor leaders and writers, giving voice to the aspirations of the immigrant working classes, had articulated a version of home ownership that linked property rights in housing to an assertion of American identity and autonomy for the industrial wage laborers. In the 1890s, the house builders who marketed ever-larger and more expensive houses on the edges of the city revised the older version of the home ownership ideal.[2] In the advertisements lining the pages of the *Chicago Daily Tribune* and *Chicago Times*, property rights in housing were linked to the aspirations and status of a new, increasingly consumer-oriented middle-class, to the manhood and independence of clerks, accountants, lawyers, and corporate administrators. Not entirely distinct from the working-class immigrants' vision, the emerging middle-class attraction to property rights in housing drew new attention to home ownership as an investment that would enhance status, secure gender order, safeguard family health, and prove, as builders asserted, a "useful investment" for aspiring and more affluent families.[3] Probably no builder-developer was more responsible for producing and exploiting a new cultural ideal of home ownership than Samuel Eberly Gross.

———

Though the native-born, urban doctors, lawyers, and small business owners had used the decor, design, and location of their homes to distinguish themselves from the immigrant working classes, few among the middle classes pursued property rights in housing with the same zeal as their immigrant neighbors in the 1870s and 1880s. The city's custom of long-term leasing of both land and housing had since midcentury provided many native-born skilled workers and lower-middle-class families with rental houses. Long-term leases, some as long as twenty-one years, coupled with an elaborate system of subleasing unimproved lots, blurred distinctions between renting and owning single-family dwellings. Even those who sought to purchase single-family dwellings tended to reject sites beyond the built-up area of the city, where acres of less expensive and undeveloped land were available. A lack of efficient transportation systems combined with a widespread view that outlying locales were less respectable home sites hampered sales of lots and houses in the very places where builders could most efficiently build single-family houses.[4]

The city's most affluent families purchased or built mansions in elite districts, like that along Prairie Avenue just south of the Loop, but were reticent to move to suburban sites outside the city. In 1889, Joseph Sears, developer of Kenilworth, purchased 223 acres of farmland, "a thick tangle of woods . . . and along the lake a cleared area under cultivation," to build the elite North Shore suburb. His neighbors along Prairie Avenue—the Pullmans, the Armours, and others—"admired but questioned Joseph Sears' courage," wrote Sears's biographer, Colleen Browne Kilner. "Only in summer did they evacuate their town houses for the North Shore. It was scarcely the place for an all-year-round residence." Drawing on the recollections of Sears's daughter, Dorothy, the biographer, with some exaggeration, calls Kenilworth "a pioneer experiment." Houses in the semirural landscape surrounding the city were not new, but elite and middle-class Chicagoans remained, through the 1880s, skeptical of the social value of residential property in suburban locales.[5]

In the early 1880s, apartments became a popular form of dwelling for the city's aspiring white-collar workers. Commercial banks began to issue mortgage bonds, generating new capital for the construction industry; with larger amounts of credit available, builders could more easily construct larger buildings. New multistory apartment buildings, built near the city's center, attracted large numbers of middle-income families, setting off what the *Tribune* called "flat fever." Lacking the income necessary to build elegant mansions and disdaining "workingman's cottages," many of the middle classes rented suites of rooms in "family hotels." By 1883, a real estate reporter noted that apartments had sprung up "almost as if by magic on every main and cross street in the city."[6]

Even some elite families debated the merits of elegant apartments versus single-family houses. In 1886 and 1887, when Mary Brewster Laflin appealed to her son Louis and his wife Josephine to move from New York back to Chicago with their newborn son Laurence, she filled her letters with descriptions of apartment hotels ("flats at The Carleton"), convenient neighborhoods, and single-family houses. Mary's husband George, who owned a slaughterhouse and some Chicago real estate, finally decided to purchase a house for the young family. The father did not buy a new house since, in his wife's opinion, "if you were building, you would find something wrong when done," and few of the new houses were in neighborhoods that Mrs. Laflin considered acceptable for her son. The choice between renting or buying a house or renting an apartment had been widely debated in the letters sent between Chicago and New York in the months before the younger Laflins moved to their Chicago home. Ownership of a single-family house was not the obvious or inevitable choice for the young, affluent family.[7]

Yet while apartment hotels filled demand for middle-class rental dwellings, an effort was under way to expand the market for single-family houses. While some businessman-builders began by targeting an existing market of skilled immigrant workers, many also sought to develop new marketing strategies to promote home ownership to those who could most easily afford single-family houses, the middle classes. Health and housing reformers provided the builders with a new language to apply to housing sales, streetcar and railroad companies improved access to undeveloped sites, municipal officials—often land speculators themselves—provided public money for park, sewer, and street construction, and newspaper advertising offered an avenue to a wider consumer market. With promotional strategies tailored to the social conditions of an industrializing city, the builders of the late nineteenth century effectively linked new transportation and construction technology to the language of health reform to encourage urban residents to purchase new single-family homes along the edge of the city's built-up area.

In the summer of 1880, the editors of the *Real Estate and Building Journal*, long disappointed by the sluggish market of the 1870s, set out to encourage investment in residential real estate. The journal, which had been founded by a group of land speculators in 1865, tracked residential and commercial sales, offering builders and speculators a guide to real estate investments. Since 1877, when the real estate market had slowed to a near halt and prices hit their lowest mark in the decade, the journal had offered cautious but optimistic accounts of real estate transactions. By August 1880, however, the journal's editors took a more aggressive approach. Recognizing that the revival of the market depended on new investments in residential real estate—from both home buyers and land speculators—the journal's editors published a series of articles designed to establish the economic value of real estate investments.

The journal's strenuous efforts to define and establish value in real estate is not surprising, perhaps, in an economy in which the social and financial value of landed property was being eclipsed by industry and commercial enterprises. General incorporation acts passed by the state legislatures in the 1840s and 1850s aimed to expand available capital for investments in railroad construction and industry. Incorporating a business and the selling of stock were becoming routine transactions. By the end of the Civil War, shares in railroad corporations, circulating through the stock market, constituted a new form of private property. By the 1880s, a growing number of manufacturing enterprises were incorporated and a few of the larger firms were offering securities for sale to the public. Stocks, bonds—all pieces of paper representing partial ownership in fluctuating business enterprises—forced capitalists, along with legislators and jurists, to reconsider the meanings and values of what counted as private property. Just as the legal system endeavored to redefine the scope of private property rights and regulations, capitalists also faced competing investment options.[8]

Well aware of the expanded meanings and forms of property, the journal moved to persuade readers of the "superiority" of land investments, commenting, "There are so many ways to look at real property, and every way convincing of its superiority over any other thing, that there is no chance left for cavil." Comparing real estate to other investments, the journal continued, "A paper on which a promissory note, draft or agreement is written is worthless when its owner fails. A mine is soon exhausted. . . . A market may become so gorged with some commodities as to cause destruction from non use of millions of dollars worth of fabrics or merchandise. On everything but real estate is written uncertainty."[9]

Yet uncertainty about how to establish value in urban land and residential buildings permeated late nineteenth-century Chicago. In the decades following the Civil War, industrial production attracted capital that earlier generations had invested in land, clouding, but certainly not obscuring, the social value of landed property. Moreover, federal fiscal policies to erase the war debt and put the national economy back on the gold standard conspired to enhance the profits of bankers and merchant-creditors, sorely injuring anyone who had gone into debt to purchase landed property—farmers, land speculators, and home buyers. In this atmosphere, residential real estate stood in a contradictory position: by 1880, land values in Chicago appeared to be climbing, but not at the same rate as corporate, mainly railroad, stock, which often was diluted to increase investor profits. Chicago was experiencing another housing shortage, yet speculators and land syndicates had flooded the market with subdivided lots priced beyond the means of wage laborers. And the handful of land syndicates that had sought to profit from subdividing large tracts of land and marketing lots for single-family homes during and just after the Civil War had either gone bankrupt or retreated from the land speculation business by the late 1870s.[10]

Indeed, speculation in city real estate had proved nearly disastrous to those who had invested just before and after the fire. By 1880, the city had such an oversupply of undeveloped lots that few speculators were willing to risk further investment in undeveloped land. As early as 1870, the supply of subdivided lots far outpaced demand for lots or houses. Even as the population of the city and surrounding region increased substantially over the next fifty years, a surplus of subdivided lots continued to flood the land market. Between 1865 and 1872, more than seventy square miles, or 33 percent of the total area of Chicago was subdivided. The result was such an oversupply of lots that few new subdivisions occurred until the early 1890s. Within the 1873 city limits, only about one-half the platted lots were occupied; from 1868 to 1873 lots enough for a population of one million living in single-family homes had been offered for sale in a city of less than 400,000 people.[11]

Attempting to direct buyers toward the oversupply of subdivided land, the journal sought to infuse value in land that many in Chicago had considered nearly worthless. The vast majority of the subdivided lots lay on the fringe of the city's built-up area, locations that were least attractive to those considering building or buying single-family houses. Although land on the edge of the city was less expensive than land near the city's center, anyone purchasing a lot in the outlying areas would pay additional costs in travel time and transportation to reach jobs in offices and factories. Yet the editors sought to encourage purchases of lots in what it called "suburban" locales, undeveloped tracts both within and outside of the city boundaries. In July 1880, the journal urged subdividers to plant trees and shrubs around their lots, commenting, "The tide of movers will set strongly suburbanward next spring, and it will be for the interest of lot owners to make them as attractive as possible."[12]

Aside from the journal's advice, several land speculators already had attempted to attract buyers to outlying areas by linking their subdivisions to interstate railroad lines and promoting their communities' "easy commute" to downtown Chicago. These efforts had met at best with mixed success. Transportation networks, long considered the primary force driving suburban development, played a complex role in the growth of the region's housing market. The arrival of interstate railroad lines running through the Chicago region in the 1850s and 1860s set off periodic booms in land speculation, but often left speculators holding undeveloped lots. The railroads generated tremendous expansion in the city's trade, manufacturing, and population. Over 100,000 new residents arrived in Chicago between 1850 and 1870, expanding settlement as far north as Chicago Avenue, south to Twelfth Street (later renamed Roosevelt Road), and beyond Halsted Street

to the west.[13] Farming villages and market towns like Barrington and Pala-
tine grew around railroad depots in the 1850s. Land speculators tended to
follow rail routes, subdividing farmland within a few years after the intercity
rail lines were laid. But the construction of intercity lines and the subsequent
subdivision of nearby land by speculators did not prompt large numbers of
Chicago residents to purchase lots and build houses in outlying areas.
Jerome Fellman's detailed study of land use patterns in nineteenth-century
Chicago found that only "isolated quarter sections" on the city's West Side
were sold within five years following interstate railroad construction. Fellman argues that "[a]lthough railroads were greeted with enthusiasm by land
subdividers . . . [m]uch of the area through which they passed was then too
remote from the central city to attract lot purchasers."[14]

With hundreds of acres of subdivided farmland on the market, several
land speculators hedged their bets by promoting their communities as resort
areas. In 1853, a young lawyer from New England, Paul Cornell, purchased
and subdivided three hundred acres of land along the lakefront south of
the city, calling the area Hyde Park. Hoping to develop an elegant resort
community, Cornell built a hotel with an outdoor bandstand and a landing
pier for excursion boats traveling the lakefront. He soon reached an agreement with the Illinois Central Railroad to schedule regular stops nearby. Ten
years later, the forty-eight-acre township of Hyde Park had nearly one thousand year-round residents; but Cornell, still not satisfied, began pushing the
state legislature to approve funding to develop a lakefront park. Similarly, a
group of Chicago businessmen who in 1868 formed the Ravenswood Land
Company and purchased property about eight miles north of Chicago built
the Sunnyside Hotel. Despite the distance from the city center, the Ravenswood lots sold quickly, jumping from $4 to $8 a foot in 1869 to $20 to $30
per foot in 1874. By the 1880s, Ravenswood was one of the city's most exclusive suburbs, with numerous lawyers, doctors, and manufacturers building houses there.[15]

Many other land speculators were not so fortunate. Seeking substantial
profits, subdividers and land speculators put lot prices beyond the reach of
the working classes, yet could not attract enough more affluent households
to home ownership in suburban areas. Despite ominous signs of at least a
few failed suburban enterprises, the journal commented in August 1880, "The
suburbs must grow. The tendency of people is toward them." Three months
later, however, The Chicago Times commented, "There are a great many so-
called suburbs whose names appear on the maps and railroad time tables, in
whose existence there is little more reality than in name." The Chicago Times

seemed to mock *the Real Estate and Building Journal's* optimistic proclamations, noting that even those speculators selling subdivided tracts near railroad depots struggled to make sales. The *Times* continued,

> As a matter of speculation, a tract of land near a line of railway has been subdivided into lots, a depot built by the owner, a name given to the prospective town, the "station" is noted on the railway time cards, a few trains are scheduled to "stop on signal or to leave passengers," and the public is advised that desirable country residence property is for sale cheap and on "time payments" and then the owner sits down to watch and wait. Sometimes he is lucky and his lots are sold; often the "streets" grow up to weeds, the windows in the depot buildings give place to boards, and the weather-beaten bumble down structure is in after years painful evidence that the town on paper was not a success.[16]

Still, in September 1880, the journal's editors, with an inaccuracy that must have been obvious to them, concluded, "[Real estate] is always fixed and has a positive merchantable value." A month later, the journal again sought to reassure land investors, asserting that landed property had "intrinsic" value. "Real estate is property, distinguished from chattels that die, wear out, burn up, decay, or take wings before their possession is realized," the editors wrote. "Real estate is *real* (italics in original) estate. Nothing else is real."[17]

But what counted as "real" was precisely the point of confusion. The *Real Estate and Building Journal* sought to distinguish among investments in industry, loans used to purchase "chattels," and landed property. As the editors surely knew, most people bought land on credit, hoping that the price of the landed property would increase, or at least remain stable, during the period of the loan repayment. A land buyer did not own the land outright until the mortgage was paid off, generally a period of six to eight years. A subdivider, or land speculator, who purchased a tract of land on credit, as most did, paid property taxes and assessment fees for paving streets until selling the lots. The speculator, then, gambled that lot prices would increase enough to cover both the initial cost of the land, interest on the loan, and taxes on the land. Moreover, the value of the land, or the price it would yield on the market, was determined by a host of economic and social forces; from the Civil War through the turn of the century, builders and speculators like Cornell sought to minimize risks and enhance property values by promoting railroad construction near subdivisions, targeting specific consumer markets, lobbying aldermen for sewer and water lines in undeveloped plots, and promoting the establishment of urban parks. Still, developers and home buyers risked losing initial capital investments when the economy slumped and land prices fell, as they did in the 1870s, mid-1880s, and 1890s. Investments in landed property were no more certain than stocks.[18]

Partial ownership in a corporation represented by a stock certificate surely appeared ephemeral when compared to a plot of land, which an investor could touch and see. Yet the city's booming industrial plants, the multilevel buildings containing ever-more complex machinery and scores of workers, would provide ample evidence of the value of a stock certificate.[19] Late nineteenth-century fiction was rife with tales of industrial entrepreneurs recognizing the "products" of their labor in the industrial plants. Robert Herrick's *Memoirs of an American Citizen* concludes with the protagonist, Van Harrington, who had arrived in Chicago with almost nothing in his pockets and made millions in the meat packing and railroad industries commenting, "I stood and gazed at the busy tracks in the railroad yards below me, at the line of high warehouses along the river. I, too, was a part of this. The thought of my brain, the labor of my body, the will within me, had gone to the making of this world." In a society that celebrated the rising industrial magnate, those who sought to make their fortunes in land speculation or home construction competed with the popular image of the successful industrialist. As Herrick clearly recognized, the ideal "American citizen" was, by the late nineteenth century, the captain of industry. Men like Cornelius Vanderbilt, John D. Rockefeller, Gustavus Swift, and Philip Armour had built great fortunes by investing in railroads, steel, and meat packing. Production, along with wealth, was increasingly associated with industrial production.[20]

Anxiety over how to value and price urban residential property derived, in part, from the ways an industrializing economy altered the customary meanings and functions of domestic property. The shift from agricultural to industrial production raised new questions about the customary value placed on domestic property. In an agricultural economy, residential property had intrinsic value as a site of production; a home sat at the center of a farm. Since the colonial period American political theorists and popular culture had celebrated the value of agricultural property, linking the productive capacity of farmland and household labor to the political independence of the head of a farming household. In the early nineteenth century, artisans and craftsmen had claimed a proprietary value in the skills, tools, and workshops, which were centered on, and often located in the same space as, the family house.[21] But the rise of factory labor and large-scale commercial enterprises had removed some wage labor from the home. Although many families continued to employ servants and sustained wage-labor relations in the home, an ideology emerged that separated the home from other sites of production. Rendering invisible the waged and unwaged labor performed within the home, the ideology of separate spheres designated the home as a site removed from production, a refuge from competitive market relations. In the rhetoric of scores of writers, the home was defined as the opposite of the market, constituted as a bastion of morality, a bulwark against the nation's competitive, often corrupt and chaotic, commercial relations. Although factory workers and their employers certainly needed shelter, the commercial value of a privately owned dwelling, of a site that was ideologically separate from market relations, was, as the editors of the *Real Estate and Building Journal* demonstrated, unclear.[22]

Though before the Civil War some writers, advice givers, and housing designers had urged well-to-do families to remove their households from the chaotic urban scene, the antebellum suburban ideal focused on particular values and virtues, paying little attention to home ownership. Andrew Jackson Downing, the landscape architect whose death in a ferry accident in 1852 cut short his prolific career, promoted residential development in semirural areas, "a home of the virtuous citizen built and loved upon new world . . . ideas and principals." A close experience of "nature" and a view of a "pastoral landscape" would, in Downing's words, secure the "independence and manliness" of citizenship. Similarly, women's advice writers like Catharine Beecher and Sarah Josepha Hale had urged wives and mothers to seek "healthy" environments for their families, houses suffused with fresh breezes, with rooms and furnishings organized around particular standards. For these writers, the advocates of the "cult of domesticity," a particular style of life, of household order, separated the respectable from the downtrodden and unhealthy family. By the 1870s, Beecher and others were suggesting that this style of life could best be acquired through a move to a semirural, a suburban, landscape. Still, property rights played a small part in the production of the proper family environment. Whether owner or tenant, and many in the 1870s and 1880s were tenants, the suburban dweller could effectively acquire a respectable home. It was for the home builders and land speculators to link respectability and health, which in the increasingly consumer-oriented late nineteenth century required a degree of affluence, to home ownership.[23]

Largely ignoring the domestic advice givers, the journal's strategy represented a remarkable shift in the ways residential property was valued. If a factory or farm carried obvious productive capacity, generating profits for capitalists and wages for workers, then a single-family home would seem to have little obvious economic value. Instead of asserting the actual productive capacity of household labor, or the cultural value placed on a well-furnished and properly organized home, the editors sought to establish a value in residential property by comparing it to ownership of nonlanded property. The journal's editors simply obscured the ideological distinction between domestic and productive sites, between respectable and unworthy homes. In their view, landed property was an investment like any other, only better. Yet the journal's broad proclamations, surely unnecessary in a community in which the value of residential property was widely acknowledged, reveal the doubt underlying their optimistic assertions. "As a rule," the journal proclaimed, "everybody is now convinced that land purchases are among the very best and surest investments and they who have means are really earnest in looking over the ground." In an economy in which investments in industry, though hardly certain, provided ever larger returns and in which an oversupply of undeveloped lots demonstrated that land speculation was no longer a quick path to wealth, the journal's editors moved to assure readers that real estate investments were sound.[24]

The journal's claims were striking, particularly to those readers who had watched prices for land and buildings plummet in the previous decade. With obvious exaggeration, the journal commented, "Nothing has so completely shown the intrinsic value of our real estate as the way it has come from the two great calamities: the fire and the reckless speculation that succeeded it."[25] No one would have been more surprised by that statement than Samuel Eberly Gross, a land speculator and builder, who nearly lost his business in the 1870s. But Gross would hardly have complained about the journal's campaign since he was among its greatest beneficiaries.

––––––––––––

Gross arrived in Chicago just after the Civil War. Born in Dauphin, Pennsylvania, on November 11, 1843, Gross had served in the Union army and, shortly after arriving in Chicago, completed a bachelor of laws degree at the old University of Chicago.[26] In 1867, he purchased some land on the North Side, hoping to make his fortune in land speculation and home construction. When the fire struck in 1871, Gross saved his enterprise by gathering his papers and rowing them to a tugboat on the Chicago River. Although the construction business boomed in the year following the fire, the economic depression of the mid-1870s nearly destroyed Gross's business. He lost several thousand dollars and determined that housing was a poor investment. Turning away from construction, Gross practiced law and wrote a play entitled *The Merchant Prince of Cornville*, which in 1902 became the subject of an internationally publicized libel suit. Gross won a lawsuit claiming that

13. S. E. Gross, Dec. 19, 1889. Chicago Historical Society.

Edmond Rostand's *Cyrano de Bergerac* was stolen from his play. As the economy recovered in the early 1880s, Gross revived his construction business and put his creative talents to work in advertising his houses.[27]

Gross was among the first, and certainly the largest and best-known, of the new generation of businessman-builders who moved to expand and speed construction of single-family houses. The younger generation merged what had in previous decades been three separate businesses—subdividing large tracts of land into individual lots, constructing houses on the lots, and providing loans to home buyers.[28] Although he continued to sell undeveloped lots, his reputation rested on his building and financing practices. Acquiring credit from commercial banks and from insurance companies, Gross could purchase a tract of land, subdivide it, purchase construction supplies in large quantities, and provide his buyers with credit to buy their houses. Large financial institutions, often based on the east coast, had provided much of the financing for the city's reconstruction after the fire, and in the 1880s commercial banks and life insurance companies began to offer credit to house builders. With borrowed capital, Gross could lower the costs of producing housing and underwrite his buyers. When Gross filed for bankruptcy in April 1908, with debts totaling more than $585,000, close to $310,000 was owed to commercial banks and life insurance companies, including $125,000 to the Provident Life and Trust Company of Philadelphia and $35,000 to the Northern Trust Company.[29]

Although neighborhood-based building associations proliferated in the 1880s, they faced new competition from businessman-builders. Gross was among the first to move to displace community networks of credit with an "easy payment plan," through which buyers could put as little as fifty dollars down and make monthly payments of fifteen to forty dollars. In the 1880s, Gross's "workingman's cottages" were priced from $1,000 to $2,000 for a four- or six-room house. Those who purchased houses from Gross would not have to turn to family, friends, or neighborhood building associations for loans.[30] Gross's financing system, which was immensely popular among skilled workers, was quickly copied by other builders. Howting & Crowhurst, a construction firm established in 1881, began selling houses on an installment plan in 1883. A year later, the firm, which employed 75 to 100 skilled and unskilled laborers, built and sold about thirty-five cottages. E. A. Cummings & Company, William Merigold, and several other home construction firms were also advertising houses sold on payment plans so that "before you know it you will have paid for the lot without any perceptible difference in your pocket book." By 1886, the *Real Estate and Building Journal* claimed, with some exaggeration, that the building associations' "sphere of usefulness was being somewhat curtailed by the construction of so many new houses, which are offered and sold at lower prices and on easy and inviting terms." The building associations, the journal claimed, could not afford to offer interest rates as low as those provided by the large-scale construction firms.[31]

Like other businessman-builders of his generation Gross gradually replaced the city's carpenter-contractors, tradesmen who around midcentury had turned their craft into small business enterprises. With large construction loans up front, Gross's firm could produce more housing at lower costs than any of the city's carpenter-contractors or individual craftsmen. By hiring laborers directly or employing carpenter-contractors to supervise parts of the construction process, Gross effectively turned what had been immigrant-controlled and community-based enterprises into a regional industry. Carpenter-contractors, unable to amass large amounts of credit to mass-produce housing, became, like the tradesmen they formerly employed, wage workers. A local builder in 1886 asserted that mass production of housing by construction firms "will naturally go ahead of the small retail and individual operations made with dear money." Even cooperative enterprises by organized tradesmen found their efforts frustrated by the combination of a lack of capital, or credit, and low-priced houses produced by Gross. In 1881 a group of skilled carpenters represented by the Trades and Labor Assembly revived a decade-old plan for a cooperative building society to employ out-of-work building trades unionists and construct housing for skilled workers. The project failed when the group found that it could not raise enough capital to build houses as cheap as those Gross was putting on the market. Four years later, a similar effort by another group of skilled carpenters was jettisoned under the same constraints.[32]

Gross and other businessman-builders further moved to speed, standardize, and lower the costs of the construction process by using factory-produced materials. Although Andrew Blackie and Samuel Smale opened the city's first sash factory in 1839, woodworking factories could not produce enough materials to compete with handcrafted, on-site carpentry work until after the Civil War. By the 1870s, however, new technology enabled the factories to use semiskilled labor to mass-produce moldings, doors, window sashes, and standard-sized lumber. In 1870, there were fifty-one planing mills and sash, door, and blind factories in Cook County, employing 2,288 workers. By 1890, 116 woodworking factories in the city employed more than 8,000 workers. Using factory-produced materials, builders could more efficiently produce houses based on standardized designs.[33]

With large quantities of precut, standardized materials available, builders could subdivide tasks on the construction site and hire less skilled labor at lower wages for each task. Instead of hiring skilled carpenters to carve and install the woodwork on site, builders could hire semiskilled pieceworkers to install precut doors, windows, or trim. The woodworking factories undermined the status of craftsmen by mass-producing materials that had formerly been hand-carved and contributed to the further breakdown of the apprenticeship system within the building trades. Master craftsmen no longer set prices for their work. Instead, builders or contractors bid out the work, hiring pieceworkers for day wages to install piecework. Most significantly, piecework dramatically increased the supply of labor for house construction since semiskilled and even unskilled laborers could be easily trained for a few tasks like stair building or framing and installing factory-made doors, windows, and trim. Almost any laborer who arrived in Chicago seeking work could hire on for a day, a week, or several months installing piecework on a construction site. Piecework undercut the status and wages of skilled tradesmen and, with more laborers available and less skill required, wages for carpentry work stagnated and then fell. Calling pieceworkers "woodbutchers," craftsmen protested the use of pieceworkers. As one letter published in the *Progressive Age* commented, "As the carpenter trade suffers more from piece work than any other cause, it is what should be first abolished." But to contractors and businessmen-builders, the use of pieceworkers was a cost-saving measure.[34]

Despite proving an obstacle to the tradesmen's cooperative schemes and undermining the status of skilled tradesmen, Gross retained the respect of skilled workers throughout the city. His ability to produce and sell houses that skilled laborers could afford apparently quelled labors' complaints about his production and hiring practices. During the 1880s, he astutely targeted an existing market of potential home buyers, the expanding population of German- and Scandinavian-born skilled workers. Touting himself as "the workingman's home builder," Gross placed advertisements in foreign-language newspapers and in the *Rights of Labor*, the newspaper published by the Knights of Labor. To further lower the cost of individual houses, Gross purchased lots just beyond the city's 1872 fire limits, a move that enabled him to use wood frame construction materials and further endeared him to the immigrant skilled workers who had protested the fire limits. Among his earliest subdivisions was Gross Park, designed for workers in the brickworks in Lake View, a suburb until 1889. In another suburb, Lake, he put up scores of four-room cottages for skilled and unskilled workers in the packing plants. Immigrant laborers seeking home ownership made ample use of Gross's long-term payment plans. In 1889, the city's Labor Party, so pleased by Gross's efforts to alleviate the housing shortage for skilled workers, nominated him as their candidate for mayor, an honor Gross quickly declined.[35]

If Gross's lower prices and easy payment plan put home ownership within the financial reach of many of the city's skilled workers, his advertising campaign functioned to broaden his market and, ultimately, to transform the significance of home ownership in Chicago. Gross used advertising to attract working-class buyers, while almost simultaneously seeking to expand the home buying market to include the city's "respectable" households headed by men working as supervisors and clerks in the city's corporations. By the mid-1890s, when the city sank into another economic depression, Gross's promotional strategies began to pay off as he shifted his business toward building larger and more expensive houses, some in newly developed suburban communities.[36]

The use of advertising was not new. Home builders had placed small ads in newspapers in eastern cities since the early nineteenth century. But Gross's promotional campaign was innovative. Brochures for Gross's subdivisions illustrate a carefully planned promotional strategy designed to appeal to a mass audience of tradesmen and businessmen. He placed large advertisements in labor-oriented newspapers and in the *Chicago Times* and the

ARCHER AVE. COTTAGES.
$8 MONTHLY PAYMENTS AND LONG TIME.

LOCATION.

These cottages are located on Hoyne Ave. and Champlain Ave., between 33d and 34th Sts., just north of Archer Ave., and a few blocks west of Ashland Ave. (see plat of property on opposite page).

DESCRIPTION.

These, for the price, are the handsomest, best built brick cottages in the City, with stone and brick trimmings, seven foot basement, lake water and large lot.

FIRST FLOOR.   BASEMENT.

TERMS.

Price $950 to $1,300; $50 to $100 cash, balance on long time and $8 monthly payments.

BRANCH OFFICE AND HOW TO GET THERE.

Branch Office for this property is located on Archer Ave. near Long John St. Open every day. Take Archer Ave. cars and transfer at Archer Ave. car barns to Brighton Park car, which takes you to the office door, or call at Main Office and be taken free to see the property.

South-east corner Dearborn and Randolph Sts.

14. Archer Avenue cottages advertisement. S. E. Gross (firm), *Illustrated Catalogue of S. E. Gross' Lots, Houses, Cottages* (Chicago: S. E. Gross, 1889), Chicago Historical Society, Gross Papers.

Chicago Daily Tribune, and he published and distributed his own yearly catalogues, providing detailed drawings and descriptions of each new subdivision. Gross used images, anecdotes, and stories framed as morality tales to
sell mass-produced and standardized houses. Drawing on images and language widely circulated in nineteenth-century American culture, Gross fash-
ioned a new vocabulary of home ownership. Moving beyond the *Real Estate
and Building Journal* editors' efforts to establish economic value in real estate
investments, Gross sought to sell single-family houses to individual buyers
by stamping the owner-occupied single-family home with a vibrant collection of weighty symbols. His campaign looked backward to antebellum
ideals, linking home ownership to individuality, autonomy, morality, and
social order. At the same time, Gross's collection of symbols, implicitly placing residential property at the heart of market relations, produced a modern
vision of home ownership.

Gross's advertisements reveal a series of paradoxes in the cultural form
that was entrusted with upholding nineteenth-century distinctions between
public and private spaces, and waged and unwaged labor.[37] His overt commodification of the home subverted the notion that the home was a refuge
from the competitive market. Using sketches of the home's interior to sell
houses, Gross took the intimate signs of domesticity into the public realm
and into capitalist market relations. Scenes of a family gathered around the
hearth and of kitchen facilities were exhibited in newspapers and plastered
on billboards. Price lists and elaborate financing mechanisms accompanied
the images. In Gross's advertisements, industrial capitalism invaded even
the most intimate aspects of family life and domestic spaces. The implica-
tion was clear: the value of the home, like commodities produced in the factory or the shop, was determined by market relations. Property in housing,
as the *Real Estate and Building Journal* had claimed, was an investment like
any other.

Yet even as Gross's advertising campaign blurred the distinctions between public and private spheres, he sought to sell an ideal of home ownership by reinforcing the ideological boundary between the public street and
the private home. In Gross's telling, the owner-occupied home offered stability and comfort, a stark contrast to the chaos of the streets. Several of his
ads compared renters to home owners, always claiming the property owner
was the more stable and respectable. Despite the city's custom of long-term
leases, Gross's advertisements suggested that tenants were forced to move
each spring. *A Home Primer for Old and Young*, a widely circulated promotional pamphlet, chronicled the lives of two men, Andrew and Benjamin.
Andrew, described as a hard worker, saves his earnings, purchases a house

15. "The First of May" advertisement. Chicago Historical Society, Gross Papers.

from Gross, and is pictured at the story's conclusion sitting comfortably by a fireplace, surrounded by a wife and children. Benjamin, by contrast, spends his evenings with "rollicking boys . . . which everyone knows must cost Benjamin money." Indebted and miserable, Benjamin, by the end of the tale, is shown on a trash-strewn street, pursued by a wife and horse-drawn wagon overflowing with their possessions. In this morality tale, renting is associated with the squalor of the urban street, with transient households, and with the humiliation of having private possessions displayed in public. Home ownership, by contrast, was linked to comfort, family unity, and stability, virtues increasingly associated with middle-class home life.[38]

In setting the owner-occupied home as a reward for hard work and temperance, Gross endowed wage work with purpose beyond the mere collection of a paycheck. As industrialization rendered production ever more complex, rational, and routine, work was no longer a source of dignity and personal fulfillment. The story of Andrew and Benjamin did not identify either man by occupation. Instead, Andrew's identity—or his character— was revealed in the attributes that enable him to purchase his home. Hardworking, temperate, and devoted to his family, Andrew is rewarded with a comfortable home. Benjamin's lack of character was illustrated by his public humiliation at the story's conclusion. Production, in Gross's tale, becomes a path to the comforts of consumption.

Expanding industrialization heightened the social significance of consumption; consumption patterns, rather than production or labor, became standards by which individual character was measured. In a city populated by recent immigrants, where longtime residents confronted strangers in the streets, shops, and workplace, Gross sought to produce an ideal of home ownership, which might serve as a means of distinguishing the respectable from the dishonorable, the upstanding character from the crowd of strangers. He proclaimed the single-family home a reward for dull and dehumanizing labor and a symbol of exemplary character. In the story of Andrew and Benjamin, Gross reconfigured the preindustrial equation of work with identity and production with the home. Gross represented home ownership as a result of a series of consumption decisions, a reward for decisions well-made.[39]

But businessman-builders like Gross were not simply promoting home ownership; they wanted potential buyers to purchase new houses, most of which were constructed on previously subdivided land edging the city. The builders found ample support in the language and ideals of domestic writers and health reformers. After the Civil War, writers like Catharine Beecher had begun to argue that not only was the organization of the home's interior important, but its location also profoundly influenced the health and morality of the household. Beecher's previous domestic tracts had not mentioned the home's location. But in *The American Woman's Home*, coauthored with her sister, Harriet Beecher Stowe, Beecher argued that household health could best be preserved by surrounding the family dwelling with grass and trees. By the 1870s, health reformers buttressed Beecher's admonitions with "scientific" principles, arguing that clean air and pure water were the basis of household health. In articles published in women's magazines, newspapers, and architectural journals, sanitary reformers linked the home's healthy environment to the morality of the household.[40]

Mary Brewster Laflin, though urging her son to live within the city, clearly believed that fresh air, cool breezes, and a house with a "yard" were necessities for Louis's family. "The houses on the North Side, in Potter Palmer's vicinity are numerous," she wrote in a note, planning his move to Chicago, "but they are in blocks, and on the made ground you dislike and a majority of them only pretty in hall and parlor." The "blocks," she observed, meant that the yards were small and inadequate. Health reformers, while encouraging municipalities to construct and expand sewer and water systems, also urged urban residents to seek "healthy" locations for their dwellings. Those locations, typically called "suburban locales" and found both outside and within the municipal boundaries, referred to a particular environment, a landscape that included yards with trees, grass, and "fresh breezes" and was removed from the "dirt and turmoil" of the city.[41]

In their books and pamphlets, health reformers constructed a healthy environment, an imagined landscape that had little in common with the undeveloped prairie and subdivided farmland surrounding Chicago. Yet as they competed for buyers, the city's businessman-builders made ample use of the health reformers' language, moving to redesign the environment surrounding their houses by promoting the construction of urban parks.[42] Advertised as providing a natural and healthy environment, the parks ultimately looked more like the hilly and forested New England landscape than the midwestern prairie.[43] Gross and other builders deployed the language of health reform in advertisements touting their developments' proximity to parkland. An 1882 advertisement for houses near Humboldt Park noted, "The land is high, dry, and rich soil and its nearness to Humboldt Park makes it very desirable for ladies and children who wish to obtain the blessings of pure air and enjoy the charms of delightful scenery. In short, there is no other part of the city where a man of moderate means can obtain a healthful home for his family which so well unites city and country advantages."[44]

Chicago's widely touted park system, circling the built-up sections of the city, became a leading attraction in builders' advertisements. With the public financing for the city's parks, long promoted by land speculators and developers and at a cost of over $46 million in municipal and state funds, real estate interests successfully directed public money toward capital improvements in privately owned land and housing. Parks, which enhanced the value of nearby land, regularly appeared in the builders' promotional campaigns. Applying the ideals of sanitary reformers, the builders' advertisements drew sharp contrast between urban and suburban living environments, even when the houses advertised were located within the city limits. A move to the fringe of the city, to a new neighborhood edging a new park, would, builders claimed, provide the household with "a choice and respectable neighborhood, away from the corrupting influences and temptations incidental to a great city and inhabited by a quiet and agreeable class of people." By the 1890s, the new parks combined with advertising campaigns emphasizing the healthy environment helped push the city's growth outward.[45]

Like the advertisements of several late nineteenth-century builders, Gross's promotional literature marketed health as a commodity; it could be purchased only when an astute builder combined the benefits of nature with the new technology of home construction. Promoting a south suburban subdivision, Gross wrote, "Nature has fitted Calumet Heights for residences for those in search of a home away from the smoke and turmoil of the city, and I propose to make it one of the healthiest and finest suburbs in Chicago." The suburb's 1,400 lots, costing $300 and up, would be fitted with six-room, two-story frame houses priced at $2,900. Each would include a bathroom with water closet and hot and cold running water. Another builder claimed his lots were "fine, high, dry and covered with beautiful natural trees." An advertisement for Grossdale, a suburban community just west of the city, noted, "The air is the purest and as the property is perfectly drained your health and that of your family will always be good." His promotional literature for Humboldt Park, a subdivision on the city's west side, guaranteed buyers "pure air and good health." In Gross's campaign, nature combined with indoor plumbing to produce a healthy environment for the home owner.[46]

As commuter rail lines made suburban houses more accessible and parks provided an attractive environment, indoor plumbing conferred new cultural and material value on the single-family home. While enhancing household health, indoor plumbing facilities added substantial construction costs, which of course were passed on to the buyer in the form of higher housing prices. In the 1880s, Gross and other builders built and marketed housing to a two-tiered consumer market: those who could and those who could not afford indoor plumbing. In the mid-1880s, C. C. Landt & Co. began building houses in Englewood, south of the city, marketing two styles: a four-room house with a backyard privy for $900 and an eight-room house with indoor bathrooms, hot and cold running water, and a marble wash bowl, for $1,900. Another builder, J. L. Cochran, who was selling lots and houses in north suburban Edgewater, boasted of spending over $375,000 "to make the improvements when the population warrants them," including "artistic homes, underground sewerage, macadamized streets." By the mid-1890s, indoor plumbing had become standard in Gross's houses, pushing up costs by more than $500. Even if indoor plumbing added to the cost of the house, it also added to the marketability since sanitary reformers had publicized the health benefits of sewers and running water.[47]

The health reformers' ideals also proved useful in marketing housing in suburbs well beyond the city limits. Joseph Sears touted the health of his North Shore suburb, Kenilworth, in his marketing campaigns. Sears, as his daughter remembered nearly seventy years later, was determined to find a "community with the atmosphere of the country and the convenience of the city." The chosen site had the "dryness of the high bluffs and sandy soil [that] would be causes for healthfulness." Sears moved his family to Kenilworth in 1890 and over the following decade installed water, sewer, and gas lines, as well as streets and sidewalks. In the early 1890s, as the city's economy struggled through economic depression, residents of neighboring suburbs believed Sears was "sinking . . . money into a swampy piece of land" (an exaggeration since the land was hardly "swampy") and bound for bankruptcy. But home ownership and homes fitted with the latest household technology attracted businessmen, professionals, and their families to large, elegant houses, and the village grew quickly. By 1904, 271 adults were listed as Kenilworth residents in the North Shore directory.[48]

Drainage, sewers, indoor plumbing, and proximity to a public park were not the sole means through which the builder manipulated the natural environment. Gross's advertising suggested that the builder's construction techniques would tame and transform the formerly remote and undesirable "suburban locales." Surrounding his houses with lawns and planting trees across the recently subdivided prairie, Gross presented nature as a commodity, refined and constructed as the builder blanketed the terrain with cottages. His advertisements pictured houses set on manicured lawns, images of a carefully tended natural environment. The builder then sold this crafted environment to the home buyer, who often was pictured standing next to the front door looking out on his newly purchased lawn. In the foreground, and usually smaller than the male home owner, are his children, and often wife, standing or playing near the edge of his property. The industrial laborer, low-level clerk, or white-collar office worker to whom Gross marketed his houses might lack authority in the workplace and lack property rights in the mechanisms of industrial production, but pictured on the doorstep of his home or at the entrance to his yard in Gross's advertisements, the home owner claimed his property rights in housing and asserted control over his domestic environment. Nature, harnessed by the builder and remade in terms that might benefit the household's health, also provided the home owner with an emblem of his independence, a term that emerged as a potent symbol in Gross's promotional campaigns.[49]

Long a central concept in American political theory, independence proved a remarkably flexible, and forceful, symbol in marketing single-family houses. Republican theory asserted that manhood and citizenship were based on the household head's ownership of productive property and control of household labor. Property, the theory claimed, freed men from the influence of employers and enabled men to function as autonomous actors in politics. By the 1880s, industrialized labor relations dramatically narrowed opportunities for wage workers and even salaried clerks and managers to claim independence through ownership of productive property or skill. Gross's promotional materials suggested that as industrialization diminished the status of labor, it heightened the significance of property rights in housing. Gross moved to redefine independence, locating it in residential neighborhoods and linking a workers' autonomy to private ownership of his dwelling. As the *Chicago Globe* commented, Gross "undertook to devise a plan by which these people, who, more than any other, needed a home of their own with the independence, self-respect, better citizenship and stronger manhood its acquisition would give, could secure and pay for a cottage and lot."[50]

As the city's trades unions fought to retain the dignity and authority of skilled labor, Gross urged male workers to look to residential property rights as a source of independence. He supported organized labor's eight-hour-day movement in 1889 by associating home ownership with labor's goals. In a series of advertisements published in the *Rights of Labor*, Gross linked leisure to independence, asserting that the strike's achievement would be additional leisure, time in which workers could enjoy the benefits of home ownership. "It's only a matter of 'time' that's the cause of the great strike now in progress," Gross's advertisement in the *Rights of Labor* proclaimed. "Eight hours is a working day. In the meantime the best thing working men can do is to select and secure a home site where they can erect a handsome little cottage and spend the 'time' to be gained by this strike with their family under their own roof—Independent and Happy." Rather than asserting the potential economic advantages of property in housing as an investment, Gross stressed the social status acquired by a man who purchased a house, appealing both to working men's vision of independence from capitalist employers and to a white-collar aspiration for independence without business ownership.[51]

Gross's advertising suggested that home ownership carried an even more significant function: reinforcing a husband's authority within his household. In Gross's somewhat convoluted scheme, property rights in housing marked an assertion of manhood and a move to reclaim male authority within the home. Gross's advertising campaigns explicitly acknowledged that industrialization wrought profound, and what he perceived as disturbing, changes in late nineteenth-century gender relations. Gross was not alone in perceiving these changes. Richard Sennett's study of Union Park, an affluent community on Chicago's West Side, found widespread concern about the increasing authority of wives and passivity of husbands in middle-class households. Theodore Dreiser illustrated these shifting patterns of authority in the opening scenes of his novel, *Sister Carrie*, set in another Chicago neighborhood. For Mary Brewster Laflin, such issues had become a common and amusing topic in women's magazines and newspapers. "I have just laid aside the Graphic after reading a long article," she wrote to her son Louis, "on the way for a wife to make herself always attractive to her husband. At any age, do you think it necessary to draw papa with any stronger cords than I now hold? Why, he would not be able to attend to his legitimate business!!!" Gross's own household was nowhere near so pleasant. It is clear that he was deeply troubled about gender relations in the city at large and in his own home in particular.[52]

Gross's views of domestic order, and disorder, were likely shaped by his wife, Emily Maude Gross, whom he married in 1874. Emily Gross was an ardent supporter of women's suffrage and a friend of Susan B. Anthony, who visited the Gross home several times in the 1880s. What Gross absorbed about women's rights from his wife or from Anthony is unknown, but the Gross's marriage was not a happy one. Gross's father in an 1886 letter advised that "a man needs to guard against being influenced by his wife—because a woman don't know things as a man does . . . and I trust and hope you will be cautious in that respect."[53] When the Grosses divorced in 1909, the *Chicago Journal* commented, "It is said now by mutual friends that Mr. Gross was ambitious for his wife to shine in society, but that Mrs. Gross was bored by society and wanted to do sociological work." The *Chicago Inter-Ocean* wrote, "While her husband wrote verse, she campaigned for the right to vote. She joined clubs and made speeches. Neither, it seems, got what he and she went after." Gross apparently was privy, reluctantly it would seem, to some of the contemporary debate over women's rights and roles within the household.[54]

Although he was not able to control his wife's activities, Gross's advertisements proclaimed that home ownership would resolve marital conflicts within the home. In another, and the most elaborate, of his promotional pamphlets, Gross reveals a central paradox in the ideological separation of masculine and feminine spheres, and of the complimentary productive and domestic sites. The story, published in 1886, suggests what many proponents of the separate spheres ideology might have seen as an unsettling truth: women's remunerative labor was a critical component in the realization of home ownership. In the story, which relates the struggles of a young Chicago couple, Lucy and Charley Graham, gender order is buttressed by home ownership, but only through a web of seemingly contradictory activities.[55]

The story begins with Charley Graham, a low-level clerk whose salary barely covers household expenses, grumbling over his family's finances. Lucy, determined to purchase a house, convinces Charley to allow her to control the couple's meager finances. Unbeknownst to her husband, Lucy visits Gross's firm, pulls together enough money for a down payment and then, secretly, launches a laundry business out of the new house, making house payments with her earnings. At the story's end, Lucy turns the title to the house over to her husband. Charley is somewhat upset to learn that Lucy has been earning money, but is mollified when she claims that the maid did most of the manual labor. And he is so pleased by the comforts of his new home and by the baby Lucy has found time to have, that he proudly overlooks this slight indiscretion. The Grahams, happy home owners, prosper. Women's wage labor, it seems, is sanctioned if it is hidden and if her earnings are used to acquire the domestic sphere.

Moreover, Lucy is described as a "modern woman"; she knows how to achieve her goal while also strengthening her husband's position in society and the home. Just before she gives Charley the title to the house and reveals her secret, Charley tells her that he has a fail-safe opportunity for advancement, which requires a $2,500 investment. Since he hasn't the money to invest, he says he will sacrifice the opportunity. The wily young Lucy then remortgages the house and, along with the title, hands him a check for $2,500. Lucy's hard and secretive labor has not only improved the couple's domestic space, but also has enhanced her husband's earnings and ultimately returned him to his position as the household's primary financial support. Rather than challenging his role within the household, she has further solidified it.

The story of the Grahams suggests the practical contradictions underlying the ideology of domesticity. The ideology rested on a fragile and easily shattered financial foundation. To achieve the status of bourgeois homemaker, Lucy Graham had to become a laborer and entrepreneur. Explicitly undermining the popular rhetoric that separated the home from the wage labor market, Lucy engaged in waged work in her home with the assistance of a paid servant. Apparently recognizing that men like Charley Graham might, for lack of investment capital, slip downward economically, Gross suggests that women's wage labor, in or out of the home, may prove a necessity. With Lucy's proud presentation of the check from the remortgaged house, Gross demonstrates that home ownership not only provides a household with a secure dwelling, but also can function to generate cash. Though working-class families had long used multiple housing loans to gain money for necessities, in Gross's tale, the cash from a remortgaged dwelling could be deployed to obtain new professional opportunities for the struggling middle-class man. Gross represented home ownership as a strategy used by aspiring middle-class families to advance in the industrial workplace. More than a cultural symbol of independence and stability, home ownership might provide the economic basis for upward mobility. He sanctioned Lucy's wage work since it allowed her to achieve her and Gross's goal: the purchase of a house.

Once the house was purchased, however, Gross moved to assure home buyers that wives would return to their specialized status within the home. Indeed, in Gross's tale, the purchase of a home reinforced a gender order prescribed by nineteenth-century standards and recently challenged by women's rights campaigners. At the story's conclusion, Lucy happily gives up her laundry business and devotes herself to her growing family. Capable and inventive entrepreneur, she willingly relinquishes control of the family finances. Domestic ideology, in Gross's rendition, is simply remodeled for the period it takes a young couple to purchase a house. Aiming to sell houses, Gross suggested and sanctioned a path to home ownership for buyers who, without their wives' earnings, could not afford a house. A few years later, when her husband becomes a successful businessman, Gross concluded that none of her "fashionable friends would ever have known that the elegant Mrs. Graham had taken in washing."[56]

Gross's fame and wealth suggest the widespread appeal of his marketing strategy. During the last two decades of the nineteenth century, Gross partly built twenty-one subdivisions and suburbs, erecting 10,000 houses and selling more than 40,000 lots. By 1900, his fortune was estimated at over five million dollars; on his death, after declaring bankruptcy in 1907, Gross left an estate of $150,000. By the turn of the century, Gross had achieved near-celebrity status in Chicago. In his 1911 novel, *Jenny Gerhardt*, Theodore Dreiser apparently used Gross as a model for Samuel E. Ross, "the real estate dealer, whose great, wooden signs might be seen everywhere on the windy stretches of prairie about the city."[57]

Dreiser's depiction of the real estate business and of the self-promoting Ross probably embellishes the cynical manipulation of the ingenious promotional strategies of the real estate man. Still, Dreiser astutely highlighted the significance of advertising in selling houses, and the lacuna between the optimistic claims of the self-aggrandizing real estate men and the risks of investing in the city's ever-vacillating real estate market. In Dreiser's portrait, the real estate dealer seeks investment capital from a young man who has been forced out of his family's highly profitable industrial enterprise. Ross "blinked his cat-like eyes" and conjured an illusion of riches to be made from a simple land deal. His potential investor, easily persuaded there "were indications of a genuine real estate boom there—healthy, natural, and permanent," hands over nearly $90,000. When rumors that a new packing-house was planned near the property, the deal soured. "[T]he mere suspicion that the packing company might invade the territory was sufficient to blight the prospects of any budding real estate deal." Ross attempted to "boom the property heavily, by means of newspaper advertising," but few lots were sold, and Ross, wanting "no more to do with it," moved on to the next deal. The young man lost most of his investment, but Ross, like Gross, continued to prosper, using aggressive and innovative advertising to expand residential real estate sales.[58]

———————

Gross's success, like that of other late nineteenth-century businessman-builders, rested on his ability to link his promotional literature to a wide array of economic and political changes in the city at large, and in the real estate market in particular. During the thirty years Gross was building houses, the construction industry, as well as land investment concerns, lurched through a series of highs and lows. Sometimes leading, often following larger economic and cultural trends, businessman-builders like Gross developed elaborate strategies to enhance the value of their land holdings and lure new segments of the population into home buying. In the late nineteenth and early twentieth centuries, builders, subdividers, and real estate investors used new technologies in transportation and in home construction to inflate land values, encourage home ownership, and enhance the position of residential property in the competitive capital market. Labor strife in the final decades of the century lowered the value of real estate in some sections of the city at the same time that builders, subdividers, and investors were moving to establish and enhance values in landed property on the city's fringe. Gross established a reputation as "the workingman's home builder," but in the 1890s, as economic conditions and public attitudes toward home ownership shifted, Gross too shifted to building houses for more affluent buyers. His success, despite a severe economic depression through the mid-1890s, suggests that he, and others, had adequately laid the foundation for a new vision of home ownership.

By 1889, when the city annexed north suburban Lake View and the township of Lake, where the packinghouses were located, rapid population growth in neighboring suburbs had pushed up land values significantly.[59] That year, thousands of laborers and clerks began to pool their savings, form land syndicates, and invest in suburban properties. After watching real estate firms achieve significant returns on their land investments for more than five years, low-wage and salaried workers began to see land speculation as a sound investment. The *Real Estate and Building Journal's* campaign of a decade earlier had apparently succeeded. Massive speculation by small-time investors forced up prices and drew even larger numbers of buyers to the land market. By the spring of 1889, rumors of the millions to be made in the land market spread through the city, and newspapers were marveling at the spiraling prices of outlying land. "Even servant girls, seamstresses and woman clerks have caught the fever, put their savings into a lump and become joint owners of suburban property," the *Tribune* commented. "Kindled by stories of large profits, they believe it is impossible to pay too much."[60]

The land boom culminated in 1890 when Congress announced in February that the World's Fair was awarded to Chicago. Land values near Jackson Park, the site selected for the fair, advanced as much as 1,000 percent in the year. Tracts partly under water south of the park were bid up from $600 to $6,000 and even as high as $15,000 an acre. The sale of lots surpassed all previous records. Gross was selling as many as five hundred lots a week; on one of his free excursions to his subdivision Grossdale, west of Chicago, twenty-seven coaches pulled by two engines were required to transport three thousand people who were eager to buy lots. Gains in land value from the beginning of 1889 to beginning of 1891 were greater than in the preceding six years, particularly in central business property and residential property on the fringe made accessible by transportation and attractive by parks.[61]

Price increases, however, were not uniform throughout the region. Land near Jackson Park was an overnight gold mine, but prices for existing housing occupied by working-class families in the city fell as owner-occupants and landlords began to compete with those selling lots and houses in outlying areas.[62] The newer houses were drawing buyers who a decade earlier might have looked in the inner city for lots or existing housing. In 1889 and 1890, price increases in suburban areas outpaced those for houses closer to the city center by more than 50 percent. Immigrant laboring families continued to flow into older, built-up areas of the city, setting off a wave of subdividing older single- and two-family houses into multiple small apartments and pushing those who could afford larger dwellings outward toward newly built housing.[63]

In December 1890, housing sales and the speculative land boom came to a halt. Real estate prices in outlying regions remained relatively high through the World's Fair in 1893, but by the mid-1890s, Chicago's economy and its real estate market had sunk into an economic depression as severe as that of the 1870s. Banks seemingly overnight began rejecting real estate loans, and many of those who had gone into debt to purchase property found they could not get a second loan to make payments on the first. The frenzied transactions that had opened the decade, pushing lot prices ever higher, wavered, leaving many struggling to make loan payments for lots whose value fell well below the amount of the loan.

Yet for an established real estate entrepreneur, like Gross, the drop in land values was not as devastating as it might have been a decade earlier. Although Gross sold only 129 lots during the week ending July 26, 1891, as compared with 529 for the same week a year before, Gross had already begun to transform his business in ways that would enable him to survive and prosper during the economic depression. In the early 1890s, Gross began shifting his production and marketing strategies away from working-class buyers and targeting a more affluent consumer. By 1892, the half-page advertisements that in previous years graced the pages of the *Rights of Labor* no longer appeared. Gross's tenth annual catalogue, published in the spring of 1891, was directed to middle-class households. While Gross continued to advertise some lower-price houses, the bulk of the houses advertised in 1891 were larger and priced well beyond the means of his working-class buyers. The tenth annual catalogue was not the first to advertise $3,000 and $4,000 houses, but it contained more of the higher-priced houses than any of the previous catalogues. Published on the heels of a market downturn, the catalogue suggests that Gross perceived that changed economic conditions might slow sales of lower-priced houses.

As factory production fell and unemployment, particularly in the trades, soared in the mid-1890s, builders like Gross survived and even prospered by selling larger and more expensive houses. In June 1889, Gross introduced a new subdivision, Grossdale, now west suburban Brookfield, with the construction of a $5,000 depot for the Chicago, Burlington & Quincy Railroad. Located thirteen miles from downtown Chicago, Grossdale was surrounded by family farms and further from the city center than any of Gross's previous subdivisions. The community's nine-room single-family homes included indoor bathrooms and were set on lots two to three times the size of a typical city lot. Priced at $4,300, Grossdale's houses marked a significant departure from the "workingman's" cottages that had launched Gross's career. During the summers of 1889 and 1890, Gross sold as many as five hundred lots a week in Grossdale. Despite faltering sales for lots throughout the city, Gross's sales were strong enough that in 1892, he subdivided another five acres and added East Grossdale, now Hollywood (a part of Brookfield), to the community and in 1894, as much of the city's real estate market ground to a halt, he put another subdivision, West Grossdale, now Congress Park (also part of Brookfield), on the market. With each of the new subdivisions, advertisements highlighted the ever larger and more expensive houses.

By the turn of the century, Gross's business had shifted fully into construction of homes for an affluent market. He continued to expand his suburban subdivisions, and between 1900 and 1904, Gross constructed Alta Vista Terrace, a subdivision of row houses designed by architect J. C. Brompton, on the city's North Side. Priced from $4,575 to $7,200, the eighteen two-story and two three-story attached townhouses were clearly aimed for a more affluent clientele than the skilled workers who had helped to build Gross's business.

––––––––––

Samuel Eberly Gross was not solely responsible for the reorientation of Chicago's housing market. A host of late nineteenth-century businessman-builders worked to encourage the city's growing middle classes to invest in residential real estate and to push the house-buying public out of the city center and into suburban locales. The businessman-builders deployed a variety of strategies. Some, like Paul Cornell, who had purchased a large tract in what became Hyde Park, used their personal and political connections to gain municipally financed parks near their subdivisions and sewer lines and commuter rail lines running through their communities. Gross too made ample use of these strategies.

Immigrant workers, of course, continued to seek home ownership both within the city's boundaries and in suburban areas. Seeing home ownership as a mark of autonomy in a labor system in which steady work was unreliable and factory labor was disconnected from pride in skill, many workers purchased houses as a means of asserting an American identity and respectability. As conflicts between labor and capital became increasingly hostile and violent in the 1880s and 1890s, housing conditions remained a central issue in labor's struggle. But as wage cuts, strikes, and massive immigration made steady employment uncertain, unskilled wage workers found home ownership an increasingly difficult goal. Builders contributed to the production of home ownership as a cultural ideal, often in language that appealed specifically to the working classes, but by the turn of the century, growing numbers of builders were constructing houses that were priced beyond the means of working-class households.[64]

By 1900, builders like Gross had helped to reorient the city's housing market and reshape its social geography. For working-class families after the turn of the century, home ownership meant a move to an urban neighborhood slightly removed from the older and increasingly crowded neighborhoods clustered along the Chicago River or to a suburban community of simple lower-priced houses. Determined to maintain ties to extended families and urban religious institutions, many formed new neighborhoods of owner-occupied single- and two-family houses on the Northwest, West, and Southwest Sides of the city. New working-class neighborhoods were built on undeveloped land within the city and formed in existing housing left by middle-class families who moved to suburban towns. The builders had established a class-segregated housing market and a pattern of mobility that would characterize Chicago and its suburban real estate markets through much of the twentieth century.[65]

Even in the 1890s, middle-class Chicagoans, as well as some of the city's wealthiest residents, continued to seek rented apartments or long-term leases on single-family homes. And capitalists continued to debate the merits of investments in landed property. But as new factories lined the banks of the Chicago River and lumber mills, meat packing plants, and steel and iron works claimed ever-larger pieces of prairie land, the urban environment began to pose new dangers, both real and imagined. Builders and real estate entrepreneurs proved particularly adept at playing on these fears, portraying the owner-occupied single-family home as a solution to the wide array of urban problems and the resolution to emerging household conflicts. The builders' aim was, of course, to sell houses. But by fashioning a new vocabulary associated with home ownership they went even further, promoting an ideal of home ownership to a population that remained, for a time, skeptical of the value of residential property. At the turn of the century, the builders' marketing strategies gained a significant boost from a new generation of housing reformers who, like the health reformers of the 1880s, saw multifamily dwellings as a threat to the morals and stability of the city's families. Urging wage-laboring Chicagoans to secure their family's privacy by moving to single-family houses, housing reformers further highlighted the potential benefits of single-family home ownership.

CHAPTER SIX

Reforming the Family Home and Improving Neighborhoods

In November 1894, Mary McDowell moved into a four-room apartment in a "wooden tenement building" in Packingtown, the sprawling immigrant community surrounding Chicago's packinghouses. McDowell, the forty-year-old daughter of a steel plant manager who moved to Evanston after the Civil War, had spent four years working at Hull House, the settlement house opened by Jane Addams five years earlier. McDowell's apartment would soon be expanded to become the University of Chicago Settlement House, a center for community organizing and education programs and a base for scores of university researchers seeking to examine the lives of McDowell's immigrant neighbors and to explain, and eliminate, the causes of poverty in the city. Within weeks after moving to Packingtown, McDowell launched a campaign to demand that the city enforce existing health department ordinances in the neighborhood's crowded, run-down dwellings. McDowell had joined the ranks of a new generation of urban reformers dedicated to eliminating what they called "the tenement problem."[1]

Like the health reformers a decade earlier, housing reformers were concerned with the effects of poverty on urban life. But the settlement house volunteers, the largely middle-class men and women who determined to improve urban living conditions by living among the poor, set a broader reform agenda. Industrialization, they believed, created an environment that threatened the "bonds of family" and caused dangerous divisions within American society. With their campaigns against child and sweated labor, for minimum-wage and maximum-hours laws, for kindergartens, playgrounds, public baths, women's suffrage, and for municipal regulations of the size and design of urban dwellings, this new generation of civic activists brought the daily struggles of urban communities into City Hall, into the state legislature, and into political debates. Reformers sought to use their studies of the poor to generate sympathy among the wealthier classes and to pressure politicians to improve housing and regulate industry. They aimed to bring together the foreign-born and the native-born, the wealthy and the impoverished, to "regard the entire life of their city as organic," proclaimed Jane Addams, to "make an effort to unify it, and to protest against its overdifferentiation." Politics would determine the physical and moral health of the community, and the network of communities, of neighborhoods organized block by block, would, the reformers hoped, become the model for a new society, a "cooperative commonwealth." By organizing immigrant laborers to work together to demand municipal resources for their communities, tenement reformers helped to cement bonds among neighbors, sharpen boundaries separating neighborhoods, and produce a vision of property in housing that both secured family privacy and linked the well-being of each individual household to that of its neighbors.[2]

Turn-of-the-century housing reformers urged on immigrants an "American standard of life," a vision that combined home ownership with the "family home," a dwelling that secured the privacy, morality, and health of parents and their children. The immigrants they sought to assist, however, had a conception of property rights in housing that undermined many of the reformers' goals. Immigrant working-class home owners and tenants who aspired to home ownership, while grateful for many of settlement house workers' achievements, often ignored the reformers' pleas to remove boarders and waged labor from their homes and sent their children to work to help sustain their households. The "American standard of life," which had rallied immigrant home owners in the 1870s and continued to inspire turn-of-the-century wage laborers, became a phrase that paradoxically both sharpened and obscured differences in the ways working-class households and their reforming neighbors conceived of the social benefits of property rights in housing. The reformers did not see home ownership as the primary solution to the city's housing problems, but in articulating a new ideal of the family home, the reformers' strategies and language often overlapped with those of businessman-builders like Samuel Eberly Gross. By defining the home as the source of social order and promoting family privacy, urban reformers contributed to a remaking of the home ownership ideal. They crystallized an increasingly rigid definition of the family home and of an American standard of family life that would have long-term consequences for the ways Americans would conceive of the home, of property values, and of housing reform through the twentieth century.

When McDowell arrived in Packingtown, she found a hardscrabble community of immigrants battling to establish themselves on low wages and irregular work, pursuing home ownership and seeking to use property rights in housing to cushion the blows of an unpredictable job market. Living in a neighborhood widely considered among the dirtiest and most impoverished in the city, tenants and home owners treated their homes as spaces for eating, sleeping, rearing children, and waged labor. By taking in lodgers to cover household expenses and sending teenage children to work for wages, the result of necessity and custom, low-wage workers spread the responsibility for maintaining their households among several laborers, making the home into a space for collective labor and living. "We are building without money," one fourteen-year-old girl who had taken a job in the packinghouses told an investigator, who added, "the heavily mortgaged house too often calls for the united wage-earning power of the entire family." Those who achieved and maintained property rights in the expanding low-wage community adeptly managed household labor and income, and with good fortune avoided illness or the death of a wage earner. Packingtown's residents—tenants, boarders, and property owners—saw the household as a cooperative and adaptable entity.[3]

From the 1890s to World War I, thousands of peasants and laborers recently arrived from villages and farms of the Russian and Austro-Hungarian empires moved into Packingtown's frame cottages, living among the Irish, German, and Canadian butchers and seeking jobs slaughtering and packaging the hundreds of live animals shipped into the yards each day. Packingtown's population increased by 75 percent in the first decade of the twentieth century and continued to grow until by 1920 more than fifty-seven thousand people lived in the three-square-mile community. From 1900 to 1910, new arrivals began to outnumber older more established residents; in 1910 those of Irish, German, and Canadian descent comprised just 28 percent of the population while the percentage of Poles, Lithuanians, Slovaks, and Bohemians had jumped from 18 to 48 percent of the population. Residents retained their national distinctiveness in the early decades of the twentieth century, building ethnic communities around churches and parochial schools. There were, for example, few marriages that crossed ethnic lines. Particular national groups clustered in residential districts, yet most blocks contained a mix of nationalities, all of European descent. While language, religion, and culture might divide the neighborhoods' households, Packing-

16. Mary McDowell, n.d. Chicago Historical Society.

town residents shared the experience of low-wage work and poor housing conditions.[4]

In the decade after McDowell arrived, the neighborhood expanded south and west until new housing, purchased and leased, pushed against the municipal garbage dump in an area McDowell came to call the "urban frontier." The dump, along with the slaughterhouses and the blood and animal waste that the packers dumped into Bubbly Creek, a branch of the Chicago River, emitted a stench that permeated the neighborhood. When Robert Hunter set out to study tenement conditions in Chicago in 1900, he deliberately excluded Packingtown, fearing that living conditions there were so bad they might prejudice his sample. "The Stock Yards District and portions of South Chicago show outside sanitary conditions as bad as any in the world," he wrote. "Indescribable filth and rubbish, together with the absence of sewerage, make the surroundings of every frame cottage abominably unsanitary."[5]

Dominated by the massive conglomerates owned by Philip Armour and Gustavus Swift, the stockyards housed more than a thousand companies, which butchered and packaged fully 90 percent of the meat sold in the United States between 1900 and 1910. Although competition among the

packers was cutthroat as growing companies moved to undersell their com-
petitors, the packing companies responded to laborers' unionization efforts
in 1894 by forming their own association, which set wages for all workers
in the yards and agreed on blacklists. A skilled butcher, typically a man of
Irish, German, or Bohemian descent, could earn as much as seventeen and
a half cents an hour, or more than $2 per day. Native-born whites, congre-
gating in those jobs designated most skilled, averaged $2.20 to $2.30 per
day. On the low end of the pay scale were recent immigrants, Polish and
Lithuanian laborers, who earned about $1.79 per day. Nearly 70 percent of
the neighborhood's household heads worked in the packinghouses, the vast
majority in low-skilled or unskilled jobs. In 1911, University of Chicago
Settlement House investigators estimated the average weekly wage for laboring men at $9.67, well below the estimated $15.40 needed to cover
weekly household expenses. Even those earning the wages of skilled workers
could not earn enough to pay rent or a mortgage and purchase food, coal,
and other necessities.[6]

Wage laborers crafted their version of the American standard of life in the
blocks of cottages, two- and three-story frame buildings that blanketed the
muddy terrain surrounding the packinghouses. Though Gross and a handful of other developers had constructed low-cost single-family dwellings
in Packingtown in the 1880s, by the turn of the century almost no new construction occurred. The builders had shifted their business to outlying
areas, where larger and more expensive dwellings generated greater profits;
with few open lots remaining in Packingtown there was little incentive or
space for new construction. More than 90 percent of Packingtown's dwellings were frame (compared to about 60 percent in the city as a whole), built
before passage of the 1902 housing ordinance, which set standard room
sizes, required at least one window in each room, and required that all apartments be equipped with a kitchen sink and private toilet. (In buildings
with apartments of fewer than two rooms, the law required one toilet for
every two apartments.) The law exempted existing buildings from most of
these requirements, leaving most Packingtown tenants and home owners
to use backyard or basement privies and to share indoor sinks with often-
unreliable running water.[7] Inside, most buildings were divided into four-
room dwellings, although some households got by in one or two rooms.
Even most cottages built for single families were by the turn of the century
used to house several households or families with several boarders. The average household, according to the 1905 Bureau of Labor survey, included
6.7 people—parents, two children, and two or three boarders. There also
were widows living with their children and a few boarders, households in-

cluding parents, grandparents, and children, and one apartment shared by eight men, one of whom cooked and cleaned while the others worked for wages. Buildings nearly filled the 25-foot-wide lots so that windows faced neighboring buildings, shedding little light and few breezes on interior rooms. Investigators for the 1905 survey noted that residents spent little money on maintaining their dwellings. Still, many hung pictures of relatives, patron saints, Christ, and the Madonna on their walls. Some could even afford rugs and curtains, some kept small pots of plants and flowers, while other households crowded into mud-floored basements. The "tenement problem," in the view of the settlement workers, included nearly all of the neighborhood's dwellings.[8]

Even as the cost of housing relative to wages increased, residents pursued property rights in housing, expressing the belief that home ownership provided autonomy, additional household income, and, as they told housing investigators, an American standard of life. Of the 284 families questioned in the 1905 Bureau of Labor survey of Packingtown, 22.5 percent were living in homes they owned. There also were some, although uncounted by investigators, who invested in rental property, using investments in tenement dwellings to generate additional household income. Those of German descent had the highest home ownership rates with three-quarters owning their homes. Germans had arrived in the city before other post–Civil War immigrant groups, established more and larger building and loan associations, and German men held a significantly larger portion of higher-paying jobs in the packinghouses. Irish and Bohemian immigrants each had home ownership rates around 50 percent. Both had lived in the city longer than the Polish and Slovak families, whose home ownership rates stood at nearly 20 percent. Of the neighborhood's largest immigrant groups, only the Lithuanians, the most recent arrivals, had home ownership rates below 10 percent. Still, the "great city frontiersmen," as McDowell called them, had "a strong desire to have a home of their own."[9]

As the ethnicity of the neighborhood's population changed in the first two decades of the twentieth century, home ownership remained a particular aspiration for immigrants, more common among the foreign-born than among the neighborhood's native-born laborers.[10] In 1914, the foreign-born made up just half of Packingtown's adult population, but immigrants accounted for about 90 percent of the home owners. By 1920, more than 58 percent of the houses in the neighborhood were owner occupied. Throughout this period, Packingtown's home ownership rates remained well above those of the city at large. Of sixteen neighborhoods canvassed by University of Chicago investigators in 1914, Packingtown ranked second in home own-

17. Children in street near stockyards, n.d. Chicago Historical Society.

ership. The first few chapters of Upton Sinclair's fictionalized portrait of the neighborhood, published in 1906, concerns the efforts of a recently arrived Lithuanian family to purchase a home, a struggle that neighborhood housing studies suggested was typical of recent arrivals.[11]

Snapshot statistics on home ownership rates in Packingtown, however, reveal little of the experiences of individual home owners. After the turn of the century, foreclosures on building loans were so common that many of those who were listed as home owners on the day an investigator or census taker knocked on their door were a year or two later renters. In particular, risks of foreclosure and loss of all money invested in the purchase of the dwelling were greater for those who bought their homes under the new "contract system." Building and loan associations, often run by neighbors and fellow-countrymen, were more likely to allow a household to miss a few payments and to permit an owner to sell the dwelling and recoup some of his investment if he could not keep up with the loan payments. But by 1905 what neighborhood residents called the contract system was flourishing in Packingtown. Under that system, a real estate speculator purchased a group of houses, provided short-term loans with monthly payments for the buyers, and then often reclaimed the house when the buyer missed a single loan payment. (Speculators, unlike commercial banks, were not covered by the state's banking and property lending laws.) Recent immigrants, unaware of the potential for job loss or injury, or simply unwilling to acknowledge those risks, and less likely to have developed a relationship with a building and loan association, were more likely to purchase a dwelling through a real estate speculator. Sinclair's account of the Rudkus family was probably representative of actual circumstances. Putting most of their savings into the purchase of a single-family house, the family soon discovered that they also had to pay interest on the loan and could not keep up with the loan payments. Within a year, the property owner foreclosed and they were forced out of the house, only to find that the house and many others on their block had been sold several times in the previous couple years with the lenders foreclosing on the buyers within six to twelve months after each sale.[12]

Home owners' struggles to pay housing loans and household expenses prompted many to subdivide apartments and houses, cramming ever larger numbers of people into ever smaller spaces.[13] With rents ranging from $6 to $15, and housing prices running from $800 to $1,500, even the best-paid laborers and their families barely earned enough to cover their housing costs, along with other necessities. The home was used to generate income and as a hedge against future uncertainties. Households of unskilled laborers, or of working-age adults who had been injured on the job or suffered from one of the many contagious diseases that plagued the neighborhood, tended to take in more boarders to cover household expenses. Noting that in the stock-yards district, income was "uncertain and work not regular," McDowell said that lodgers helped to soften the blow "if a strike or serious sickness or death occurs or a period of unemployment." On the edges of the neighborhood, where speculators built new two-story frame houses and quickly sold them to the most recent arrivals, McDowell and her volunteer investigators found that "the population of six houses was equal to many blocks where only single family houses were built." As she well knew, these "frontier" houses built "on the edge of the prairie" were single-family cottages, but their owners, in order to pay off housing loans, had taken in boarders and "unless the nine dollars extra are paid every month, all will be lost."[14]

Whether taking in lodgers or not, home owners and tenants working for less than two dollars a day relied on the contributions of all household members to achieve the American standard of life. "The daughter of the foreign born mother is expected as early as the law permits, to add to the family income," McDowell wrote, "because the father's wages are not sufficient to meet the needs of the growing standard of living."[15] A survey of nine hundred families in the stockyards district conducted between November 1911 and September 1912 found that while the girls were "struggling to keep up with American standards and avoid being classed as 'foreigners,'" 65 percent left school at age fourteen, when they could under law, and some sooner, to seek employment. Among the reasons offered by their parents, "the need of money and the ambition to own property" ranked second, just below the "peasant belief that education is the privilege of the 'upper classes.'" Not all Packingtown residents believed their children's education should be sacrificed for the well-being of the home. A Bohemian stockyards laborer, hoping for a more comfortable life for his children, contended, "People who have learned nothing do the dirty work of the world. I want my children to have a chance at a clean job. That's why I send them to school." Still, in most families "hard pressed by poverty" children were "made to feel that [they] must earn money enough to make some cash return" for the cost of maintaining the household.[16]

In Packingtown, residential property ownership was a strategy for low-wage workers to "draw an income," to establish some economic security, and to claim some autonomy in an industrial city. It was, as residents repeatedly told investigators, the "highest mark of prosperity." In the jam-packed community surrounding the Union Stock Yard, dwellings housed parents, children, grandparents, uncles, and aunts and often lodgers paying weekly fees for bed and board. Residents relied on the labor and wages of several adults and of teenage children to maintain their households. The home, whether frame cottage or two-room dwelling in a three-story building was, as Packingtown residents demonstrated, a communal structure serving multiple purposes, a conception of the home and of the social value of home ownership that would deeply disturb the settlement workers who sought to transform their neighbors' living conditions.[17]

In autumn 1894, when Mary McDowell moved into an apartment on Gross Avenue, the neighborhood was still recovering from a violent strike four months earlier. In July, packinghouse butchers had walked off the job in support of the strikers at the Pullman car works several miles southeast of the yards. Though no workers from other packinghouse departments joined the nine-week strike, thousands of people poured into the neighborhood's streets for four days in early July, torching boxcars and confronting state militiamen and police who were called in to quell the riot. In all, four people were killed and seventeen injured, and more than eighty million dollars of property was destroyed. "Disorder reigned back of the yards that autumn," McDowell wrote. "[B]lood had been shed, the regular army was encamped at Ashland and Gross Avenues, and the people were left cowed and hopeless."[18] McDowell set out to revive the community, to bring residents together to fight to improve the material conditions of life in Packingtown. Like settlement workers across the city in the late nineteenth and early twentieth centuries, McDowell would help to strengthen the bonds among residents, to create a sense of neighborhood as a unified and influential political force within the city. Property rights in housing, central to the ideals of immigrant Packingtown laborers, would prove a useful but just as often neglected feature in the reformers' campaigns against the "tenement problem."

Though the Pullman strike had sparked the violence, the angry crowds were spurred by long months of layoffs and wage cuts touched off by falling demand for meat products in the nationwide economic depression beginning in the winter of 1893. Women and children had joined the mobs, leading the *Tribune* to complain that the neighborhood's children were "steeped in the spirit of insurrection." The community's newest arrivals, Lithuanians and Slovaks, joined Polish, German, and Irish laborers in protesting the effects of their employers' cutthroat tactics. "In the mob the jargon of foreign tongues was conspicuous and the latent hatred of capital found full effervescence," the *Drovers Journal* commented. The neighborhood, the *Tribune* warned, verged on revolution. By fall, the butchers' union was destroyed, the strike leaders were permanently blacklisted, and the neighborhood's muddy streets were filled with tramps and jobless laborers.[19]

The failed Pullman strike angered and radicalized Hull House volunteers. Many were influenced by the militant rhetoric of labor organizers and the depression, which swept through Chicago's industries in the winter of 1893 and 1894, gave renewed impetus to many of the women who worked with the city's reform organizations. McDowell, whose father, a former abolitionist, was always able to provide a comfortable living for his family, was immediately and deeply affected by what she saw in the neighborhood that fall. "That very word, 'job,' came into my vocabulary in '94," she later wrote, "and has since become almost a sacred word, for I have learned that it means to my neighbors food, clothes, shelter and a chance to be human."[20] When the packinghouse workers walked off the job in 1904, McDowell supported the strike. The two-month strike of 1904, like the strike a decade earlier, ended with the firing of strike leaders, a cut in pay for wage laborers, and the destruction of the movement to organize packinghouse workers. The movement would not be revived until the late 1910s. For her support of the striking workers, McDowell was, as Gustavus Swift's son Harold later remembered, vilified as the "she-devil back of the yards."[21]

McDowell was hardly the divisive or threatening presence Swift imagined. Instead, she aimed to use the settlement house to bring people of varied classes and nationalities together to "creat[e] an environment for greater understanding" for all citizens of the city.[22] Influenced by Addams's critique of competitive capitalism and by a vision of Christianity as a force for humanitarian action and social improvement, McDowell, like many settlement volunteers, believed her task was to mitigate the direct and increasingly violent confrontations between workers and their employers. The settlement workers' goals and views on the potential of reform were, in part, shaped by their social positions; some of those who volunteered their time were the wives and daughters of the city's elite.[23] Yet settlement volunteers believed that the individualistic ethos of industrial capitalism threatened the bonds of community linking all of Chicago's residents. McDowell spoke of social cooperation among the city's diverging social classes, urging a recognition that the "population of foreign origin . . . share the destinies of Chicago and the United States." The task of the settlement, McDowell later commented, "is to be the wise, understanding, and generous neighbor."[24]

Though McDowell launched the settlement as a private venture under Jane Addams's guidance, the University of Chicago soon incorporated it and established a board of directors to oversee its work. Using the settlement as an extended classroom, university officials treated the surrounding community as a kind of laboratory, a site to be examined and quantified and on which students might test emerging theories of social order and social change. The students who worked at the settlement house conducted scores of studies, producing graphs and statistics on all aspects of the community's life. They walked from door to door, questioning residents about their home life: the availability of sinks, toilets, and running water in their dwellings, the number of people in their households, and relationships among household members. Students commented on curtains, furnishings, cleanliness, and sleeping spaces in their neighbors' dwellings. Producing voluminous amounts of knowledge about the city's wage laboring poor, students and settlement house volunteers could claim an intimate knowledge of the living conditions of their neighbors and of housing problems in the city.[25]

Highlighting the connections among housing, industrial working conditions, wages, and leisure activities, social surveys produced by settlement house volunteers helped to give McDowell's "neighborliness" spatial meaning. By mapping neighborhood boundaries and urging residents to work together to improve living and working conditions in the community, settlement volunteers strengthened existing neighborhood improvement groups and organized new ones. Home owners on the West and North Sides of the city had established neighborhood improvement organizations in the 1880s to demand municipal services, like sewer and water lines. Packingtown, with its ever expanding population, its unruly mix of nationalities and religions, of skilled and unskilled laborers, was largely unorganized until the mid-1890s. Then the strike, combined with the work of the settlement volunteers, spawned a variety of block clubs and neighborhood groups, some dedicated to education and cultural pursuits, others to cleaning alleys and fighting for garbage pickups, a labor union for the "girls and women" working in the packinghouses, and a variety of "neighborhood improvement associations."[26]

To McDowell, housing was embedded in a network of social relations: wages, family order, municipal politics all gave rise to the "tenement problem," all pervaded even the minutest details of urban living. On several occasions McDowell marched into the dwelling of a drunken husband and demanded that he stop threatening his wife and children; she also testified in hearings before the City Council (formerly known as the Common Council); she aided striking workers and campaigned for "reform-minded" candidates in City Council elections. Wage-labor relations on the packinghouse floor were as much her concern as family relations in the tenement dwelling, since both households and packinghouses shaped the life of the community. "The turn of the machine cannot be the truth of living men," McDowell wrote. "Life cannot be separated into parts, it must be seen as a whole and seen clearly."[27] Battling the "tenement problem" required organizing tenants and home owners to demonstrate their "voting strength" before the aldermen and gain "mass justice," McDowell wrote. Furious about the lack of sewer and water lines along many Packingtown streets, McDowell regularly led groups of women to meet with the commissioner of public works in City Hall. "I found the commissioner so human," she later wrote, "that when we gave the number of children for whom these mothers had to carry water from a fire plug a block away" he agreed to push the City Council to finance sewer and water lines on their block. Neighborhood, in terms of both its geography and social needs, was, in the broadest sense, a political institution.[28]

Following the precedent set by West Side property owners to demand sewers and water lines along their streets in the 1880s, property in housing further became the basis for rights-based claims on municipal resources, claims most effectively made by associations, or "combinations," of home owners. At about the same time that McDowell was organizing neighborhood women, Addams, more articulate and perhaps more politically astute than McDowell, explicitly used property relations to mobilize Hull House's neighbors in the Nineteenth Ward. Addams grafted an immigrant vision of property (where property produced household income) onto the emerging middle-class view of home ownership (where property investment generated future profits) to mobilize neighboring home owners. Contending that immigrant property owners had a "common aim" in "enhanc[ing] property values," Addams set up the Nineteenth Ward Improvement Association to pressure the council to allocate funds for paving neighborhood streets, which had "long remained a shocking mass of wet, dilapidated cedar blocks, where children were sometimes mired as they floated a surviving block in the water." The association effectively challenged the city's assessment system by demonstrating that the streets had been destroyed by "heavily loaded wagons of an adjacent factory," winning public money to cover half the costs of repaving the streets and cutting property owners' assessments by half.[29]

These efforts, however, further strained the resources of impoverished tenants and separated the interests and rights of property owners from those of the less fortunate and propertyless. While regularly employed and skilled home owners and tenants, able to pay hookup fees water and street paving assessments, were grateful for McDowell's campaigns, sewer and water lines increased the cost of housing to place "additional burdens on our poorer families." The reformers' campaigns to improve the neighborhoods' health and ease the work of cleaning the home had the unintended consequence of increasing housing costs. As sewer and water lines were installed along their streets, tenants and struggling property owners were forced to use their homes to generate additional income, moving into ever smaller and more crowded dwellings. "The mere consistent enforcement of existing laws and efforts to their advance," Adams wrote, "often placed Hull-House, at least temporarily, into strained relations with its neighbors."[30]

Still, a common interest in improving streets and maintaining their homes, combined with Addams's and McDowell's ability to apply political pressure on municipal officials, brought neighborhood home owners together despite differences of nationality and religion. "So far as a Settlement can discern and bring to local consciousness neighborhood needs which are common needs, and can give vigorous help to the municipal measures through which such needs shall be met," Addams wrote, reflecting on the role of the settlement, "it fulfills its most valuable function." An individualist strategy for economic advancement for some Chicagoans, home ownership proved an equally significant communal tactic for demanding municipal services, improvements that, as residents came to realize, could stabilize or enhance property values.[31]

While residents gathered in neighborhood organizations to fight for improvements in their local communities, the politically active and cooperating neighborhood also served as a model for the larger society. In organizing residents of different nationalities, in urging their neighbors to conceive of

Leaving the Dump
1905

18. "Leaving the dump, 1905." Chicago Historical Society.

their individual interests as linked to the interests of the larger community,
McDowell, Addams, and others sought to create a template for social relations in the city and the nation. The basic building block for this new "civic
cooperation" would be, in the housing reformers' approach, the family
home, "[h]omes where sunshine, fresh air and space with a touch of beauty
are, where the children sleep in rooms apart from the adults." These "essen-

tials," McDowell wrote, "must become necessities in every city and every industrial community if we are to conserve the national health and morals of our family life." If settlement house workers aimed to change urban society, then, they believed, they must make urban dwellings into "family homes." Under their guidance, the dwellings of the urban poor and working classes would become "respectable" family homes, something almost unrecognizable to the city's poorer residents and difficult for them to achieve.[32]

Well into the 1890s, the family home remained a fairly flexible institution, used for a variety of purposes and sheltering varied and often unrelated individuals. A household might include parents, children, servants, and boarders as well as other relatives of the household members. Though a pervasive ideology marked a distinct separation between domestic and productive sites, feminine and masculine spheres of activity, in day-to-day social practices, the boundary between home and work was fluid or nonexistent. Servants worked for wages in working- and middle-class homes and growing numbers of poor and laboring women did piecework in their dwellings, eliminating any pretense of a separation between domestic and wage labor spaces. Industrialization prompted many low-wage immigrant workers to use dwelling spaces in ways that directly challenged the separate spheres ideology, yet the rapid structural changes in the nation's economy and the resulting deterioration in housing conditions also raised new questions about the social function of property rights in housing.[33]

In the industrializing city, rents and housing prices typically determined the numbers of people living in a single dwelling. As housing prices increased relative to wages, as growing numbers of builders targeted more affluent house buyers by including indoor plumbing and larger interior spaces in new houses, those lower-middle-class and working-class buyers who aspired to home ownership often took in boarders to help cover housing costs and save money for a house purchase. A woman's labor in the home, preparing meals and beds for boarders, helped the family to meet its shelter needs while boarders shared beds and living space with family members. Students surveying tenement conditions for the Citizens Association in 1884 found many cases of large families taking in several boarders in small apartments. On Holt Street, for example, a family of five, along with eight boarders, lived in four rooms. On DeKoven Street, eight people lived in two rooms, four sleeping in the kitchen and four in the bedroom. As surveys of housing conditions demonstrated, the interior dwelling spaces of wage-laboring households served multiple functions, as any room could be used for sleeping, eating, preparing food, and gatherings of friends and relatives.[34]

Even as immigrant wage laborers pursued home ownership, the social value of owner-occupied housing for laboring families was further challenged in the 1880s by an experiment launched southwest of the city. The model town built by sleeping car tycoon George Pullman looked, to many of the city's businessmen, like a solution to both labor unrest and inadequate housing. After purchasing 3,500 acres twelve miles southwest of downtown Chicago, Pullman had invested eight million dollars to build an entire town, including brick houses for 12,000 people, workshops, schools, and a library. An architect and landscape designer had laid out the town. Sewer lines, paved streets, and landscaped lawns surrounded tidy brick houses. The Pullman Palace Car Company was both employer and landlord, and Pullman expected to make a profit of 6 percent on renting the houses.[35]

A cross between a company town and a model tenement, Pullman was in the 1880s a "showplace for private enterprise." It seemed to exemplify its founder's belief that capitalism worked and that the wage system was fundamentally fair. Poor housing, Pullman believed, resulted from unscrupulous landlords charging unreasonable rents for unsanitary tenements. By providing his labor force with decent dwellings, Pullman expected to improve productivity among his workers and, probably most importantly, eliminate a primary source of labor strife. As a benevolent, but profiting, landlord, Pullman believed that he could demonstrate that unions, strikes, industrial warfare, and slums could be made obsolete. Pullman's experiment had the added benefit of providing the manufacturer with an accessible supply of labor, dependent on him for both housing and jobs, a benefit that did not escape the notice of labor organizers. "With wonderful shrewdness [Pullman] takes the very best means of insuring a steady and docile class of workingmen," a *Progressive Age* writer noted, "as past experience has taught them that when men are as it were 'anchored to the soil' they are not in a position to take exception to any indignity that may be put upon them." Workers living in Pullman were separated from union organizers in other parts of the city, from alternative sources of employment, and from dwellings outside Pullman's rental market. Pullman had fully integrated housing and wage work.[36]

Despite the complaints from organized labor, Chicago's Citizen's Association, led by men like Marshall Field, pointed to Pullman's apparent success in constructing decent rental housing for wage laborers. The association's 1884 report on tenement housing affirmed Pullman's logic: wages were fair and housing reform could and should prove profitable to the city's business leaders. The association proclaimed that the prescription for the tenement problem was "model tenements," for-profit rental apartments owned and managed by local businessmen. Using Pullman along with model tenement projects in London and in northeastern cities as examples, the association urged the "provision of comfortable and convenient tenements for their [the working classes'] use at a moderate rent."[37] Though it repeatedly called for the construction of model tenements, and published building designs and business plans, the association was not able to find "interested capitalists" willing to invest in low-cost rental housing. When Pullman erupted in strikes and violence in 1894, the city's business leaders shelved the for-profit model tenement plans.

Yet Pullman did spur efforts to improve tenement conditions and re-newed debates over how best to house "the working man." Three years after the bloody strike, a group of settlement workers and wealthy patrons of char-itable causes gathered at the Northwestern University Settlement to discuss Chicago's "tenement problem." During three days of conferences, Addams argued for the construction of "small cottages," but while most agreed single-family houses were the best solution, they also contended "land costs rendered the ideal a practical impossibility." The group determined to call on the city government to conduct an official census of tenements and en-force building codes and to urge the city's "capitalists" to construct model tenements. The meeting resulted in the establishment of a permanent com-mittee, led by Jane Addams, Graham Taylor, and Mrs. Henry Wade Rogers (the major financial donor to the Northwestern University Settlement). In 1900, the committee called a weeklong conference, inviting some of the na-tion's best-known tenement reformers, including Jacob Riis and Laurence Veiller of New York City, and renamed itself the City Homes Association. The new organization, led and bankrolled by one of the city's wealthiest women, Cyrus McCormick's daughter, Anita McCormick Blaine, launched a wide-ranging and energetic reform program. Of its broad array of reform activi-ties, only one, the construction of low-cost rental dwellings for wage-laboring families, "produced no tangible results."[38]

The Model Tenement Committee developed plans for large multiunit rental buildings for workingmen "on sound business principle," a plan that generated some debate over the importance of a free market in housing. While committee members affirmed existing tenement regulations and Health Department inspections of tenement dwellings, some opposed di-rect intervention, by private entrepreneurs or by government, in home con-struction. One member commented that even "philanthropy that pays" was unnecessary in the housing market. Possibly thinking of the violent outburst in Pullman, another member noted, "There is not only no need for philanthropic enterprises in this line, but such enterprises are positively harmful." The committee, however, supported the Health Department's "war on bad tenements," which resulted in the demolition of buildings. No property owners went to court to fight the razing of old buildings, probably grateful that the city paid the costs of demolition leaving them better able to sell or avoid taxes on the already low-valued property. Clearance of old run-down buildings opened spaces for neighborhood parks and playgrounds, which gained the reformers' support. The city established more than ninety new parks and over one hundred municipal playgrounds in the first decades of the twentieth century. But without new housing for low-wage workers, thousands of families were left to seek shelter in increasingly crowded existing buildings.[39]

In the early twentieth century, the city's business leaders pushed for zoning laws to regulate new construction while proposals for model tenements would come largely from settlement workers who, like Mary McDowell, expressed continued concern over the urgent needs of working-class families for low-cost housing. In 1912, McDowell issued a proposal for a model tenement. She solicited financial support and business advice from architects, bankers, and a manager at Swift and Company, but was unable to find investors for her project.[40] Instead, while members of the City Club, a civic organization that included among its members many of the city's business and professional leaders, continued to search for "methods for inexpensive construction of sanitary homes for working men," the organization devoted its political influence to pushing for a "zone system" to allow the city to "abate nuisances, [and] make structural changes in buildings." With a move toward using municipal resources to regulate land uses in a zoning system modeled on New York City's 1914 ordinance, the City Club sought to improve urban life by using zoning to stabilize property values and encourage private investment in landed property. Zoning ordinances would provide "a well considered plan," without risking municipal or private capital in low-cost housing, risks that had proved overwhelming in the Pullman strike.[41]

Recognizing the tenement residents' lack of resources, McDowell, Addams, and other settlement workers had sought to offer an alternative to the lone individual confronting the shelter market. When they promoted the construction of model tenements financed by private investors, they sought to socialize the costs of worker housing. But without investors with capital or government subsidies for housing these strategies failed. Housing reformers like McDowell continued to argue for government intervention in the real estate market, for building inspections and for holding landlords responsible for the "sanitation" of their properties. The relatively high rates of home ownership in places like Packingtown suggested to the reformers that property rights in housing alone would not secure healthy and moral environments for working-class families.

As they worked to strengthen bonds of community among wage-laboring households, they also directed much of their, and the public's, attention to the immigrant household. After the turn of the century, the immigrant tenants' and home owners' uses of their homes, the multiple functions for single rooms, the varied and often unrelated residents sharing space and contributing to the household economy would increasingly conflict with the reformers' vision of the "American family home." Formerly an institution flexible enough to serve the needs and affirm the values of a diverse urban population, the home became a space whose meaning and function were disputed. Though settlement workers did not gain significant government intervention in the housing market, the reformers were increasingly able to dictate the terms of the American standard of life.

———————

In the tumultuous years around the turn of the century, the health reformers' scientific rhetoric was merged with ideas about family relations to produce a new conception of the function of the family home. The "tenement problem"—the two- or three-family dwellings subdivided into multiple apartments, the grimy dark basements housing destitute families, the ramshackle frame cottages lining mud-clogged alleys, and, most significantly, the households including a chaotic mix of parents, children, boarders, and distant relatives—was, in the reformers' view, strangling the urban community. Unable to marshal broad support for government-funded housing, McDowell, Addams, and their coworkers helped to strengthen enforcement of existing Health Department regulations and add new building codes to city ordinances. The reformers were probably most successful in heightening public awareness of what many considered the greatest "housing evil," the intermingling of unrelated adults and children in a single household. While the crowding of many individuals and families into a few small rooms was a long-standing concern of people working to improve urban health and housing, turn-of-the-century reformers linked the problem of inadequate housing to the need to secure the privacy of parents and children. The family, Graham Taylor commented, was the basic "unit of settlement work."[42] Ultimately, in formulating solutions to the tenement problem that stressed the privacy of the family, those who sought to improve housing conditions for wage laborers crystallized an increasingly rigid definition of the home.

From the 1890s through the 1920s, none of the various causes of the tenement problem was more widely discussed than "overcrowding." In his prizewinning essay, *The Housing of the Poor in American Cities*, Marcus T. Reynolds, an economist who later published a guide to corporate investing, claimed "overcrowding is at the root of all these evils . . . which are inseparably connected with the tenement-house system, which affect the wealth, morality and the very being of the nation." In 1901, when Robert Hunter, a settlement volunteer and socialist, completed his massive study of tenement conditions in Chicago, he devoted an entire chapter to "The Overcrowded Population." Though Hunter expressed surprise at the large numbers of tenements lacking indoor plumbing and sewer hookups, he assumed that overcrowding was a well-known cause of the tenement problem.[43]

More than twenty years later, Grace Abbott, a former Hull House resident and recently appointed director of the Children's Bureau, would take up a similar refrain, demonstrating the depth and enduring concern of reformers over overcrowding. In a 1924 national radio address, Abbott referred to a series of the bureau's studies that, she said, showed a direct correlation between high infant morality rates and overcrowded tenement housing. The studies had isolated overcrowding and identified it as the central factor in determining household health. "Eliminating by statistical method other factors which affect the baby's chance to live and which are frequently associated with bad housing—poverty, race or nationality, employment of mothers, type of feeding, etc," she said, "the evidence shows that the infant death rate among babies born to homes in which two or more persons per room live is twice as high as among babies in the least crowded homes."[44]

Indeed, all that frightened and motivated the disparate group of progressive reformers could be traced to overcrowded tenements. Eliding distinctions between threats to household health and "immoral" behavior, the reformers argued that overcrowding generated a laundry list of dangers both moral and medical. "After all, the social problems created by bad housing may be more serious than the health problem," one prominent reformer commented.[45] Merging concerns over household health with family morality, settlement house workers worried that typhoid and tuberculosis were "fostered by inadequate rooms and breathing spaces," just as overcrowding led to an early and dangerous sexualization of immigrant children. "No attempt at decency in the separation of the sexes—boys, girls, elder brothers, sisters, father and mother all sleeping together in one room," wrote one reformer. "The picture is not one of beauty, nor fit for calm contemplation." Children's exposure to unrelated adults, probably the reformers' greatest concern, the sharing of beds and of "family" spaces with adults not their parents, would, in Addams's view, lead to crime and unregulated sexual activity. "The surprisingly large number of delinquent girls . . . become criminally involved with their own fathers and uncles," Addams wrote. "It is these subtle evils of wretched and inadequate housing which are often most disastrous."[46] When a family of six or eight lived in two or three rooms, it was common for boys and girls to share beds and dress and undress in the same room. "Eating, sleeping, giving birth to children, the nursing and rearing of children, the care for the sick and the care for the dying are all managed after some painful fashion in these cramped living quarters," Hunter commented. He added, "A little imagination will show you how difficult or impossible delicacy or decency is in such narrow quarters."[47]

The cause of overcrowding was what reformers called "the lodger evil," the boarder paying rent and augmenting a struggling family's household income. The lodger "problem," McDowell asserted "is more nearly than any other, a menace to the health and morals of the family." Writing about juvenile delinquents, Bowen stated "the lodger problem "is always found dangerous to family life." A report on Chicago's housing published by the Commercial Club urged the enforcement of the city's building and sanitary ordinances, but never mentioned wages or rents. Instead, the report stated "The overcrowding of small family apartments with lodgers also breaks down all family privacy and often leads to gross immorality." The lodger, usually a fellow countryman, whose rent helped the cover household expenses and who shared living and sleeping spaces with other members of the household, threatened the sexual purity and morality of children, and thus good citizenship, of the biologically-related family.[48]

Overcrowded living conditions probably did prove a threat to household health by exposing more children, as well as adults, to contagious disease. But this was the case only when disease was already present; overcrowding alone did not cause epidemics. The germ theory of disease, which almost none of the reformers' writings about housing conditions mentioned, would have provided a scientific basis for their concerns. In addition, worries about "decency" and the "moral condition of the home" were not new to late nineteenth-century bourgeoisie. New York City's housing reformers had in the 1820s associated immorality with poor housing conditions. But turn of the century housing reformers, addressing both lodgers and sweated labor, added a new concern to the older morality-based domestic ideology: family privacy.

Worries about privacy were splashed across the housing reformers' writings. As McDowell asserted, housing reformers should seek to provide homes that "insure to each child sunshine, fresh air, and *privacy*" (emphasis in original).[49] Both Hunter and Reynolds identified "loss of privacy" among the "evils" caused by overcrowded tenements. Neither father nor brother, the lodger, who shared intimate domestic space with children, might disrupt lines of authority within the family, exposing children to activities like gambling and crime. The lodger, the settlement house workers worried, brought all of the vices of the neighborhood into the most intimate spaces and relationships of the home. Louise de Koven Bowen's thorough study of the juvenile court system in Chicago cited overcrowded tenements and the resulting loss of privacy as a primary cause of juvenile delinquency. The emerging rhetoric of privacy suggested that "saving children," preventing illegal and immoral behavior, required that children live under the direct supervision of mothers and fathers, that the lines of authority within the family not be confused by allowing multiple adults in the household.[50]

The reformers' rhetorical emphasis on overcrowding and the resulting demands for family privacy were part of a bourgeois vocabulary that crossed racial lines and cemented alliances between African-American and native-born white middle-class reformers.[51] In his 1919 report on housing conditions for the city's black residents, the African-American sociologist Charles S. Duke noted that taking in lodgers proved a serious threat to the household. "The situation amounts practically to the colored householders' home not being a home but in fact a home and a hotel combined with its corresponding shameful lack of privacy and opportunity for immorality."[52] Like their white counterparts, African-American housing reformers tended to link immorality and health, arguing for a remaking of the household dwelling into a "family home." Chicago reformers were not alone in articulating this new definition of the family home. Reformers in New York, Boston, and Philadelphia also associated the family home with the single-family house and with family privacy. "The normal method of housing the working population in our cities is in small houses, each house occupied by a separate family," wrote New York housing reformer Lawrence Veiller, "often with a small bit of land, with privacy for all, and with a secure sense of individuality and opportunity for real domestic life."[53]

The late nineteenth-century emphasis on privacy within the family dwelling targeted bourgeois as well as wage-laboring households. In the mid nineteenth century, Catharine Beecher had argued that domestic servants threatened "women's profession" with "dishonor" by providing services better performed by housewives. By the 1890s, Beecher's argument against servants had been replaced by arguments that emphasized family privacy and the "industrialization" of domestic service. Most middle-class and elite families retained their servants, but after 1870, as women began to find jobs in clerical work, department stores, and manufacturing, many complained about the difficulties of hiring "good servants." In 1889, the *Chicago Housekeeper* linked the "servant problem" to the danger of a "loss of privacy" for the family. Addams was more explicit, calling the domestic servant an "alien" within the household. She argued that the custom of live-in servants threatened the moral character of servants who were "isolated" from their own families and impinged on the privacy of their employers' households. Addams urged "modern" families to treat domestic servants like industrial workers, allowing their servants to live in separate households and work a set number of hours.[54]

The reformers' vision of a family home and family privacy was assumed by more affluent families. Mary Brewster Laflin, urging her son and daughter-in-law to move to Chicago, repeatedly wrote about the problem of finding adequate servants and a nurse for their infant son. Noting that "it is easy to find them [servants] in a city—and get good ones," despite her recent frustration with a cook who left for better-paying employment in a commercial laundry, Laflin added that the house can be "put in order" without the burden of live-in servants. Women like Laflin supported local women's groups, which, at the turn of the century, sponsored studies of domestic service while domestic advice givers advocated removing servants' dwelling spaces from the family home.[55]

What did the housing reformers mean when they discussed privacy? Although the reformers were quite specific when they discussed measurements for the size of rooms and per person cubic feet of dwelling space, their views of "privacy" remained vague. No reformer, for example, ever suggested that each child should have his or her own bedroom. But privacy involved a careful charting of the uses of the dwelling's interior space. Housing reformers urged families to separate sleeping from "living" rooms and to provide separate sleeping quarters for boys and girls, parents and children. Most importantly, privacy required removing the "lodger evil," the unrelated single men and women who paid for bed space in the family home.

The ideology of separate spheres had emerged earlier in the nineteenth century, but not until the 1890s did those concerned with housing conditions emphasize the private family as a distinct unit in need of physical space for its protection.[56] As they redefined the "family home," reformers stressed a particular definition of family, two married heterosexual adults and their biologically related children. Addams linked the home to the nebulous "right" to privacy, emphasizing the privacy of the family, not of its individual members. She argued that industrialization had transformed the household, replacing the "medieval affair of journeymen, apprentices, and maidens who spun and brewed" with "the family proper." The family home, in her view, should be the dwelling for "those who love each other and live together in ties of affection and consanguinity." Affective ties, more than contractual agreements between laborers, defined the family. That version of the family would exclude the lodger and the domestic servant. "Privacy," it seemed, highlighted the relationships of residents and uses of interior spaces of the home. No longer simply a shelter for adults laboring to sustain a household, a house, in the reformers' views, had become a "family home."[57]

The irony, of course, was that many of the women reformers who sought to reorder the working-class household and redefine the family home were themselves living outside the restraints and structures of the heterosexual family, living in dwellings that housed a variety of nonfamily members. Neither Mary McDowell nor Jane Addams ever married, and nor did many of the other women working in the settlement house movement. Instead, some had long-standing relationships with women and all constructed alternative-type homes, houses used by a variety of individuals who were not biologically or legally related: settlement houses. But they argued that for their neighbors, whether poor or affluent, the American standard of life required family privacy in a "family home."[58] As they urged families to eliminate boarders and wage labor within the home, the reformers' tactics ultimately functioned to narrow the definition of the home and heighten public awareness of the potential benefits of home ownership, closing off other possible avenues for providing for the shelter and household needs of both middle- and working-class families.

———————

Immigrant wage laborers' determination to own residential property put housing reformers in a difficult and contradictory position. While housing reformers tended to view home ownership as part of an American standard of life to which immigrant workers should aspire, settlement house workers also contended that their neighbors' strategies for acquiring residential property were an obstacle to improving housing conditions. Addams blamed the neighborhood's landlords, typically wage laborers who had struggled to acquire property and often subdivided single-family dwellings, for blocking efforts to improve housing conditions. "One of the most discouraging features about the present system of tenement houses is that many are owned by sordid and ignorant immigrants," she commented. "The theory that wealth brings responsibility, that possession entails at length education and refinement, in these cases fails utterly."[59] McDowell, overlooking the immigrant wage laborers who invested savings in multifamily tenements, blamed "absentee land-owners who held on to the land for future specula- tion" for the overcrowded, flood-plagued dwellings in which her neighbors lived. While grateful for much of the reformers' work, wage laborers in the packinghouses, struggling to sustain themselves and often to purchase neighborhood property, rejected much of the reformers' advice. "Hard- headed peasants," one reformer wrote, considered both family privacy and their children's education "a luxury either for the well-to-do or for those whom some mysterious power has placed above the common people."[60]

The pursuit of property rights in housing, moreover, often led to a dete- rioration of living conditions for the building owners, which worried and sometimes angered housing reformers. An Italian man and his wife, for ex- ample, saved for several years to make a down payment on a house on Chicago's West Side in 1912. The couple, worried they were "getting too old to work" and believing they could "live on the income" from tenants, moved into the basement of the two-story frame building, a damp space "too dark to rent." Though home owners regularly told tenement reformers that home owning made them "real Americans," most also said they made "heavy sac- rifices to become property-owners and landlords," sacrifices like moving their families into "dark and sometimes damp basement flats" or taking chil- dren out of school "to go to work at the earliest legal working age." Working- class families' strategies for acquiring property rights quickly became a source of tension between reformers and their neighbors.[61]

To the settlement workers' surprise, their strongest allies in fighting over- crowding were the neighborhood's youth, the generation of young men and women born in the United States and raised by immigrant parents. The younger generation, "making their own standards through the natural law of imitation which leads them to break away from the older ideals of the home" and working for wages in factories, department stores, and offices, used their contributions to the household income to pressure parents for "a higher standard of living at home." Faced with reformers' efforts to reorder her household and with her children's desires to live "according to the Amer- ican standard," a Slovak woman told her daughter, "You are not a rich Amer- ican." Yet her daughter, like many Packingtown teenagers, sought to spend her earnings on "fashionable" clothes and evenings in the dance halls, and to become "American" through the elimination of lodgers from her family's rented dwelling. Some young people even "hasten[ed] marriage to escape the "unbearable condition" of living with "seven or eight people in four rooms." "It is a significant fact," wrote one investigator of housing conditions in Packingtown, "that the rebellion against overcrowding comes from the young people and not the parents."[62]

The younger generation's opposition to the "lodger evil," though gratifying to McDowell, meant that households were even more dependent on their children's wages, an outcome that alarmed the housing reformers. When a father's wages fell below two dollars a day or when mothers were widowed, deserted, or left with injured or ill husbands, daughters were significantly more likely to enter wage work. Yet the aspiration for property in housing remained a central factor in the decisions made by working-class families. "Some of the children, principally Italians, Bohemians and Germans are sent to work by their parents out of sheer excess of thrift," commented Hull House resident Florence Kelley, "perhaps in order to pay off a mortgage on some tenement house." The reformers' attempts to eliminate overcrowding, as settlement workers discovered, meant that growing numbers of younger women and men left school to work to earn an American standard of living. Immigrant workers and their children sought to become American, but often on their own terms.[63]

Of possibly greater significance for Chicago's changing housing markets, the reformers' struggle to limit overcrowding confronted the property rights claims of tenement and boarding, or lodging, house owners. While the tenants themselves found little legal ground to improve living conditions, propertied Chicagoans who sought to generate profits from managing multiple dwelling sites resisted government efforts to regulate the uses of their properties. The reformers gained a short-lived victory in 1899 with the passage of an amendment to the state board of health act, which barred more than six persons from occupying the same room for "sleeping purposes" and put all lodging houses under the direct control of the Department of Health. Lodging house owners, citing contract law and their private property rights, stood on firmer legal ground than the tenement dweller who rented a bed to a boarder. In November 1899, J. A. Bailey, the owner of a lodging house, was arrested, convicted, and fined twenty-five dollars for permitting nineteen people to sleep in one large room. Bailey appealed the conviction and in April 1901, the state Supreme Court ruled the amended law void. In its decision, the court stated that the right to receive lodgers "is a liberty and also a property right," one that cannot under the state constitution be restricted or abridged.[64]

The effort to restrict crowding in tenement dwellings was revived in the following years, and municipal legislation passed in 1902 added regulations that further distinguished the property rights of tenement dwellers from those of commercial lodging houses. The legislation required four hundred cubic feet of air space for each occupant over twelve years and two hundred cubic feet for each person under twelve in any tenement dwelling. Though some City Council members opposed the bill, which applied primarily to future construction, few wanted to be seen as opposing Anita McCormick Blaine's call for dwellings that would provide "an effective motherhood, of a happy childhood, of the integrity and the promise and happiness of family life." The bill passed forty-seven to seven. By then, increasing public concern for the health and morals of the laboring classes, for "improved standards for family" dwellings, for, as Blaine suggested, privacy for the family, overrode some property rights claims.[65]

With the court's 1902 ruling, boardinghouses became the reformers' chosen dwellings for the single men and women who arrived in the city seeking work. Even critics of model tenements supported construction of "lodging houses," a "paying" enterprise that might replace the use of police stations for housing "tramps" and the homeless. The depression of the 1890s had generated a burgeoning population of homeless laborers, who regularly spent the night in parks, police stations, and even on the steps of City Hall. In 1901, the City Homes Association proposed the construction of a boardinghouse maintained by the city. A municipally managed lodging house, the association contended, could take the job of housing the poor away from the police. The city announced a plan to construct a lodging house in 1901, but a year later, when public funding proved inadequate, the association raised $5,000 and opened Chicago's first municipal lodging house. Two years later, it was taken over by the city. It became a model for other lodging enterprises, which strictly supervised lodgers and often required men who could not pay for their lodging to work off their fees on the premises. Although some religious organizations, like the Salvation Army, had run lodging houses before 1900, the number of lodging houses in the city, most privately run, grew significantly after the turn of the century. Often uncomfortable, poorly furnished, and rigidly regulated, lodging houses provided young, single men and women a legal and low-cost alternative to renting bed space in an already crowded tenement dwelling.[66]

Though some immigrant wage-laboring families resisted the reformers' campaign against lodgers, by the 1910s fewer families were taking in boarders and there was a sharp decline in the number of boarders living in family dwellings in the 1910s and 1920s. Edith Abbott's 1935 study of Chicago's tenements reviewed a series of door-to-door canvasses of immigrant neighborhoods, finding that the proportion of lodgers in the city dropped from nearly 15 percent to 8 percent between the mid-1910s and the mid-1920s;

in Packingtown that number fell from nearly 30 percent to about 9 percent.[67] The reformers' antilodger campaign was not the sole cause of the decline in the number of boarders in family homes. The expanding availability of jobs in manufacturing combined with a growing number of married women seeking wage work outside the home likely helped an increasing number of wage-laboring families to subsist without taking in boarders. With the outbreak of war in Europe and the resulting cutoff of immigration from Europe, foreign-born families were less likely to be pressed by fellow countrymen to provide lodging.[68]

Yet Chicago's population continued to grow during and after World War I, as native-born African-American and white workers moved to the city seeking jobs in war-related industries, and the decline in numbers of lodgers in family dwellings reached beyond immigrant neighborhoods. During the period of the largest expansion of Chicago's African-American population and in an increasingly tight housing market, proportionately fewer African-American households took in lodgers than in previous decades. On the West Side, the proportion of lodgers in the total population declined slightly from 14 to 11 percent between 1912 and the midtwenties, and in the Black Belt on the South Side, the proportion fell from 31 to 22 percent in the same period. Some recent arrivals continued to find shelter in family dwellings, but increasingly single young men and women, both native born and foreign born, moved into lodging houses and rented single rooms. Dwelling space was still hard to find, and fewer families opened their homes to boarders.[69]

———————

Exposing and then critically analyzing the varied networks of economic, and perhaps emotional, support that helped to sustain immigrant wage laborers and African-Americans living in tenement dwellings, the reformers urged a reordering of community relations that emphasized the individual family unit. While approaching the neighborhood as a cohesive unit, they argued that the community drew its moral and physical strength from individualized family dwellings, from their version of an "American standard of life." Reformers like Addams and McDowell set new and more rigid standards for the relationships among the household members, envisioning a "family home" that was not simply a shelter, but rather a site that separated parents and children—what we might call the nuclear family—from the rest of the city. They established the "privacy" of biologically related household members as the American standard, the model for healthy and moral housing, a standard that overlapped with and buttressed the promotional campaigns of businessman-builders like Samuel Eberly Gross. Reformers' campaigns, with their housing surveys and detailed neighborhood maps, highlighted the material conditions of city housing, but of equal importance, had a profound impact on the ideological construction of the family home. Struggling to improve living conditions in impoverished urban neighborhoods, tenement reformers inadvertently fueled Americans' desire for and celebration of single-family home ownership.

By focusing attention on relations among individuals inside the home, turn-of-the-century reformers tended to overlook what would become the most critical and divisive of Chicago's housing problems: the increasingly rigid racial segregation of its neighborhoods. Nor did the city's housing reformers view racial discrimination in housing as a significant obstacle to solving the city's tenement problem.[70] Black settlement workers, and some whites, like Mary McDowell and Jane Addams, noted the deteriorating living conditions in the Black Belt. But as wage laborers, black and white, struggled to stretch inadequate wages to cover rents or home purchases, competition for low-cost housing increasingly occurred along racial lines. Black and white housing reformers were well aware of the racial boundaries separating their neighborhoods, yet not until the competition for housing, and for jobs, erupted in a bloody riot in 1919 would any of the reformers see those boundaries as a significant obstacle to solving the city's housing problems. Indeed, some of the housing reformers proposals functioned to buttress racial bias in the housing market and further solidify racial divisions.

CHAPTER SEVEN

Drawing the "Color Line":
The Roots of Residential Segregation

In 1903, when a "respectable" black minister was denied housing on Chicago's North Side, *Co-operation*, the weekly journal published by the Chicago Bureau of Charities commented that racial discrimination in the city's housing market had sadly become common. The journal noted that the unfortunate fact was that "persons of undoubted worth [were] shunned and made to feel that character went for nothing and that the color of their skin was a reproach to them." The minister, however, responded by referring to the advice of the black educator, Booker T. Washington, urging black men to acquire property so that "[their] dual position, that of [men] of character plus [men] of property will command respect and honor from the whites." The minister's advice was repeated in the city's black-owned newspapers and in essays published by middle-class African-American housing reformers. His association of respectability and home ownership was by the turn of the century fast becoming commonplace among the city's middle classes, both black and white. The pursuit of home ownership by growing numbers of black Chicagoans, however, fueled the increasingly rigid racial segregation of the city's residential neighborhoods. Property rights in housing, long desired by working-class immigrants, enshrined by reformers as a solution to the city's health and housing problems, and touted by builders as securing gender order and establishing middle-class status, would in the early twentieth century enflame racial violence and further divide the city along racial lines.[1]

For black Chicagoans, home ownership proved a tricky and dangerous pursuit. In the decade and a half after 1900, real estate operators and lending institutions effectively redrew the social landscape of the city, producing a "color line" that determined real estate values and separated the homes of white Chicagoans from those of African-Americans. Creditors tended to

Built-up area
Parks and cemeteries
Areas of significant black population
Elevated lines
Railroads

Oakton
Touhy
Devon
Peterson

Milwaukee
Lincoln
C I T Y   L I M I T S

Lawrence

Harlem
Irving Park
Narragansett
Central
Cicero
Belmont
Crawford (Pulaski)
Elston
Kedzie
Western
Ashland
Clark
Halsted
Fullerton

LAKE
MICHIGAN

North
Chicago
Madison
Lake
Desplaines River
Roosevelt (12th)
Hull House
22nd (Cermak)
31st
Ogden
Archer
Black Belt
Vernon Avenue
Binga Bank
Pershing
Sanitary & Ship Canal
Pershing (39th)
Stock Yards
Back of the Yards
47th
Hyde Park
Univ of Chicago
Archer
55th
Central
Cicero
Crawford (Pulaski)
Kedzie
Western
Ashland
Halsted
63rd
71st
C I T Y   L I M I T S
Harlem
79th
Columbus
Cottage Grove
Stony Island
South Chicago
Yates
South Shore

N
ONE MILE

87th
95th
103rd
Pullman
Lake Calumet
111th
106th
Torrence
Calumet River
119th
127th
C I T Y   L I M I T S

Maps by Chicago CartoGraphics

19. Map of Chicago, 1919.

refuse to finance the purchase of properties occupied by black tenants while real estate operators developed elaborate schemes to cement the bonds of community among home owners of European descent. African-Americans who could afford to purchase single-family houses outside of increasingly run-down black neighborhoods often were the first to face long-simmering white hostilities. By the 1910s, when Chicago's black population doubled in less than ten years, rising demand for housing and struggles over the racial character of neighborhoods resulted in recurring violence. In the sweltering summer of 1919, a bloody race riot erupted. As historian William M. Tuttle says, "the riot should have surprised few people."[2]

Despite the small article about the minister in *Co-operation*, racial segregation was rarely mentioned in the journal. As the city's settlement house workers pursued investigations of living conditions in immigrant communities and organized wage laborers of varied nationalities to demand municipal regulations of housing, they rarely acknowledged the increasingly rigid racial boundaries dividing Chicago's citizens. Possibly the only student of the urban scene to complete a study of housing conditions among Chicago's small but growing black population in the early years of the twentieth century was Monroe Nathan Work, a graduate student at the University of Chicago. Work's masters thesis, completed in 1902, was never published. His research, though limited, might have proved useful to Chicago's housing reformers. Work noted that black Chicagoans "seeking to avoid segregation and excessive rents" turned to "property ownership." And, wrapping up thirty pages of analysis of property ownership rates, rental fees, and occupational data on black Chicagoans, Work commented, "the most pressing problem that at present confronts him [the Negro of Chicago] appears to be the Housing Problem."[3]

———

At the turn of the century, the majority of the city's 30,000 African-Americans were newcomers, recent migrants from "the small towns and country districts of the South." Just over 1,000 "refugees from slavery" had settled in the city before the Civil War. The African-American population grew slowly until 1890, when black Chicagoans made up just over 1 percent of the city's 1.7 million people. Then, an ever-growing stream of black Americans flowed into the city. Among them were the ministers, lawyers, and educators who briefly during Reconstruction held positions in southern state legislatures and Congress. Many others, fleeing the system of sharecropping and the regimes of terror in the American south, landed in Chicago. "The restless educated and half-educated who were not contented to live life on southern terms" arrived in Chicago after 1890, expanding the city's tiny black population by the thousands and then by the tens of thousands in the early twentieth century.[4]

Most found jobs in low-wage, unskilled, and often unreliable work in businesses and homes owned by white men. A handful of African-American entrepreneurs and professionals catered to their neighbors' needs, creating a fairly insular community largely removed from the strike-weary immigrant neighborhoods. Black men were listed in the 1900 census as laborers, porters, janitors, clerks, cooks, and waiters. There were a few musicians, some lawyers and doctors, bootblacks, barbers, and at least one ball player. Some black men worked in low-wage jobs in the packinghouses, but until the 1910s, black men generally found work in industry as "scabs" when European-born laborers walked off the job, the first to be fired when the strike ended. Although some married women worked at home, caring for young children and looking after the needs of lodgers, a large portion of black married women worked for wages outside their households. Some found jobs as seamstresses and hairdressers, but the vast majority of wage-earning black women, married and unmarried, worked as servants in the homes of white Chicagoans. Wage-laboring African-Americans, earning significantly less than their working-class counterparts newly arrived from Eastern and Southern Europe, were less likely to acquire the cash to invest in home ownership.[5]

Affluent black Chicagoans, particularly those who owned their homes, would be among the most vocal and outraged opponents of the tactics of white real estate men. Many of these "old settlers," the city's tiny black elite, like the lawyer, S. Laing Williams and his wife Fannie Barrier Williams, had arrived in Chicago before 1890. The Williamses lived on Forty-second Place off of Grand Boulevard, which was home to some of the city's well-to-do native-born, Irish, and German Jewish families. Another prominent lawyer, Lloyd Garrison Wheeler, who moved to Chicago before the end of the Civil War and later was a close friend of Booker T. Washington, in the 1890s resided with his family at 4344 South Langley Avenue, in a neighborhood of affluent native-born and German households. Members of civic reform organizations and advocates of racial uplift through the nineteenth-century values of respectability, thrift, and hard-work, Chicago's black elite mingled in white business affairs, politics, and social reform work. Separating themselves geographically and socially from the regularly employed and small business owners who made up a "respectable" black middle class and from struggling working-class African-Americans, affluent black men and women increasingly affirmed the social value of property rights in housing.[6]

Despite the apparent economic success of Chicago's black elite and despite the Illinois legislature's ban on school segregation in 1874 and of racial discrimination in public accommodations a decade later, racial segregation of residential neighborhoods remained the general custom from the late nineteenth century through the twentieth. In 1900, enclaves of black families settled around Chicago with small groups of families living in single-family cottages along Lake Street from Ashland to Western Avenues and near Halsted and Adams Streets on the West Side, and south of Madison Street and west of State Street just east of the Chicago River. Clusters of single men lived in rooming houses near the city's southern border. More than half of the city's African-American population lived in what was called the Black Belt, a narrow corridor stretching more than three miles south from the downtown railroad yards to just below Thirty-ninth Street.[7] A neighborhood that included the poorest and some of the most affluent of Chicago's African-Americans, the Black Belt was possibly the only section of the city whose population spoke one language and could trace its roots to a single region, the American south. "The good and bad" lived in "close proximity," as Richard T. Wright put it, not only in the same community, but "indeed in the same house, often in the same room."[8] The census of 1900 shows a smattering of immigrants from Bohemia, Russia, Ireland, and Italy living among American-born black people on several Black Belt blocks. By 1910, when the city's black population hit nearly 44,000, the Black Belt had absorbed more than 10,000 people in less than twenty years, and European immigrants had largely separated themselves from black Chicago.[9]

Though home to some of the city's middle class and most "respectable" black families, the Black Belt was long associated in the minds of most Chicagoans with vice. The connection between vice and wage-laboring African-American neighborhoods probably predates the fire, yet the Black Belt's reputation was further tarnished in the 1890s following the appearance in Chicago of British journalist and moral reformer William T. Stead. In the wake of Stead's famous 1893 speech exhorting Chicagoans to remove houses of prostitution, gambling dens, and saloons from their midst, the newly formed Civic Federation moved to "clean up" the municipality. Although most of the city's saloons were untouched, police officials responded to the reform campaign by "segregating" overt gambling and prostitution to the few blocks just south of Harrison Street, an area occupied by some black Chicagoans and edging an enclave housing three of the city's largest African American churches and their congregations.[10]

Stead's sensational account of vice in the city, *If Christ Came to Chicago!*, set off a "battle between the segregationists, who believed in a legal Red-light District, and the non-segregationists who wished to abolish it." At least one

black minister accused police officials and reformers of "driving these un-
fortunates [prostitutes and gamblers] to the very doors of Quinn Chapel, the
Olivet Baptist and Bethel churches." Since it was impossible, and politically
untenable, to close down all gambling and prostitution in the city, police
segregated it.[11] "Segregating vice" did not solve the city's "vice problem," nor
did it remove gambling or prostitution from other sections of the city. But
it did leave some of the most infamous "houses" to flourish in a largely
African-American neighborhood. Long after the legal red light district was
broken up, the Black Belt retained the stigma of vice.

Middle-class African-Americans, in particular, were angered both by the
stigma and by the reality of vice in their community. Regularly employed
professionals earning enough to finance well-maintained homes, as well as
postal clerks, Pullman porters, and hotel waiters considered the open displays of gamblers and prostitutes and the drunks spilling out of Black Belt
saloons particularly insulting. "The huddling together of the good and the
bad, compelling the decent element of the colored people to witness the
brazen display of vice of all kinds in front of their homes and in the faces of
their children," commented Fannie Barrier Williams, "are trying conditions
under which to remain socially clean and respectable."[12]

The vast majority of black Chicagoans, arriving in the city in the wake of
the construction boom of the 1880s and early 1890s, rented living space in
existing older dwellings, particularly in the Black Belt. White real estate investors had either built frame houses as investment properties or purchased
the dwellings when middle-class and wage-laboring white families left to
buy new houses near parks and on the edge of the city.[13] In 1912, Alzada P.
Comstock, a sociologist, made a house-by-house survey of two black districts, five blocks in the Black Belt and a section of the West Side near Lake
Street. Comstock reported that housing conditions in African-American
neighborhoods were the most deteriorated, crowded, and unsanitary in the
city. Chicago's black families tended to live in two-story frame houses origi-
nally built for one family, but subdivided into two, three, or four two- or
four-room flats. Outside, stairways and porches "seem to be almost falling
apart." Inside was worse. Comstock's investigators found few houses fitted
with indoor plumbing. Most were marred by "broken down doors, unsteady
flooring, and general dilapidation." If the decay continued, Comstock concluded, "Chicago will have its 'devastated area' without the assistance of the
violence of modern warfare."[14]

Deterioration of African-American neighborhoods had begun long before Comstock's investigators arrived and would continue unabated for decades. Most of the housing she explored was owned by white real estate

speculators who lived outside the neighborhood, and most was built before the 1902 housing ordinance. Back alley and basement privies remained into the 1910s; even when indoor plumbing was installed, investigators reported that "water has not been running in [the] toilet since last winter." Well aware that black wage-laborers had few choices over where to rent dwelling spaces, property owners could easily fill the most run-down buildings with black tenants. Though tenants complained about housing conditions, property owners found they could collect rents without investing money in repairing or improving property in African-American neighborhoods. As soon as a black family moved into a building, "[t]he wealthy owner of a large battery of flats . . . immediately dispense[d] with his efficient janitor service and his corps of house repairers." Decaying housing led to falling property values, and as the value of their real estate investments fell, property owners saw little reason to invest capital in repairs or improvements. It was a seemingly inevitable downward spiral of falling values and deteriorated housing. As Charles S. Duke in his 1919 study of housing available to Chicago's African-Americans noted, "This failure on the part of property owners on the south side to make the necessary repairs for colored tenants and the failure to provide efficient janitor service is the outstanding cause of the rapid deterioration of property in this district and the fall of real estate values."[15]

One prominent exception was the African-American real estate entrepreneur and banker, Jesse Binga, whose successful businesses, located at the corner of State Street and Thirty-fifth Street, marketed housing directly to black Chicagoans with advertisements in the *Broad Ax* and the *Chicago Defender,* African-American-owned newspapers. In the early twentieth century, Binga, following the pattern set by Gross and other businessman-builders, provided loans to buyers and managed several South Side rental properties. He sold houses priced from $2,000 to $9,000. But Binga alone could not provide enough capital in the form of housing loans for all of those who sought to purchase Black Belt housing; equally importantly, the handful of rental buildings managed by his firm were among the very few owned or managed by a locally owned real estate firm.[16] Many other Black Belt properties, owned by white investors and typically left without capital investments in maintenance or improvements, set the pattern of falling property values and deteriorated housing in the neighborhood.

Falling property values did nothing to lighten the burden of rents. Rather, racial segregation combined with the influx of black laborers pushed rents higher even as dwellings fell into disrepair. Black tenants, Work found, were charged 10 to 50 percent more in rent than wage laborers of European descent. "The consequent limited area in which the Negro is compelled to

20. Visiting nurse and five children, interior of tenement, n.d. Chicago Historical Society.

live," he commented, fueled demand for housing and spurred rent increases. "In general," he added, black Chicagoans "are compelled to rent whatever is offered, and at the price demanded. The rapid increase in the Negro population without a corresponding increase in the area of the district in which the Negroes can rent property, causes a great deal of competition among them . . . and a consequent raising of the rent price." A decade later, Comstock found that rents paid by African-Americans were "appreciably higher than that paid by any other nationality." By then, competition for housing had spurred white real estate operators to gradually push the "color line" south, with little or no benefit for black Chicagoans.[17]

Provoking and playing on the fears of white home owners, real estate brokers and land speculators found they could reap large profits by expanding the boundaries of the Black Belt and the West Side's African-American community. Property values would not automatically plummet when a black family moved into a white-only neighborhood, but the tactics of many real estate dealers convinced wage-laboring and middle-class whites that black neighbors signaled a drop in property values. It wasn't a difficult argument to make: real estate men simply pointed to the Black Belt, where housing was in serious disrepair and property values were falling. A white family, particularly recent immigrants, who had invested all of their savings into a home purchase and might still be paying off a housing loan would likely be frightened by the prospect that the value of their investment would fall and they would be unable to acquire a second or third loan on the property. (While the Black Belt did not expand significantly into immigrant neighborhoods on the South Side until the mid twentieth century, brokers used these tactics in West Side immigrant communities surrounding clusters of African-American households.) The emotional and financial security of home owning, many were convinced, would be destroyed by African-American neighbors.[18]

Real estate brokers and land speculators stood to gain significant profits by frightening owners into selling their cottages and two- or three-flats. Pushing east of State Street into comfortable enclaves of middle-class white households and south of Thirty-ninth Street into the largely affluent Kenwood and later Hyde Park neighborhoods, speculators convinced frightened white property owners to sell quickly and for low prices, then resold the properties to black buyers at inflated prices. "It is said that one firm has cleared up nearly $1,500,000 in the past five years in speculating with white owners who are sacrificing their property from the fact that some colored man has bought or rented in the immediate vicinity," Binga commented to a *Chicago Defender* reporter in 1915. The appearance of a black resident was used "as a lead pipe on the owners" to persuade them to sell at "a low figure then to market it to negroes at an advance of from $500 on residences to $5 on rents on flats and apartment buildings."[19] Real estate salesmen also earned significant profits from multiple rapid sales. Salesmen earned a commission on each property sold. Those working with black buyers and tenants learned that they could generate a series of commissions rapidly by "turning over" houses owned by frightened white families.

Brokers employed these strategies in middle-class and working-class white neighborhoods, successfully appealing to the city's home owners' worries about property values. After the turn of the century, Italian immigrants on the West Side, as Jane Addams recognized, increasingly saw ownership of tenement property as a long-term investment and were increasingly concerned about the assessed value of their property. Sewers and street paving "enhanced value," she noted, urging Italian tenement owners to invest some capital in maintaining their buildings. While she was not always able to persuade her neighbors to improve living conditions in rental dwellings, the American standard of life was, as Addams recognized, increasingly conceived as a long-term investment. "In immigrant neighborhoods," wrote Edith Abbott in her massive study of tenement conditions in Chicago, "the purchase of any kind of house, an income-producing tenement or cottage, or even an empty lot in an undesirable neighborhood, is looked upon as a 'safe' investment." For working-class Chicagoans, Italians near Hull House and Eastern Europeans in the packinghouse district, who achieved home ownership only through subdividing houses and renting space to boarders and tenant families, the prospect of falling property values meant losing value and potential income on property that had required great sacrifice to acquire.[20]

Speculators and real estate brokers employed a variety of strategies to frighten white property owners into believing property values were falling and into selling out quickly. White real estate salesmen, often called "blockbusters," typically worked through African-American subagents. There were some legitimate black real estate operators who worked with middle-class black buyers. Others were known as "curbstone brokers," whose job was to recruit impoverished black families and move them into a white-only neighborhood. If black families could not be found to buy the surrounding houses, white speculators would swoop in to purchase several properties. They might further subdivide the dwellings, renting a few rooms to wage-laboring and impoverished black families. And they could raise rents without investing any capital in improvements. New black tenants and home owners, realizing that they had to stretch their meager earnings to cover housing expenses, took in boarders to add to the household's income. The result was that a block of single-family dwellings previously owned by white families had, sometimes within one year, become a block of slowly deteriorating multifamily dwellings occupied by struggling black tenants and home owners. The brokers and speculators who had provoked the racial transition used white fears and black aspirations to fill their bank accounts.[21]

Along with projections of falling property values, realtors produced a particularly crude image of black tenants to force nearby whites to sell. Clearly exacerbating white racism, realtors picked out the most recent arrivals from the rural south and encouraged, often paid, them to embody racist stereotypes of black buffoonery and ignorance. In the summer of 1900, realtors applied this strategy to a block of Vernon Avenue, just east of the Black Belt. In July, "a colored man" appeared on the exclusively white block, announcing that he was authorized to sell the brick two-flat at number 3342, which had been vacant for a year. After workmen remodeled the building, dividing each apartment in two and adding a rear stairway, three black families moved in. As the *Chicago Inter-Ocean* noted, the black tenants sat on the porch each evening, enjoying "the breezes that blow through the streets so carefully nurtured on Vernon Avenue." Every morning a "black 'sandwichman' shuffled out of the basement apartment" wearing clanking boards proclaiming "Wear Never-Rip Pants." The visibility of the black residents, their obviously overcrowded dwellings, and their low-wage jobs drove their white neighbors to a state of "nervous prostration." The whites rallied and fought off the "invasion" for a few years. But a decade later, Vernon Avenue housed only black families.[22]

Vernon Avenue's new tenants and home owners, however, belied the image of black Chicago so insidiously cultivated by real estate men. In 1908, the socially conscious Richard T. Wright Jr. described this block of Vernon Avenue as "one of the most beautiful" in the Black Belt. "Many of these houses," he continued, "have small lawns in front of them . . . and shade trees between the sidewalk and the street, which add much to the appearance of the street and the comfort of the residents." The tidy brick houses had sold for between $3,500 and $14,000 to "Negro business and professional men." Even Archibald J. Carey, a powerful minister and politician, lived on the 3400 block of Vernon Avenue. Property rights in housing, even in a racially segregated block, had become a mark of status for the black middle classes.[23]

Not all middle-class African-Americans were as fortunate as those living on Vernon Avenue. Hoping to escape the deterioration and high rents in the Black Belt, a black family might purchase a house on a nearby white-only block. The "fortunate Negro" might claim "with a degree of exultation, 'We don't live in a colored neighborhood,' or 'We live in a white neighborhood.'" Then the realty agent would double-cross his black customer, frightening white owners into selling to speculators who moved impoverished black tenants into the newly subdivided neighboring dwellings. The black middle-class family would find itself again surrounded by impoverished African-Americans unable to maintain their rented dwellings.[24]

Despite the urging of black professionals and urban reformers, home owners remained a tiny portion of the growing African-American population, and black Chicagoans were less likely than their white counterparts to own their homes. Home ownership rates among black Chicagoans, though small, increased steadily after 1890. In 1900, 362 African-American households owned residential property, a 39 percent increase over the previous ten years. Many owned two or more pieces of real estate, typically a dwelling and vacant lot, or two or three dwellings. The vast majority of black-owned dwellings were valued at less than $2,000, suggesting that those dwellings were one- or two-story frame houses. Those who owned two or more properties tended to subdivide single-family dwellings, renting rooms and small apartments to other black families and placing advertisements in black-owned newspapers, typically announcing, "Good Colored Tenants Always Appreciated."[25]

Some black families, seeking homes with lawns and near industrial jobs, sought housing outside the city limits. Just five thousand black people lived in suburban Chicago in 1910, mostly in a handful of largely white suburban communities. Some, often household servants, lived in affluent north suburban Evanston. About one fifth of black suburbanites lived in Harvey, Aurora, and Joliet, communities south and west of Chicago where steel and railroad jobs attracted working-class black and white residents. Most significantly, black suburban residents lived in African-American enclaves located within communities that housed primarily white residents.[26]

In the city, since the number of black-owned dwellings was small, the amount of capital generated by property ownership and circulated through the Black Belt in the form of rent payments was small. Still, African-American renters used their homes to generate additional income by taking in lodgers. For African-American families, paying higher rent than any other wage laborers, rents paid by boarders provided a needed addition to household income. Comstock's study in 1912 as well as studies of black households in 1920 found that dwellings housing black families tended to include substantially higher numbers of boarders than those housing families of European descent. The reason, as Charles S. Duke noted in 1919, was high rents and higher costs for property purchases in black-only neighborhoods.[27]

Though black Chicagoans earned, on average, significantly less than white Chicagoans, the low level of home ownership in largely black neighborhoods was likely caused by the lack of capital available for loans on property in African-American neighborhoods. Lower wages, higher rents, and higher purchase prices certainly made it more difficult for black Chicagoans to accumulate capital for down payments on residential property, but a lack of credit proved a near insurmountable obstacle even for those who earned enough to save for a down payment. Some property owners acquired housing loans from building and loan associations and after 1908 from real estate entrepreneur Jesse Binga. Yet the majority of African-American home owners purchased dwellings on the contract system through local real estate dealers who tended to put higher prices on property in black neighborhoods and to charge black purchasers higher interest rates than those for white home buyers. (Black real estate dealers were likely simply passing on higher interest rates that they were charged by commercial banks.) Black home buyers faced a double barrier: it was hard for a black person to find a loan for any property, and it was near impossible for anyone, white or black, to acquire a loan to purchase property in the Black Belt. As residential property in the Black Belt continued to deteriorate, and property values plummeted, fewer creditors would lend money for property purchases there. "Real estate operators complain that it is almost impossible to obtain any kind of a loan on property occupied by colored people from any bank or real estate loan broker," noted Duke in 1919, "except with the greatest of difficulty."[28]

Yet black Chicagoans, particularly those with steady employment and aspirations for social mobility, desperately sought to purchase housing. Since loans for property in areas already occupied by African-Americans were unavailable, aspiring black families looked to property outside of black-only neighborhoods. Living conditions in the Black Belt, where frame houses were packed and decaying, gave added impetus to those who sought a decent, well-kept house. Whether housing activists themselves or influenced by the rhetoric of the reformers, black families sought single-family dwellings that would secure family privacy and preserve household health. "The Negro of the better sort is prospering," the *Chicago Record-Herald* editorialized in 1911. "He demands and can pay for a better home with more favorable surroundings than he could afford a few years ago. Hence, the Negro 'invasions' of neighborhoods hitherto white."[29] But moving outside of the Black Belt or the handful of African-American enclaves on the West Side was not easy. Even when a black man had money to purchase property outside the Black Belt, "he would find, when his lot was ready for him, that he would be unwelcome to his neighbors of a lighter skin. Even as a renter he is only acceptable in regions devoted to his race."[30]

Recognizing that white neighbors might pressure property owners or real estate men to refuse to sell to a black family, some African-Americans kept their identity a secret until the transaction was complete. In 1910, for example, a black woman purchased a West Side lot near a park and contracted for the construction of a small cottage. "It was not until she moved into the complete house that the neighbors discovered that a colored family had acquired the property there." Reaction was swift and tragic. After a "crusade of insults and threats," a mob of masked men broke into the house at night, "told the family to keep quiet or they would be murdered; then they tore down the newly built house, destroying everything in it."[31]

The lesson taught by block–busters both contributed to and reinforced the racism that permeated late nineteenth-century America. Black Chicagoans typically complained that "foreigners learn how to cuss, count and say 'nigger' as soon as they get here." Comstock noted that "colored people of all positions in life found it nearly impossible to escape the relatively small and well-defined areas" to which Chicago relegated all black people. "The explanation for this condition of affairs among the colored people," Comstock concluded, was "comparatively simple." White people could not stand having "colored people living on white residence streets, colored children attending schools with white children, or entering into other semi-social relations with them."[32]

By the early twentieth century, the growing numbers of black Chicagoans seeking housing in previously white neighborhoods prompted organized resistance from white property owners. The block clubs and neighborhood associations formed by immigrant home owners to improve their communities turned to "indignation meetings in which hysterical protestations were registered" when a black family moved nearby. Threats mounted and violence often resulted. When a black family moved to Champlain Avenue in 1911, white neighbors responded with a "judicious use of a wagon load of bricks, broke a few heads and then vanished." Describing the attack as "something as nearly approaching the operations of the Ku Klux Klan as Chicago has seen in many years," the *Record-Herald* noted that the brick throwers were part of a "committee, supposed to be Champlain avenue property owners."[33] By 1915, the *Chicago Defender*, reporting on another attack by white property owners on an African-American family that had purchased a house on a previously white-only block, commented, "to recount the large number of lone families 'of color' in erstwhile exclusive white neighborhoods is too long a story for a newspaper article. Their entry in these particular sections caused the same rumpus" as had the 1915 sale of a house to a black businessman and his wife. Even before the mass migration of southern African-Americans to Chicago during World War I, black Chicagoans faced organized campaigns to define and enforce racial boundaries of neighborhoods.[34]

Among the first targets of racially motivated violence were the financially secure African-American professionals—ministers, doctors, entrepreneurs, and those with steady, decent-paying jobs. The black middle classes tended to have saved enough for a down payment on a single-family dwelling and were more likely to seek property in "respectable" neighborhoods outside the Black Belt.[35] When several African-American families bought houses in Hyde Park, the comfortable, tree-lined community surrounding the new University of Chicago, in 1909, white Hyde Parkers launched a campaign to remove them. As Allan Spear notes, white Hyde Parkers had long been acquainted with African-Americans who were employed as house servants and hotel workers. But when black families began to buy houses there, the Hyde Park Improvement Protective Club, a combination of two separate groups that merged in the fall of 1908 and was headed by a prominent lawyer,

Francis Harper, quickly responded. Outraged club members issued a manifesto, demanding that African-Americans remain in the "so-called Districts," that landlords hire only white janitors, and that real estate agents refuse to sell property in white blocks to black buyers. Threatening to boycott any real estate firm that defied its edict, the club appointed a committee to purchase property owned by black families in white blocks and to offer cash payments to black tenants who would give up their leases. "The districts which are now white," Harper proclaimed, "must remain white. There will be no compromises."[36]

The "householders' warfare" had been going on for a couple years. Most disturbing to many middle-class black Chicagoans was that opposition came from "respectable" whites, men and women with whom "refined" black families shared values. As early as 1906, Fannie Barrier Williams warned Chicagoans of the dangerous example set by Hyde Park's "public spirited citizens." Williams had lived on the South Side for fifteen years. In 1889, she and her husband, S. Laing Williams, were living at 2905 S. Wabash Ave. By 1898, they had moved to 4203 S. St. Lawrence Ave. in the well-to-do Kenwood neighborhood. Though she could understand why "refined people" would fight to rid their neighborhoods of unlicensed saloons and gambling dens, she resented being pushed from her home. The Hyde Parkers were searching out "Negroes of the better class" and "pushing these people into the dark corners, alleys, and back streets." In Williams view, middle-class black Chicagoans faced discrimination more disturbing than that found in the south, where race prejudice was "so dominant." At least in the south, she charged, "the best people do not band themselves together to keep Negroes in the alleys and in unsanitary and unhealthy streets."[37]

By 1909, black residents of Hyde Park and Kenwood were organizing to resist the efforts of the neighborhood improvement association. Their leaders framed the conflict in language that referred well beyond the issues of housing and the city's "color line." For black Chicagoans, as for European immigrants, access to residential property ownership was a fundamental right of American citizens. The Rev. D. P. Roberts, pastor of Quinn Chapel, reminded his parishioners of the history of American race relations, noting, "The white people of this country made their mistake in 1620 and they will have to put up with the results." Roberts went on to assert that black Chicagoans were "American citizens" with "rights and privileges, which can't be ignored." Among those rights, he asserted, was to buy "property where they thought best." He concluded that home ownership already had led to the gradual acceptance of African-Americans in other cities and "[t]he same thing will come about here." Yet when black Hyde Park residents sought to resist the club's campaign by refusing to move out of the neighborhood, white vandals broke into at least one black home, smashing furniture and shattering windows.[38]

The club's campaign was successful in the short term. But white home owners began leaving the neighborhood. In 1916, as African-Americans, despite the constant threats and harassment, continued purchasing houses and renting apartments in Hyde Park, white property owners again rallied to protect falling property values. One pamphlet called "every white person Property Owner in Hyde Park" to a meeting to "[p]rotect your property." By then, it was too late. In 1918, African-Americans made up nearly one-third of the neighborhood's residents, and residential property, some complained, had lost some of its market value.[39]

By the late 1910s, violent attacks on black home owners or renters, often the most affluent of the city's black residents, were common and terrifying occurrences. Class status or "respectability" proved little protection for black professionals and business owners who sought elegant homes among families of similar wealth. For his efforts to sell and rent property to black Chicagoans, Binga, the real estate entrepreneur who amassed a fortune in the 1910s and, after ten years planning, opened a bank on State Street in 1921, faced near-weekly threats. His house, "a spacious home at 5922 South Park," in an all-white area, was firebombed at least five times in the late 1910s. Police reported that the bombings were caused by the "racial feeling" of white men who complained that "Binga rented too many flats to negroes in high-class residence districts." After a November 1919 bomb sizzled and went out, police reported that neighbors complained that the Binga's "$30,000 home is in a white neighborhood." Despite supposed police surveillance of the house, a final bomb in June 1920 almost destroyed the front of the house and "smashed windows throughout the block." Black bankers and businessmen living in nearby largely white and middle-class Hyde Park faced threats and similar violence. No arrests were ever made, and police made few "precautions to prevent bombings," even when the attacks "were well planned and systematically carried out."[40]

Immigrant working-class Chicagoans too used threats and violence to bar African-Americans from their communities. In 1913, residents of the South Side Englewood neighborhood organized a "neighborhood improvement association" to force a white man married to a black woman to sell his property. And on the city's West Side, where black families had lived among whites since the 1880s, white "neighborhood improvement groups" launched campaigns against recently arrived black home owners in the early 1910s.[41]

Contending that the income of their neighbors mattered less than the racial identity of their community, white Hyde Parkers and first- and second-generation immigrant West Siders helped to fashion a distinctive, and increasingly potent, standard for evaluating residential property. Representing the individual interests of white property owners, neighborhood improvement organizations in Hyde Park and other Chicago neighborhoods asserted proprietary claims to lots and dwellings their members did not own. They expanded property rights beyond the legal definition of rights to uses of property to a communal assertion of rights to maintain value in the neighborhood's land and dwellings.[42] Members of white neighborhood organizations clearly disagreed with the era's free-market capitalists, who claimed that property, including landed property, was a commodity whose value was determined by the socially neutral market forces of supply and demand. Property values, white neighborhood groups proclaimed, were determined by both the assessed value of the individual dwelling and the social identity of residents in surrounding dwellings. Value, always a subjective measure, acquired a racial character.

Banding together under the banner of "preserving" property values, white neighborhood organizations asserted a "public" interest in preventing black Chicagoans from purchasing property in white-only neighborhoods. With their campaigns, neighborhood organizations demonstrated that private property functioned as what legal scholar Gregory S. Alexander calls "property as propriety," or as serving a "public good." Efforts to bar African-Americans from purchasing houses and to restrict the business activities of realtors rested on the belief that property, in Alexander's words, served as "the material foundation for creating and maintaining the proper social order."[43] In Hyde Park and elsewhere, the public interest was equated with the interests of white property owners. Turn-of-the-century business practices and free-market advocates had gone a long way toward erasing all claims to a public interest in property regulations. Yet the community organizations seeking to enforce racial segregation of the housing market breathed new life into the public interest conception of property. Their efforts to intervene in the housing market, justified as serving the public good, defined the public interest in racial terms.

While the commodification of the family home had served the interests of house builders, white neighborhood organizations asserted that the family home was not simply a market commodity. The neighborhood organizations claimed that the value of the house was linked to the surrounding neighborhood. Property, Hyde Park residents realized, generated social relationships aside from the provision of shelter. Within a few weeks after several black families moved to the neighborhood, the Hyde Park Improvement Protective Club boasted 350 members, "including some of the wealthiest dwellers on the South Side." Its campaign against black home owners expanded to cover other neighborhood institutions. In its annual report in 1909, the club called for separate playgrounds and tennis courts for African-Americans in Washington Park and for the segregation of the public schools. "It is only a question of time," a club spokesman predicted, "when there will be separate schools for Negroes throughout Illinois."[44] Asserting a neighborhood-wide interest in regulating the market for individual houses, the club's members assumed municipal support for their actions. And they were right. Chicago's officials never moved to halt campaigns against black home owners or tenants. Even the obviously illegal physical assaults on black residents and bombings of African-American homes generated, at best, a minor police response and few arrests.[45]

Members of white home owner organizations were not the only early twentieth-century advocates of government regulation of private property in the public interest. Though not intending to provide a justification for racial segregation, Chicago's Progressive Era reformers in many different arenas argued that government should and could serve a larger public interest by intervening in market relations. Whether aiming to improve living conditions among the poor in urban centers or to break up corporate monopolies, many of those aligned with reform movements asserted a public interest in government regulation of market relations. Indeed, proponents of racial segregation typically fought legal challenges to segregation ordinances by arguing that the state had an interest in maintaining public peace. The police power of the state, segregation's supporters argued, could and should be used to serve the larger public interest by eliminating potential racial conflicts.[46]

Closer to the experiences of Chicagoans, settlement house workers devoted much energy to bringing individual tenants and home owners together to demand improvements in housing conditions. Settlement house workers were particularly effective at fashioning social bonds across differences in nationality, language, and culture.[47] In several West Side neighborhoods and in Packingtown, settlement volunteers effectively encouraged working-class home owners to demand municipal services, like sewers and street cleaning, based on property rights claims, and the consequent level of property taxes paid by the neighborhood's home owners as a group. Housing reformers clearly were not encouraging racial segregation. Yet the invigorated sense of community that inspired neighborhood groups to demand municipally financed playgrounds and public baths could also spark demands for racially segregated facilities. Ida B. Wells-Barnett recognized this problem when she found that many of the nurseries established by urban reform groups rejected black children. Wells-Barnett responded by opening a nursery for African-American children. But as she knew, black Chicagoans, plagued by low levels of property ownership and low-wage jobs, lacked the financial muscle and political influence to solve what Work had called their "most pressing problem," inadequate housing.[48]

Plummeting Black Belt property values and the treacherous tactics of block-busters resonated beyond neighborhood skirmishes over racial boundaries. In the 1910s and 1920s, an influential group of economists launched a series of community studies of property values. Hoping to expand the nation's home ownership rates, the economists sought to develop ways to expand access to and lighten the burden of home loans. Their proposals, which became the basis for New Deal housing programs and as a result shaped the American housing market for decades after, grew out of rigorous analysis of the causes of instability in early twentieth-century urban neighborhoods. Though clearly not advocating racial determinants in commercial lending policies, the economists' recommendations exacerbated residential segregation and added new barriers to home ownership among African-Americans.

The recognized leader of the new generation of urban economists was Richard T. Ely, a cofounder of the American Economic Association in 1886 and founding chair of the famous School of Economics, Political Science and History at the University of Wisconsin. Ely was a prolific writer and vocal advocate for a dramatic shift in the substance and theory of economics. A proponent of the social gospel that inspired many urban reformers, Ely believed that economic scholarship should engage contemporary social and ethical issues. He argued that classical economics with its emphasis on universal principles and abstract theory was not applicable to an industrializing society. Instead, he urged economists to launch empirical studies of living and working conditions, deriving both economic theory and practical solutions to social problems from "objective" investigation of social conditions. Ely inspired a generation of scholars in economics, history, and the law. His students included John R. Commons, Helen Munchow, and others who later took jobs in the Roosevelt administration. In 1920, he founded the controversial Institute for Research in Land Economics and Public Utilities at Wisconsin, but was forced to move it to Northwestern University in 1925. During the 1920s, the institute's research staff compiled a wide array of influential studies of Chicago's real estate market.[49]

Ely was an early and avid proponent of home ownership. "There is no question," he wrote, "that home ownership is a safeguard against poverty, and it aids thrift and prosperity for the man. Indeed, a home owner is almost invariably a good citizen."[50] At issue was how to cultivate more "good citizens." One of the earliest institute studies of urban land uses found a slight increase in owner-occupied housing across the country between 1890 and 1920. More significant to Ely's concerns, the study found a dramatic increase in the percentage of owner-occupied dwellings that were mortgaged and an increase in the ratio of debt to assessed property value. More people were taking larger loans to buy houses. And the study found that home buyers were beginning to acquire loans from large financial institutions, rather than from individuals. To Ely and his researchers, these changes suggested that home ownership rates could be further increased by expanding access to home loans. To encourage banks and corporate creditors to provide a greater number of home loans, Ely's researchers sought to lower the risk, or the perception of risk, of losing money on a home mortgage.[51]

Among the numerous policy recommendations issued by the institute's researchers was a revolutionary change in the ways residential property was assessed for mortgage purposes. Giving full articulation to the conception of property value that white neighborhood groups had recognized, the economists argued that the value of residential property depended on a variety of factors, including the buyers' income, neighborhood employment patterns, and projected uses and values of surrounding properties. Home loans, then, should be based on a risk assessment that took into account the future employment and earnings of the buyer and projections of the market value of surrounding properties. The economists effectively shifted the attention of potential lenders away from an assessment of the dwelling to the less precise evaluation of the surrounding neighborhood. Using what the Federal Housing Administration later called a "neighborhood location rating," institutional lenders began to allocate mortgages according to what Marc A. Weiss calls "complex calculations of seemingly unpredictable factors," like the stability of local employers and the financial security of neighboring home owners and tenants. The result was that white middle-class families seeking single-family houses in newly built suburban locales easily acquired mortgages while black families hoping to purchase a dwelling in an older African-American neighborhood found it almost impossible to get a house loan. The system, institutionalized by the Federal Housing Administration in the 1930s, designated African-American neighborhoods with their decayed housing stock and falling property values as areas of such high risk that few lenders would loan to those who might have bought the properties, and the

FHA was unwilling to insure mortgages in impoverished black communities. Without access to mortgage capital, black Americans could do little to improve housing conditions in urban African-American neighborhoods.[52]

In a sense, Ely's researchers were right. In Chicago at least, the value of a dwelling was determined by its location defined in terms of the dwelling's geographic and demographic features. By the time the institute's staff stumbled on this insight, Chicago's real estate salesmen, speculators, and white property owners had proclaimed that value was profoundly influenced by the race of a neighborhood's tenants and owners. By refusing to invest capital in improving their properties, white owners of Black Belt property had created the paradigm to which federal policy makers, lenders, and white Chicagoans referred: housing occupied by African-Americans depressed real estate values. Almost no one seemed to see that this value system functioned to further weaken property values in African-American neighborhoods, to further strain the resources of black families seeking decent housing, and to produce and reinforce white racism.

———————

In late June 1919, Ida B. Wells-Barnett mailed a letter to the *Chicago Daily Tribune*. The letter, published on July 7, urged city officials to take action to halt the growing number of increasingly brutal attacks on black Chicagoans.[53] Wells-Barnett, a journalist and lecturer born in Holly Springs, Mississippi on the eve of emancipation, was well-acquainted with the horrors of white violence against African-Americans. After three black friends were lynched in Memphis in 1892, Wells-Barnett had launched an international campaign against lynching. Moving to Chicago after her newspaper offices were firebombed and her life was threatened, she married a prominent black lawyer and newspaper owner, Ferdinand Barnett, and after giving birth to four children, retired from the lecture circuit. She had revived her career in November 1909 after a white mob in Cairo, Illinois, lynched William "Frog" James. Accused of raping and murdering a white woman, James was being held by the county sheriff, who offered no resistance to the mob, simply returning to his office while the prisoner was hanged, shot, and burned. The violence was particularly disturbing since a state law passed in 1905 called for the dismissal of a sheriff or deputy who allowed the lynching of a person in his custody. An outraged Wells-Barnett headed to the southern Illinois town to investigate, launching a successful campaign for the sheriff's dismissal. She wrote a detailed report, which her husband presented to Illinois governor Charles S. Dineen, who a week later refused to reinstate the sheriff.[54]

Living in Chicago through the 1910s, Wells-Barnett watched as the city's black population jumped from less than 50,000 in 1910 to nearly 110,000 in 1920. The war in Europe placed new demands on American industry, and for the first time, Chicago's manufacturers had opened their doors to black laborers. Southern-born black people had flowed into the city, seeking jobs in war-related industries and homes in communities free of the terror that reigned in the south. At the war's end, as veterans returned from overseas and the revved-up wartime economy hit a slowdown, black workers were among the first laid off. As they faced off in hostile competition for jobs, black and white Chicagoans struggled to find decent housing in increasingly jam-packed working-class neighborhoods. The color line rippled through the congested South Side, bulging eastward wherever blockbusters followed by desperate black families pushed into long-standing white blocks.[55]

In her letter to the *Tribune*, Wells-Barnett noted that sparks were already flying: a "race riot" the previous week that left one black man dead, "a half dozen attacks upon Negro children, and one on the Thirty-fifth street car Tuesday in which four white men beat one colored man," and "especially . . . the bombing of Negro homes and the indifference of the white public to these outrages" were, she said, "preliminary outbreaks" of a coming riot. Chicago, she commented, "is trying to rival the south in its race hatred against the Negro." This was a rhetorical flourish; she knew that northern and midwestern cities were also sites of racial violence. Two years earlier, ten whites and thirty-nine blacks, "many of them the victims of unspeakable horror," had been killed in a race riot in East St. Louis, and riots had exploded in New York in 1900 and in Springfield, Illinois, in 1908. Calling on city officials and white Chicagoans to halt the "law breakers" before "further disaster has occurred," she concluded, "I implore Chicago to set the wheels of justice in motion before it is too late."[56]

Three weeks later the sparks exploded. As temperatures soared into the nineties on Sunday, July 27, two separate incidents ignited five days of racial violence. First, a white crowd attempted to prevent a group of black people from using the beach along Lake Michigan at Twenty-ninth Street, setting off a confrontation between white and black bathers. Then, word came of the drowning of Eugene Williams, a black teenager who had been swimming with three friends nearby. Williams was hit in the head by a rock thrown— with or without the intention of hitting him, it was never clear—by a white man standing on the breakwater at Twenty-sixth Street. While divers recovered Williams's body, rumors circulated and anger mounted. When the police arrived at the beach, outraged black Chicagoans threw bricks and rocks, and then a black man, James Crawford, drew a pistol and fired into a cluster

21. Crowds of black Chicagoans in street in front of Jesse Binga's bank during the 1919 riot.
Chicago Historical Society.

of policemen, wounding one. A black officer returned fire, fatally injuring Crawford. Other pistol shots were heard, and the race war had begun.[57]

Rioting raged, largely uncontrolled, for five days. The violence burst beyond the boundaries of the Black Belt and spread into the North and West Sides and through the city's downtown. The toll was stunning: police officers fatally wounded seven black men. Angry mobs and gunmen murdered an additional sixteen African-Americans and fifteen whites. Well over 537 Chicagoans were injured, and 1,000 were left homeless. The culmination of more than a decade of bloody conflict over white home owners' efforts to prevent black families from living outside the Black Belt and over low-wage jobs in the city's industries, the riot demonstrated that the city's social landscape was clearly divided along racial lines.[58]

In the following months, a commission appointed by the governor investigated the causes of the violence. In its nearly seven-hundred-page report, the commission stated again and again that anger over a shortage of decent housing in the Black Belt and surrounding white neighborhoods lay at the riot's core. Housing was not the sole cause. The massive migration of rural African-Americans to Chicago during the war, competition for jobs, and home-grown racism played crucial roles. But, the commissioners noted, "friction in industry was less than might have been expected. . . . In housing, however, there was a different story." Since home construction came to a near halt during the war, "and it was a physical impossibility for a doubled Negro population to live in the space it occupied in 1915," African-Americans began moving out of the Black Belt into nearby neighborhoods that had been "exclusively white." The commission concluded that "insufficiency in amount and quality of housing" was "an all-important factor in Chicago's race problem."[59]

Black Chicagoans were even more explicit. Even as the street fighting raged, T. Arnold Hill of the Chicago Urban League reported that growing pressure on the city's housing market was "undoubtedly at the bottom" of the "general feeling of unrest which has been hovering over Chicago for two or more months." Members of the Urban League, which met migrants from the south at the train station and helped them find housing, were well aware of the housing crisis. In the summer of 1917, the league had surveyed the real estate dealers who supplied dwellings to African-Americans. Out of 664 black applicants, real estate men reported that they were able to find housing for only 50. Hill attributed the riot to "the bombing of homes of colored persons who have recently moved into white districts, an attempt to enforce segregation by certain real estate agents and organizations with which they are connected, the unwarranted killing of Negroes in outlying districts, the recurrence of violence in Washington park, and the widespread belief on the part of Negroes that the police have winked at these conditions."[60]

————

Hill's reaction hit on the immediate causes of the riot. In a broader sense, however, the riot's roots could be found in the development of the city's reform movements and residential real estate markets through the previous half-century. In designating ownership of a single-family home a solution to labor conflict, shifting gender relations, inadequate urban sanitation, and child and sweated labor, health reformers, builders, labor leaders, and settlement volunteers had gradually narrowed the range of conceivable solutions to the problem of a lack of decent low-cost housing in an industrializing city. Builders had shifted their markets toward ever larger more expensive single-family houses, and even as housing prices increased, reformers urged wage laborers to reject the strategies that had allowed them to use their homes for a variety of income-producing purposes. Though many—reformers, immigrants, middle-class black and white Chicagoans—believed home owner-ship was a measure of an American standard of living, that standard re-mained beyond the financial reach of large numbers of Chicago residents. For some, particularly black Americans, the obstacle was a lack of housing loans, for others it was low-wage jobs. By the 1910s, African-Americans of all classes and unskilled workers of European descent had little choice but to compete for inadequate dwelling space in an increasingly constricted real estate market.

The lack of housing that low-wage workers could afford was not a result of population growth alone. In a sense, builders and reformers, and the more affluent buyers they encouraged, had created the housing shortage for lower-wage workers. Builders, seeking greater profits on housing, had turned to constructing larger houses with more expensive amenities and marketed their houses to more affluent buyers. Reformers had urged middle- and working-class families to secure family privacy and health by moving into single-family homes on the urban fringe. Both had contributed to the ex-pansion of the single-family housing market by drawing ever-larger num-bers of middle-class families into home ownership. Seeing property in hous-ing as a source of health, privacy, and gender order and as an investment that would yield future returns, middle-class home owners and their vision of home ownership gradually came to dominate the city's housing market. They too helped to define property in housing as an investment whose value could and should be enhanced.

For immigrant wage laborers, home ownership had never been an em-bodiment of American individualism. Rather, buying a house and attempt-ing to preserve its value was a communitywide enterprise. Pursuing home ownership on low wages and irregular employment, immigrant workers re-lied on local networks of credit and capital to finance a home purchase. Con-fronted with a municipal government unwilling to invest city funds in working-class neighborhoods, home owners had banded together to fight for sewer and water lines and more efficient municipal services. They recog-nized that property rights in housing could be used to assert rights-based claims to government resources. Skilled workers able to afford indoor plumbing increasingly separated their houses and neighborhoods from those of low-wage, unskilled laborers. Home ownership gradually came to distinguish the households of skilled from those of unskilled wage laborers, dividing the working classes and separating their neighborhoods. When as-sessments of housing value were racialized, home owners—and the white middle classes and native born often established a model for race conflict—again banded together to preserve the value of their houses and neighborhoods. As the housing of the unskilled deteriorated, skilled workers and even some low-wage immigrants increasingly conceived of their property rights as the right to a return on their investment, as the right to augment value in property by controlling the uses of neighboring properties and establishing race- and class-segregated communities.

Home owners' proprietary claims to their communities redrew neighborhood boundaries and produced a new social landscape in the industrial city. By 1919, the skilled and the unskilled, the black and the white, no longer lived side by side in Chicago. Instead, as bankers, builders, and real estate brokers increasingly applied a mix of material conditions and demographics, particularly race, as criteria to set the value of a house, white home owners fought to maintain property values by barring anyone whose racial identity was different from their own from moving into their neighborhood. The long-held working-class aspiration to home ownership, the conception of property rights in housing as income producing and of the home as a malleable institution serving multiple purposes, was gradually replaced by an increasingly inflexible version of the American family home and of the social value of property rights in housing. The emergence of the single-family, owner-occupied house as a symbol of the American dream, an ideal inspired by immigrant wage laborers struggling to survive on low wages in an industrializing city, left twentieth-century Chicago sharply divided along class and racial lines.

"Private initiative has failed lamentably," wrote Edith Elmer Wood in her 1919 study of the nation's housing markets. "Unskilled workers cannot be supplied with decent homes under existing economic conditions on a business basis." In an investigation reminiscent of those issued by late nineteenth-century tenement reformers, she demonstrated that the nation's housing market, rather than providing decent shelter for all, left growing numbers of poor families condemned to "insanitary" and run-down rental dwellings. Her argument, however, would prove more prescient, and ulti-mately more persuasive, than that of reformers thirty years earlier.[1] Born in 1871, Wood married a naval officer and was raising four children when she became interested in housing while investigating the living conditions of impoverished women in Washington, D.C., in 1911. Three years later, she moved to New York, where she earned a doctorate from Columbia Univer-sity and published her study, titled *The Housing of the Unskilled Wage Earner*. It was an explicit critique of the free market in residential real estate and of the assumption that with equal opportunity all individuals could achieve the American dream of an owner-occupied house. Wood's landmark book, widely read by those concerned with housing and urban society, resonated through 1920s-era debates about housing policies and through New Deal administrators' plans for government intervention in the Depression-era housing markets. But coming on the heels of a half-century-long transfor-mation in the ways urban Americans conceived of the family home and of the social value of property rights in housing, Wood's call for a national housing policy and for government-funded rental housing ran up against al-ready deeply held beliefs about the social functions and meanings of home ownership.[2]

Wood applauded the decades of work by housing reformers, noting their achievements had added rooms with light and ventilation to thousands of multifamily dwellings. The construction of scores of single-family houses built according to new standards established by reformers improved living conditions for many Americans. But "restrictive legislation" was, in her view, just a partial solution. What was needed was "constructive housing legislation," federal, state, and municipal programs designed to provide affordable housing for unskilled workers, for those who could not afford to purchase their homes. By 1920, approximately 45 percent of American families owned their homes, but as Wood noted, workers who formerly used property rights in housing to augment household income found that after the turn of the century their wages were too low relative to housing prices to acquire their homes. "There is a very real economic line between those who have the necessary capital or necessary credit to buy land and build homes for themselves," she wrote, "and those who have not."[3]

Wood was not alone in recognizing a housing problem facing many American workers. Herbert Hoover, the newly appointed secretary of commerce who spent much of the decade promoting home ownership, privately commented in 1921 that "on present wage levels and present building costs" there was "utterly no hope" of working-class families buying their own homes. Socialists in Milwaukee, labor leaders in New York City, and housing reformers in several other industrial cities came up with plans; in some cases, whole communities built with a mix of government and private funds to house low-wage workers. Some, like the cooperative housing built by the Amalgamated Clothing Workers Union in the Bronx, survived for decades; other such communities dissolved during the Great Depression.[4] Each project and proposal suggested the profound and continuing need for government investment in housing for low-wage workers.

Some of these ideas would take root in the 1930s, when Franklin Roosevelt's New Deal administration, faced with unprecedented economic turmoil, would provide federal funding for large multifamily rental buildings designed for the urban working classes. Better funded and more widely used were New Deal programs that aimed to buttress the private housing market: mortgage insurance for buyers and builders and, a few years later, government-sponsored low-interest loans for single-family home buyers, typically in new suburban communities. The result, as Gail Radford argues, was a two-tiered housing market: one, the underfunded and poorly designed multifamily rental housing for the urban poor; the other, well-funded programs subsidizing private bankers and builders constructing single-family homes on the urban fringe. New Deal and postwar federal housing programs—from mortgage insurance for single-family homes to highway construction—significantly expanded home ownership rates across the United States. Those programs, cementing the American infatuation with home ownership and further restricting alternative solutions to America's housing problems, simply fueled a long-term cultural shift that had begun in the late nineteenth century.[5]

Even at the turn of the century, a single-family house set on a tidy yard was fast becoming a mark of household health, respectability, and morality. During the final quarter of the nineteenth century, the construction of municipally funded sewer and water systems had enhanced the value of some properties, in particular undeveloped lots edging the built-up sections of the city, and helped fuel a new market in single-family houses. In the 1890s, builders had standardized designs for single-family houses to include bathrooms, indoor plumbing, and separate sleeping and "living" quarters, as well as a yard surrounding the house. Their advertising campaigns, stressing the social autonomy of the home owner, played on and intersected with the ideals of health and housing reformers to draw an increasing number of middle-class families out of apartment hotels and into single-family urban neighborhoods and suburban communities. Most significantly, the new home ownership ideal promoted by builders and social reformers suggested that property rights in housing was an investment that, like ownership of other forms of property, would yield future profits.

Investments in residential real estate would prove profitable for some, but not for all. Housing prices, pushed up by the costs of sewer and water connections, by indoor plumbing, and by builders marketing houses to more affluent buyers, had increased relative to the wages of both skilled and unskilled workers.[6] As immigrant wage laborers struggled to purchase houses and to maintain value in their homes, they gradually expanded their proprietary claims to include their neighborhoods. When realtors and builders linked race to real estate values, white Chicagoans, both working and middle class, moved to preserve value in their homes by preventing African-Americans from purchasing houses in their neighborhoods. Federal housing programs, in particular mortgages insured by the Federal Housing Administration, reinforced the racial boundaries established by white neighborhood groups. Providing capital for builders and buyers on the urban fringe, federal programs continued to divert bank loans out of working-class and particularly African-American urban neighborhoods. The use of racial identity of residents to assess property values meant that some urban neighborhoods were by midcentury starved for capital; home owners in those neighborhoods watched as their property values fell and their investments in housing disappeared. Federal government efforts to expand the nation's home ownership rates benefited some home owners and communities at the tragic expense of many others.[7]

For those who could afford to purchase a house and had the good fortune to watch their property value increase in the mid to late twentieth century, home ownership—in a paradox rarely recognized—was fast becoming a strategy for surviving in a postindustrial economy. Less than a century after the Brophys and their neighbors used property in housing to augment low industrial wages, home ownership was once again used to buttress households of falling or stagnant income, blue- and white-collar workers whose jobs were exported to lower-wage societies or eliminated in corporate mergers and cutbacks. Home owners of both the working and middle classes refinanced their homes, using second and sometimes third mortgages to cover daily consumption and often to compensate for large occasional expenses (health care costs for a sudden illness or a child's college education), which salaries and wages alone could not meet. Real estate was a means to wealth sometimes, but more often to household stability when jobs were temporary, employment was unreliable, and earnings were not sufficient to maintain a family's social status.

––––––––

Significant rates of home ownership among twentieth-century Americans have been used to suggest that America is a classless society. Yet in Chicago home ownership did not catapult working-class people or their children into salaried occupations or provide the education or social networks to give them middle-class standing. Instead, the vast expansion of home ownership and aspirations for property in housing among the middle classes in the twentieth century simply obscured the continuing differences in economic and cultural resources among the nation's social groups. A working-class conception of home ownership persisted, but the dominant views of home ownership had so changed by the 1920s that home ownership could be touted as a sign of social mobility and the achievement of the American dream. That different and distinctive conceptions of the meaning and economic functions of home ownership remained meant little when public officials pointed to expanding home ownership rates as a sign of American affluence, of the strength of the nation's economy, and of the effectiveness of public policies that encouraged home ownership through the private market. Home ownership then served as a mechanism to resolve fundamental contradictions in American society: the rhetoric of equal opportunity and upward social mobility with the persistent numbers of low-wage, impoverished, and propertyless Americans. The irony is that in the late nineteenth century, a period in which class conflict was pronounced, vocal, and visible, the meanings of home ownership changed in ways that would function to cover over continuing class differences.

The tragedy, as Wood recognized, was that increasing numbers of people, often invisible to policy makers and politicians, were unable to afford decent housing. As new amenities pushed up single-family housing prices, un-skilled laborers gradually dropped out of the community of home owners and, despite continued high rates of home ownership among the upper lev-els of the working classes, home ownership was increasingly beyond the financial means of low-waged and unskilled workers. The gradual transfor-mation of the meanings of the family home, the increased emphasis on fam-ily privacy and household health, and, most importantly, the growing em-phasis on property rights in new housing of standardized design and in semirural locations left those living on low-wage jobs in urban centers with-out the means to find adequate shelter.

America's future, Wood concluded, "our own brand of citizenship in health, in intelligence, in morals, in individual efficiency, in patriotism," rests on the government's ability to make housing affordable for those shut out of the private housing markets. Wood's detailed study, tracking the grad-ual deterioration of housing conditions in poor neighborhoods, claimed that without massive government investment in low-cost multifamily dwellings, a growing number of Americans would be unable to afford any shelter at all. Home ownership had become the American dream, she com-mented, but it could not solve the nation's housing problems. Wood's re-port, published more than eighty years ago, the same year as Chicago's race riot, proved sadly prophetic.[8]

NOTES

ABBREVIATIONS

CHS   Chicago Historical Society
GP   S. E. Gross Papers, Correspondence, and Clippings, Chicago Historical Society
ISARD   Illinois State Archives Regional Depository, Northeastern Illinois University, Chicago
MC   Mary McDowell Collection, Chicago Historical Society
NL   Newberry Library, Chicago
NYPL   New York Public Library
RDH   Report of the Department of Health of the City of Chicago; e.g., "RDH 1886" means the report for 1886. Note that in some years "Annual" was part of the title, although it was not always issued annually. Archived at the Harold Washington Library Center, Chicago.

INTRODUCTION

1. The phrase "American dream" dates back at least to James Truslow Adams's *The Epic of America*. Adams and others have conceived of the American dream as an ideology of upward social mobility as well as of material well-being, embodied in home ownership. I am here linking the term to the ideals of late nineteenth-century urban industrial laborers and in particular to their use of an "American standard of life." See Adams, *The Epic of America* (Boston: Little, Brown, and Company, 1932) 410.

2. Much has been written on republican ideology. See, for example, Eric Foner, *Free Soil, Free Labor, Free Men: The Ideology of the Republican Party before the Civil War* (New York: Oxford University Press, 1970); Linda K. Kerber, *Women of the Republic: Intellect and Ideology in Revolutionary America* (Chapel Hill: University of North Carolina Press, 1980); and Sean Wilentz, *Chants Democratic: New York City and the Rise of the American Working Class, 1788–1850* (New York: Oxford University Press, 1984). As many scholars have noted, liberal political theory also was on the rise in the early nineteenth century. As the rhetoric of wage laborers in Chicago demonstrates, working men too applied the language of liberalism to their version of home ownership, especially when it came to claims to the right to own property. Still, these men saw home ownership as more of a communal than an individualist strategy for surviving in the industrial city. See, for example, Eric Foner, *Who Owns History? Rethinking the Past in a Changing World* (New York: Hill and Wang, 2002) 123–24.

3. A great deal of scholarship has been produced on the rise of waged labor and market relations in antebellum America. See, for example: Christopher Clark, *The Roots of Rural Capitalism, Western Massachusetts, 1780–1860* (Ithaca: Cornell University Press, 1990); Paul Gilje, "The Rise of Capitalism in the Early Republic," in *Wages of Independence*, Paul Gilje, ed. (Madison, WI: Madison House, 1997); Jonathan Prude, *The Coming of the Industrial Order: Town and Factory Life in Rural Massachusetts, 1810–1860* (New York: Cambridge University Press, 1983); Christine Stansell, *City of Women: Sex and Class in New York, 1789–1860* (Urbana: University of Illinois Press, 1987); Wilentz, *Chants Democratic.*

4. For more on the cult of domesticity and the emergence of an ideology of separate spheres see Jeanne Boydston, *Home and Work: Housework, Wages, and the Ideology of Labor in the Early Republic* (New York: Oxford University Press, 1990); Kerber, *Women of the Republic*; Kathryn Kish Sklar, *Catharine Beecher: A Study in American Domesticity* (New Haven: Yale University Press, 1973); Alice Kessler-Harris, *Out to Work: A History of Wage-Earning Women in the United States* (New York: Oxford University Press, 1982). For an analysis of wage labor relations within the home see Elizabeth Blackmar, *Manhattan for Rent, 1785–1850* (Ithaca: Cornell University Press, 1989) 110–13.

5. Morton J. Horwitz, *The Transformation of American Law, 1870–1960* (New York: Oxford University Press, 1992) 145–46; Martin J. Sklar, *The Corporate Reconstruction of American Capitalism, 1890–1916* (New York: Cambridge University Press, 1988); Lawrence M. Friedman, *A History of American Law*, 2nd ed. (New York: Simon & Schuster, 1985) 512–17; Allen Trachtenberg, *The Incorporation of America: Culture and Society in the Gilded Age* (New York: Hill and Wang, 1982); Thorstein Veblen, *The Theory of Business Enterprise* (New York: C. Scribner's Sons, 1904); Charles Francis Adams, "A Chapter of Erie," in *High Finance in the Sixties*, Frederick C. Hicks, ed. (1929) 114–16. Corporations had existed in the colonial era as a means of passing property from a group of owners across generations, typically used by churches and philanthropies. In the early nineteenth century, states often approved corporate structures for entities that "served a public interest" such as building roads or canals. That social purpose changed in the 1840s and 1850s when state legislatures began passing general incorporation acts, simplifying the process of incorporating by allowing a group of investors to form a corporation without the passage of a bill in the state legislature. Still, it was not until the final decades of the nineteenth century that the corporation replaced individual ownership or partnerships as the primary mechanism for doing business.

6. John R. Commons, *Legal Foundations of Capitalism* (New York: Macmillan, 1924) 16; Corbin cited in Horwitz, *The Transformation of American Law* 156. The courts moved away from the Lockean definition of property as a prepolitical natural right. This shift, as Horwitz argues, generated a series of contradictions in property, business and labor law. Jeremy Waldron, *The Right to Private Property* (New York: Oxford University Press, 1988). Economists of the late nineteenth century engaged in similar debates over what counted as property and how property acquired value. See, for example, Richard T. Ely, *Property and Contract in Its Relations to the Distribution of Wealth* (New York: Macmillan, 1914); Henry Carter Adams, *The Relation of the State to Industrial Action and Economics and Jurisprudence* (New York: Columbia University Press, 1954); Robert L. Hale, *Freedom through Law: Public Control of Private Government Power* (New York: Columbia University Press, 1952). For a wonderful study of the Progressive Era economists' efforts to shift the ways property was conceived in politics and public

policy, see Barbara H. Fried, *The Progressive Assault on Laissez Faire: Robert Hale and the First Law and Economics Movement* (Cambridge: Harvard University Press, 1998).

7.　There is a small but growing literature on working-class home ownership in the late nineteenth century, and much debate over its significance. Stephan Thernstrom's pathbreaking study found that Irish workers in Boston were willing to sacrifice their children's education, and so access to social mobility, to purchase houses. Home ownership, he argues, did not provide a path to middle-class status. Even more than Thernstrom, Olivier Zunz emphasizes ethnicity as a determinant in home ownership patterns among working-class immigrants in Detroit. Approaching the issue from a completely different perspective, Elliot D. Sclar, Matthew Edel, and Daniel Luria contend that working-class home ownership served the interest of industrial capitalists who sought a stable and docile workforce. More persuasive arguments come from the urban geographer Richard Harris and a handful of others who contend that for turn-of-the-century wage laborers, home ownership carried meanings and social functions that were distinct and different from those of the urban middle classes. See Stephan Thernstrom, *Poverty and Progress: Social Mobility in a Nineteenth Century City* (New York: Atheneum, 1970); Olivier Zunz, *The Changing Face of Inequality: Urbanization, Industrial Development, and Immigrants in Detroit, 1880–1920* (Chicago: University of Chicago Press, 1982); Matthew Edel, Elliot D. Sclar, and Daniel Luria, *Shaky Palaces: Homeownership and Social Mobility in Boston's Suburbanization* (New York: Columbia University Press, 1984); Daniel Luria, "Wealth, Capital, and Power: The Social Meaning of Home Ownership," *Journal of Interdisciplinary History* 8 (1976) 261–82; Michael J. Doucet and John C. Weaver, "Material Culture and the North American House: The Era of the Common Man, 1870–1920," *Journal of American History* 72 (1985) 561–64; Richard Harris, *Unplanned Suburbs: Toronto's American Tragedy, 1900–1950* (Baltimore: Johns Hopkins University Press, 1996); Harris, "Working-Class Home Ownership in the American Metropolis," *Journal of Urban History* 1 (1990) 46–69. Significantly, Harris and Chris Hamnett note that home ownership was not a peculiarly American dream, but rather also was an important ideal in Australia and Canada. Harris and Chris Hamnett, "The Myth of the Promised Land: The Social Diffusion of Home Ownership in Britain and North America," *Annals of the Association of American Geographers* 77 (1987) 173–90. Other scholars studying the working classes or immigrant groups in late nineteenth-century cities, including Chicago, have noted the significant home ownership rates among the immigrant working classes. See Eric Sandweiss, *St. Louis: The Evolution of an American Urban Landscape* (Philadelphia: Temple University Press, 2001) 260–61; Ileen A. DeVault, *Sons and Daughters of Labor: Class and Clerical Work in Turn-of-the-Century Pittsburgh* (Ithaca: Cornell University Press, 1990) 88–89; Roger Simon, *The City Building Process: Housing and Services in New Milwaukee Neighborhoods, 1880–1910* (Philadelphia: American Philosophical Society, 1996); Robin Einhorn, *Property Rules: Political Economy in Chicago, 1833–1872* (Chicago: University of Chicago Press, 1991); Gwendolyn Wright, *Moralism and the Model Home: Domestic Architecture and Cultural Conflict in Chicago, 1873–1913* (Chicago: University of Chicago Press, 1980); Joseph C. Bigott, *From Cottage to Bungalow: Houses and the Working Class in Metropolitan Chicago, 1869–1929* (Chicago: University of Chicago Press, 2001). A wonderful study of the cultural meanings of home ownership in the twentieth century is Constance Perrin, *Everything in Its place: Social Order and Land Use in America* (Princeton: Princeton University Press, 1977).

8.　On suburbanization, see Sam Bass Warner, Jr., *The Private City: Philadelphia in Three*

212 / Notes to pp. 5–6

Periods of Its Growth (Philadelphia: University of Pennsylvania Press, 1968); Warner, *Streetcar Suburbs: The Process of Growth in Boston, 1870–1900* (Cambridge: Harvard University Press, 1962); Henry C. Binford, *The First Suburbs: Residential Communities on the Boston Periphery, 1815–1860* (Chicago: University of Chicago Press, 1985); Kenneth T. Jackson, *Crabgrass Frontier: The Suburbanization of the United States* (New York: Oxford University Press, 1985); Margaret Marsh, *Suburban Lives* (New Brunswick: Rutgers University Press, 1990); Michael H. Ebner, *Creating Chicago's North Shore: A Suburban History* (Chicago: University of Chicago Press, 1988); Ann Durkin Keating, *Building Chicago: Suburban Developers and the Creation of a Divided Metropolis* (Columbus: Ohio State University Press, 1988); David Schuyler, *The New Urban Landscape: The Redefinition of City Form in Nineteenth-Century America* (Baltimore: Johns Hopkins University Press, 1986) 149–66; John R. Stillgoe, *Borderland: Origins of the American Suburb, 1820–1939* (New Haven: Yale University Press, 1988).

9. Some scholars, inaccurately I believe, have suggested that home ownership was equated with middle-class status. See Clifford Edward Clark Jr., *The American Family Home, 1800–1960* (Chapel Hill: University of North Carolina Press, 1986); Jan Cohn, *The Palace or the Poorhouse: The American House as a Cultural Symbol* (East Lansing: Michigan State University Press, 1979).

10. C. B. Macpherson, "The Meaning of Property," in *Property: Mainstream and Critical Positions,* C. B. Macpherson, ed. (Toronto: University of Toronto Press, 1978) 1–4; Horwitz, *The Transformation of American Law.* Among other excellent studies that explore changing meanings of property see Einhorn, *Property Rules;* Fried, *The Progressive Assault on Laissez Faire;* Amy Dru Stanley, *From Bondage to Contract: Wage Labor, Marriage, and the Market in the Age of Slave Emancipation* (New York: Cambridge University Press, 1998); Fernand Braudel, *The Wheels of Commerce: Civilization and Capitalism, 15th–18th Centuries* (Berkeley: University of California Press, 1992). There is some scholarly debate over this assertion. Some classical economists argue that property, no matter the society or historic moment, retained acknowledged value. Other scholars, some historians and some political scientists, argue that property—its value and meaning—was central to American ideals from the earliest history of the nation. For a discussion of these debates see Waldron, *The Right to Private Property.* On property as a natural right outside of politics or society, see William Blackstone, *Commentaries on the Laws of England* (New York: Garland, 1978) 1:138–41; John Locke, *Second Treatise of Government,* ed. J. W. Gough (Oxford: Blackwell, 1946) 14–27.

11. My understanding of class as dynamic and relational, emerging out of struggles between workers and employers in industrializing capitalist societies and shaped by both wage labor relations and community life, is informed by the work of Karl Marx, E. P. Thompson, and Antonio Gramsci. Karl Marx, *Capital: A Critique of Political Economy* (New York: International Publishers, 1967) 1: 702–15; Antonio Gramsci, "Political Struggle and Military War," in *Selections from the Prison Notebooks of Antonio Gramsci,* Quintin Hoare and Geoffrey N. Smith, eds. (New York: International Publishers, 1987) 229–238; Gramsci, "Americanism and Fordism," in *Selections from the Prison Notebooks* 279–318; Thompson, *The Making of the English Working Class* (London: V. Gollancz, 1963) 9–14 (in particular). The work of Pierre Bourdieu, Mary Douglas, and Clifford Geertz has shaped my understanding of the interrelationships between ideas and material conditions, of culture as the ineffable but powerful glue that connects individuals and communities. See Bourdieu, *Distinction: A Social Critique of the Judgement of Taste* (Cambridge: Harvard University Press, 1984); Mary Douglas, *Implicit Meanings: Essays in Anthropology* (Boston: Routledge, 1975) 210–30. More spe-

cifically, several geographers offer provocative and useful insight on the relationship between capitalist economic development and the spatial development of cities; see Allan R. Pred, *The Spatial Dynamics of U.S. Urban Industrial Growth, 1880–1914: Interpretive and Theoretical Essays* (Cambridge: MIT Press, 1966); David Harvey, *The Urbanization of Capital: Studies in the History and Theory of Capitalist Urbanization* (Baltimore: John Hopkins University Press, 1985).

12. Class distinctions were complex and often blurred. Ileen DeVault, for example, argues that men clerks of all types, not women, identified with management and looked forward to promotion. Susan Porter Benson, in her study of department store clerks, found that clerks believed their jobs gave them a veneer of elite status and more respect from supervisors than most forms of blue collar work, but still maintained a sense of class difference. DeVault, *Sons and Daughters of Labor* 78; Susan Porter Benson, *Counter Cultures: Saleswomen, Managers, and Customers in American Department Stores, 1890–1940* (Urbana: University of Illinois Press, 1986). See also Stuart Blumin, *The Emergence of the Middle Class: Social Experience in the American City, 1760–1900* (New York: Cambridge University Press, 1989) 258–85. Among the numerous and excellent studies of class fragmentation by race, skill, gender, and ethnicity see Lizabeth Cohen, *Making a New Deal: Industrial Workers in Chicago, 1919–1939* (New York: Cambridge University Press, 1990); David Roediger, *The Wages of Whiteness: Race and the Making of the American Working Class* (London: Verso, 1991); Roy Rosenzweig, *Eight Hours for What We Will: Workers and Leisure in an Industrial City, 1870–1920* (New York: Cambridge University Press, 1983); Steven J. Ross, *Workers on the Edge: Work, Leisure, and Politics in Industrializing Cincinnati, 1788–1890* (New York: Columbia University Press, 1985); Daniel J. Walkowitz, *Worker City, Company Town: Iron and Cotton Worker Protest in Troy and Cohoes, New York, 1855–1884* (Urbana: University of Illinois Press, 1978). Several studies of home ownership rates in late nineteenth-century American cities have argued that ethnicity was as significant a determinant of home ownership as class. My research on Chicago, however, suggests that the working classes of all nationalities pursued home ownership and, even more, that housing type and uses of property ownership were fairly similar across national differences.

13. On the importance of the largely immigrant character of the working classes, see Herbert G. Gutman and Ira Berlin, "Class Composition and the Development of the American Working Class, 1840–1890," in *Power and Culture: Essays on the American Working Class* (New York: New Press, 1987) 382–83.

14. By middle class, I do not mean bourgeoisie in a Marxist sense. Here, the middle classes were instead those who rested, often uncomfortably, in the middle strata of urban society, neither the elite who owned and ran large corporations nor those who worked for hourly wages in factories, department stores, packinghouses, or the trades. A useful study that focuses on the bourgeoisie is Sven Beckert, *The Monied Metropolis: New York City and the Consolidation of the American Bourgeoisie, 1850–1896* (New York: Cambridge University Press, 2001). For uses of the term "middle class" that parallel mine, see Blumin, *The Emergence of the Middle Class*; Benson, *Counter Cultures*; Paul E. Johnson, *A Shopkeeper's Millennium: Society and Revivals in Rochester, New York, 1815–1837* (New York: Hill and Wang, 1978); Mary Ryan, *The Cradle of the Middle Class: The Family in Oneida County, New York, 1780–1865* (New York: Cambridge University Press, 1981). For a discussion of the lower middle class see Arno J. Mayer, "The Lower Middle Class as a Historical Problem," *Journal of Modern History* 47 (Sept.1975) 409–36.

15. On the persistence of a working-class ideal of home ownership in the twentieth cen-

tury, see Becky Nicolaides, *My Blue Heaven: Life and Politics in the Working-Class Suburbs of Los Angeles, 1920–1965* (Chicago: University of Chicago Press, 2002); Harris, *Unplanned Suburbs;* Harris, "Chicago's Other Suburbs," *Geographical Review* 84 (1994) 394–410; Lisa McGurr, *Suburban Warriors: The Origins of the New American Right* (Princeton: Princeton University Press, 2001); Mike Davis, *Prisoners of the American Dream: Politics and Economy in the History of the U.S. Working Class* (London: Verso, 1986). On African-American suburbs, see Andrew Wiese, *Places of Their Own: African American Suburbanization in the Twentieth Century* (Chicago: University of Chicago Press, 2004).

16. Contemporary investigators were well aware of the difficulties lower-working-class families faced in finding housing in the teens. See, for example: Edith Elmer Wood, *The Housing of the Unskilled Wage Earner: America's Next Problem* (New York: Macmillan, 1919); Edith Abbott, *The Tenements of Chicago, 1908–1935* (Chicago: University of Chicago Press, 1936).

17. Among the many excellent histories of Chicago in this period see William Cronon, *Nature's Metropolis: Chicago and the Great West* (New York: W. W. Norton, 1991); Donald L. Miller, *City of the Century: The Epic of Chicago and the Making of America* (New York: Simon & Schuster, 1996); Ann Durkin Keating, *Building Chicago: Suburban Developers and the Creation of a Divided Metropolis* (Columbus: Ohio State University Press, 1988); Harold M. Mayer and Richard C. Wade, *Chicago: Growth of a Metropolis* (Chicago: University of Chicago Press, 1969); Christine Meisner Rosen, *The Limits of Power: Great Fires and the Process of City Growth in America* (New York: Cambridge University Press, 1986); Daniel Bluestone, *Constructing Chicago* (New Haven: Yale University Press, 1991); Thomas Lee Philpott, *The Slum and the Ghetto: Immigrants, Blacks, and Reformers in Chicago, 1880–1930* (New York: Oxford University Press, 1978); Robin Faith Bachin, *Building the South Side: Urban Space and Civic Culture, 1890–1919* (Chicago: University of Chicago Press, 2004).

18. There are too many studies of immigrants in Chicago to list here. Among the most incisive are: Dominic Pacyga, *Polish Immigrants and Industrial Chicago: Workers on the South Side, 1880–1922* (Columbus: Ohio State University Press, 1991); *Ethnic Chicago,* Melvin G. Holli and Peter d'A. Jones, eds. (Grand Rapids: Eerdmans, 1984); Juan R. Garcia, *Mexicans in the Midwest, 1900–1932* (Tucson: University of Arizona Press, 1996); John M. Allswang, *A House for All Peoples: Ethnic Politics in Chicago, 1890–1936* (Lexington: University of Kentucky Press, 1971); Humbert S. Nelli, *Italians in Chicago, 1880–1930: A Study in Ethnic Mobility* (New York: Oxford University Press, 1970); Thomas A. Guglielmo, *White on Arrival: Italians, Race, Color, and Power in Chicago, 1890–1945* (New York: Oxford University Press, 2003). On African-American migration to the city, see Allan H. Spear, *Black Chicago: The Making of a Negro Ghetto, 1890–1920* (Chicago: University of Chicago Press, 1967); William M. Tuttle, Jr., *Race Riot: Chicago in the Red Summer of 1919* (New York: Atheneum, 1970); James R. Grossman, *Land of Hope: Chicago, Black Southerners, and the Great Migration* (Chicago: University of Chicago Press, 1989); St. Clair Drake and Horace R. Cayton, *Black Metropolis: A Study of Negro Life in a Northern City* (New York: Harcourt, Brace, 1945).

19. On the rise of organized labor in Chicago, see James R. Barrett, *Work and Community in the Jungle: Chicago's Packinghouse Workers, 1894–1922* (Urbana: University of Illinois Press, 1987); Leon Fink, *Workingmen's Democracy: The Knights of Labor and American Politics* (Urbana: University of Illinois Press, 1983); Eric L. Hisch, *Urban Revolt: Ethnic Politics in the Nineteenth-Century Chicago Labor Movement* (Berkeley: University of California Press, 1990); Richard Schneirov, *Labor and Urban Politics: Class Conflicts*

and the Origins of Modern Liberalism in Chicago, 1864–97 (Urbana: University of Illinois Press, 1998); Carl Smith, *Urban Disorder and the Shape of Belief: The Great Chicago Fire, the Haymarket Bomb, and the Model Town of Pullman* (Chicago: University of Chicago Press, 1995).

20. Among the many excellent studies of Progressive Era reformers in Chicago, see Jane Addams, *Twenty Years at Hull-House* (New York: Penguin, 1961); Allen F. Davis, *Spearheads for Reform: The Social Settlements and the Progressive Movement, 1890–1914* (New York: Oxford University Press, 1967); Alan Dawley, *Struggles for Justice: Social Responsibility and the Liberal State* (Cambridge: Harvard University Press, 1991); Lela B. Costin, *Two Sisters for Social Justice: A Biography of Grace and Edith Abbott* (Urbana: University of Illinois Press, 1983); Louise C. Wade, *Graham Taylor, Pioneer for Social Justice, 1851–1938* (Chicago: University of Chicago Press, 1964); Jean Bethke Elshtain, *Jane Addams and the Dream of American Democracy: A Life* (New York: Basic Books, 2002); Maureen A. Flanagan, *Seeing with Their Hearts: Chicago Women and the Vision of the Good City, 1871–1933* (Princeton: Princeton University Press, 2002); Kathryn Kish Sklar, *Florence Kelley and the Nation's Work: The Rise of Women's Political Culture, 1830–1900* (New Haven: Yale University Press, 1995); Alice O'Connor, *Poverty Knowledge: Social Science, Social Policy, and the Poor in Twentieth-Century U.S. History* (Princeton: Princeton University Press, 2001); Gwendolyn Wright, *Moralism and the Model Home: Domestic Architecture and Cultural Conflict in Chicago, 1873–1913* (Chicago: University of Chicago Press, 1980); Michael Willrich, *City of Courts: Socializing Justice in Progressive Era Chicago* (New York: Cambridge University Press, 2003); Robert H. Wiebe, *The Search for Order, 1877–1920* (New York: Hill and Wang, 1967).

CHAPTER ONE

1. *Chicago Times,* Jan. 16, 1872, 1; *Chicago Daily Tribune,* Jan. 16, 1872, 1,2; Karen Sawislak, *Smoldering City: Chicagoans and the Great Fire, 1871–1874* (Chicago: University of Chicago Press, 1995) 29, 149.

2. Sawislak, *Smoldering City* 135–36; Richard Schneirov, *Labor and Urban Politics: Class Conflict and the Origins of Modern Liberalism in Chicago, 1864–97* (Urbana: University of Illinois Press, 1998) 50–51. For a history of the *Chicago Daily Tribune, see* Philip Kinsley, *The Chicago Tribune: Its First Hundred Years* (New York: A. A. Knopf, 1943); John Tebbel, *An American Dynasty* (New York: Doubleday, 1947); Richard Norton Smith, *The Colonel: The Life and Legend of Robert R. McCormick, 1880–1955* (Boston: Houghton Mifflin, 1997).

3. *Chicago Daily Tribune,* Jan. 16, 1872, 2; *Chicago Times,* Jan. 16, 1872.

4. *Chicago Times,* Jan. 16, 1872, 1.

5. *Chicago Daily Tribune,* Jan. 16, 1872, 2.

6. *Chicago Daily Tribune,* Jan. 16, 1872, 2; Alfred Theodore Andreas, *History of Chicago* (New York: Arno, 1975) 2:49.

7. This account of the protest comes from the *Chicago Daily Tribune,* Jan. 16, 17, and 18, 1872, and the *Chicago Times,* Jan. 17, 1872. See also Christine Meisner Rosen, *The Limits of Power: Great Fires and the Process of City Growth in America* (New York: Cambridge University Press, 1986) 102–3; Sawislak, *Smoldering City* 148–53; John B. Jentz, "Class and Politics in an Emerging Industrial City: Chicago in the 1860s and 1870s," *Journal of Urban History* 17 (1991) 238–40; Emily Clark, "Own Your Own Home: S. E. Gross, the Great Domestic Promoter," in *The American Home: Material Culture, Domestic Space and Family Life,* Eleanor McD. Thompson, ed. (Winterthur, DE: Henry Francis Du Pont Winterthur Museum, 1996). Hesing later claimed the bricks

were thrown by "streetloafers and urchins," but no other evidence supports or refutes that claim. *Chicago Daily Tribune*, Jan. 18, 1872, 4.

8. A second fire, not nearly as devastating as the first, in 1874 led to a reworking of the fire limits ordinance, banning new wood frame construction in the city limits. By then, however, many frame houses had already been built.

9. Jentz, "Class and Politics in an Emerging Industrial City" 233–34; Kathleen D. Mc-Carthy, *Noblesse Oblige: Charity and Cultural Philanthropy in Chicago, 1849–1929* (Chicago: University of Chicago Press, 1982) 53–54, 65–67.

10. Richard Harris makes a similar point about home ownership rates among the working classes in Toronto. Harris, *Unplanned Suburbs: Toronto's American Tragedy, 1900–1950* (Baltimore: Johns Hopkins University Press, 1996) 8.

11. Robin Einhorn, *Property Rules: Political Economy in Chicago, 1833–1872* (Chicago: University of Chicago Press, 1991) 249–56. Einhorn has analyzed a database constructed by the Origins of Chicago's Industrial Working Class Project under the direction of John B. Jentz and Richard Schneirov and based at the Newberry Library. For a full discussion of the data see Einhorn's appendix. Also see Richard Schneirov, *Labor and Urban Politics: Class Conflict and the Origins of Modern Liberalism in Chicago, 1864–97* (Urbana: University of Illinois Press, 1998) 50. Among those who owned property valued at less than $1,000, German-born men had the highest ownership rates of any ethnic group in the city. Perry Duis writes that by 1890, 35 percent of Chicagoans owned their homes. Duis, *Challenging Chicago: Coping with Everyday Life, 1837–1920* (Urbana: University of Illinois Press, 1998) 74. For more on high rates of home ownership among working-class immigrants in nineteenth-century cities, see Olivier Zunz, *The Changing Face of Inequality: Urbanization, Industrial Development, and Immigrants in Detroit, 1880–1920* (Chicago: University of Chicago Press, 1982); Stephan Thernstrom, *Poverty and Progress: Social Mobility in a Nineteenth Century City* (New York: Atheneum, 1970); and Matthew Edel, Elliot D. Sclar, and Daniel Luria, *Shaky Palaces: Homeownership and Social Mobility in Boston's Suburbanization* (New York: Columbia University Press, 1984); Eric Sandweiss, *St. Louis: The Evolution of an American Urban Landscape* (Philadelphia: Temple University Press, 2001) 260–61; Ileen A. De-Vault, *Sons and Daughters of Labor: Class and Clerical Work in Turn-of-the-Century Pittsburgh* (Ithaca: Cornell University Press, 1990) 88–89; Michael J. Doucet and John C. Weaver, "Material Culture and the North American House: The Era of the Common Man, 1870–1920," *Journal of American History* 72 (1985) 561–64; Roger Simon, *The City Building Process: Housing and Services in New Milwaukee Neighborhoods, 1880–1910* (Philadelphia: American Philosophical Society, 1996).

12. Property Tract Records, Cook County Treasurer's Office, Chicago; Robinson's Fire Insurance Map, 1886, CHS; Louise Montgomery, *The American Girl in the Stockyards District* (Chicago: University of Chicago Press, 1913) 4.

13. George F. Yates diary (manuscript), entry dated Aug. 13, 1884, CHS. While 37 percent of skilled and unskilled workers owned some property in 1870, just 27 percent of low-income white-collar workers and 38 percent of high-income white-collar workers owned property. Einhorn, *Property Rules* 249–56.

14. *Chicago Daily Tribune*, Oct. 28, 1883. This is not to deny the growth of middle-class suburbs in the late nineteenth century. See Michael H. Ebner, *Creating Chicago's North Shore: A Suburban History* (Chicago: University of Chicago Press, 1988); Ann Durkin Keating, *Building Chicago: Suburban Developers and the Creation of a Divided Metropolis* (Columbus: Ohio State University Press, 1988). Scholars have typically seen the expansion of suburbs marketed to middle-class households, those of men employed in

the professions and well-paid managerial positions in corporations, as a sign of the middle classes separating themselves geographically from the growing classes of manual laborers and lower-paid white-collar workers. Yet the aspiration for and achievement of home ownership within the city marked another distinction, one that separated the European born from the native born and the more affluent salaried workers from skilled and unskilled manual laborers. That distinction is evident in census and property records for Chicago. Moreover, evidence from Chicago and other cities suggests that suburbanization did not always or necessarily imply a pursuit of home ownership. Nearly half the suburban residents in Sam Bass Warner's study of Boston's suburbs were renters. Similarly, Margaret Marsh found that suburbanization in mid-nineteenth-century Philadelphia represented the pursuit of a particular way of life, not of home ownership. On suburbanization and the middle classes, see Sam Bass Warner, Jr., *Streetcar Suburbs: The Process of Growth in Boston, 1870–1900* (Cambridge: Harvard University Press, 1962); Margaret Marsh, *Suburban Lives* (New Brunswick: Rutgers University Press, 1990) 87; Kenneth T. Jackson, *Crabgrass Frontier: The Suburbanization of the United States* (New York: Oxford University Press, 1985); Stuart Blumin, *The Emergence of the Middle Class: Social Experience in the American City, 1760–1900* (New York: Cambridge University Press, 1989) 275–85.

15. Daniel Bluestone, "Chicago's Mecca Flat Blues," *Journal of the Society of Architectural Historians* 57 (1999) 382–403; Bessie Louise Pierce, *A History of Chicago*, vol. 3, *The Rise of a Modern City, 1871–1893* (New York: Alfred A. Knopf, 1957) 57; Einhorn, *Property Rules* 249–56.

16. See rental and sales advertisements in the *Chicago Daily Tribune*, which ran pages of advertisements for housing in each issue. Martin J. Sklar, *The Corporate Reconstruction of American Capitalism, 1890–1916* (New York: Cambridge University Press, 1988). Sklar traces the rise of corporate investments among the middle classes and the shift toward the corporation as a primary mechanism for business organization. Late nineteenth-century middle classes were clearly divided on question of profitable investments. Some—land speculators, developers, and real estate salesmen—viewed residential property as an investment at least as good as corporate stock. See chap. 5 of this book; Ileen A. DeVault, *Sons and Daughters of Labor: Class and Clerical Work in Turn of the Century Pittsburgh* (Ithaca: Cornell University Press, 1990) 22–23. DeVault argues that young native-born white men working as clerks in offices, unlike women, continued to see their jobs as a stepping-stone to better-paid employment and identified with management as opposed to factory workers. This may help to explain the low levels of home ownership among this group, which rested uncomfortably near the lower rungs of the middle classes.

17. Richard Sennett, *Families against the City: Middle Class Homes of Industrial Chicago, 1872–1890* (Cambridge: Harvard University Press, 1970) 25–39. The fiction of late nineteenth-century Chicago similarly reveals the middle-class inclination to rent single-family houses, or even small brick cottages, saving capital for investment in business enterprises. See, for example, Henry B. Fuller, *The Cliff Dwellers, A Novel* (New York: Harper & Bros., 1893); Robert Herrick, *The Memoirs of an American Citizen* (New York: Macmillan, 1905); Theodore Dreiser, *Jenny Gerhardt* (New York: Penguin, 1989).

18. Homer Hoyt, *One Hundred Years of Land Values in Chicago: The Relationship of the Growth of Chicago to the Rise of Its Land Values, 1830–1933* (Chicago: University of Chicago Press, 1933) 74–81.

19. *Chicago Daily Tribune*, Jan. 15, 1872.

20. *Chicago Daily Tribune*, Jan. 19, 1872, 4.

218 / Notes to pp. 22–27

21. "Petition of Northsiders," Chicago Common Council Proceedings, 400 1872/181 B, ISARD. The petition is reprinted in the Chicago Times, Jan. 16, 1872; Rosen, The Limits of Power 101; Sawislak, Smoldering City 144.

22. On home life as a measure of the fairness of contract relations in work, see Amy Dru Stanley, *From Bondage to Contract: Wage Labor, Marriage, and the Market in the Age of Slave Emancipation* (New York: Cambridge University Press, 1998) 138–74. Stanley argues that control of household labor, the ability to remove a wife and daughters from wage work and divert their energies to maintaining the household, was central to workers' efforts to distinguish themselves from chattel slaves. See also David Montgomery, *The Fall of the House of Labor: The Workplace, the State, and American Labor Activism, 1865–1925* (New York: Cambridge University Press, 1987) 136–38; Lawrence B. Glickman, *A Living Wage: American Workers and the Making of Consumer Society* (Ithaca: Cornell University Press, 1997) 57–77. Comfortable, a word widely used by labor leaders and their supporters, did not have a well-accepted meaning. What counted as a "comfortable" home was largely determined by the views and values of individual writers or speakers.

23. *Progressive Age,* Oct. 8, 1881.

24. *Chicago Daily Tribune,* Jan. 16, 1872, 2; *Chicago Times,* Jan. 16, 1872, 1; Jentz, "Class Politics in an Emerging Industrial City" 245. For more on labor organizing in Chicago, see Richard Schneirov, *Labor and Urban Politics: Class Conflict and the Origins of Modern Liberalism in Chicago, 1864–97* (Urbana: University of Illinois Press, 1998); Leon Fink, *Workingmen's Democracy: The Knights of Labor and American Politics* (Urbana: University of Illinois Press, 1983); Eric L. Hisch, *Urban Revolt: Ethnic Politics in the Nineteenth-Century Chicago Labor Movement* (Berkeley: University of California Press, 1990).

25. *Chicago Times,* Jan. 16, 1872, 1; Schneirov, *Labor and Urban Politics* 26–27; Sawislak, *Smoldering City* 60–61.

26. *Chicago Daily Tribune,* Jan. 16, 1872.

27. *Chicago Daily Tribune,* Jan. 18, 1872.

28. *Chicago Daily Tribune,* Jan. 16 and 17, 1872.

29. Sawislak, *Smoldering City* 152–53; *Chicago Times,* Jan. 19, 1872; *Chicago Times,* Jan. 21, 1872.

30. *Chicago Daily Tribune,* Jan. 18, 1872; Rosen, *Limits of Power* 99–100; Sawislak, *Smoldering City* 151; Andreas, *History of Chicago* 2:50–51. For more on Medill's election and political constituency see Pierce, *A History of Chicago* 3:340–41.

31. *Chicago Daily Tribune,* Jan. 20, 1872; *Chicago Republican,* Jan. 18, 1872.

32. Quoted in Sawislak, *Smoldering City* 154, which offers this analysis of Rapp's speech. The linking of the rights of citizenship to home ownership became even more vivid in the 1880s when home builders sponsored Fourth of July picnic celebrations on recently subdivided urban and suburban land, chartering commuter trains to carry hundreds of immigrant and laboring families to "look over the site" and purchase lots and houses. For an article on one such excursion, see *Chicago Daily Tribune,* July 5, 1888, 2.

33. John Higham, *Strangers in the Land: Patterns of American Nativism, 1860–1925* (New York: Athenaeum, 1963) 4; Pierce, *A History of Chicago* 3:20–49.

34. *Chicago Daily Tribune,* Jan. 19, 1872.

35. Jentz, "Class and Politics in an Emerging Industrial City" 236.

36. *Chicago Daily Tribune,* Jan. 19, 1872.

37. *Chicago Daily Tribune,* Jan. 18, 1872, 4; Sawislak, *Smoldering City* 153–54.

38. *Chicago Daily Tribune,* Jan. 18, 1872, 4; Sawislak, *Smoldering City* 156–58.

39. *Chicago Republican,* Jan. 18, 1872 See also *Illinois Staats-Zeitung,* Jan. 18, 1872, quoted in Jentz, "Class and Politics in an Emerging Industrial City" 240. Hesing's assertions of the potential harmony of interest between workers and their employers were not unusual. The Knights of Labor on one side and employers like Andrew Carnegie on the other expressed similar hopes for cooperation between laborers and capitalists. See, for example, Andrew Carnegie, "An Employer's View of the Labor Question," in *The Gospel of Wealth and Other Timely Essays,* Edward C. Kirkland, ed. (Cambridge: Harvard University Press, 1962 [orig. publ. April 1886]).

40. Jentz, "Class and Politics in an Emerging Industrial City" 237, 241.

41. *Chicago Daily Tribune,* Jan. 19, 1872, 4. A record of the debates leading up to the passage of the ordinance can be found in Chicago Common Council Proceedings 399 1872/177 B, ISARD.

42. *Chicago Daily Tribune,* Jan. 21, 1872, 2; *Chicago Times,* Jan. 21, 1972. The *Times* called the restaurant "Raggio's." The restaurant was located at the corner of Clark and Center (later renamed Armitage) Streets.

43. Homer Hoyt, *One Hundred Years of Land Values in Chicago: The Relationship of the Growth of Chicago to the Rise of Its Land Values, 1830–1933* (Chicago: University of Chicago Press, 1933) 67–74.

44. *Chicago Daily Tribune,* Jan. 21, 1872, 2.

45. *Chicago Daily Tribune,* Jan. 21, 1872, 2; *Chicago Times,* Jan. 21, 1872; Edwards, *Directory of the City of Chicago for 1870* (Chicago City Directories), reel 14, NYPL; *The Lakeside Annual Directory of the City of Chicago for 1874–6* (Chicago: Williams, Donnelly & Co., 1876) reel 18, University of Illinois at Chicago library.

46. *Chicago Daily Tribune,* Jan. 21, 1872; *Lakeside Annual Directory 1874–6,* reel 18, NYPL.

47. *Chicago Daily Tribune,* Jan. 21, 1872, 2.

48. On nuisance laws, see Jon C. Teaford, *Municipal Revolution in America: Origins of Modern Urban Government, 1650–1825* (Chicago: University of Chicago Press, 1975), 102–9. As Elizabeth Blackmar notes, early nineteenth-century urban governments enacted new ordinances under the auspices of nuisance laws that would also encourage greater investment in urban property. Blackmar, "Accountability for Public Heath: Regulating the Housing Market in Nineteenth-Century New York City," in *Hives of Sickness: Public Health and Epidemics in New York City,* David Rosner, ed. (New Brunswick: Rutgers University Press, 1995) 45–46. John R. Commons traced the growing dominance under law of this conception of property as profit generating. He showed how a series of federal and state cases gradually established the sanctity of "highest and best uses" for balancing competing claims to property. See Commons, *Legal Foundations of Capitalism* (New York: Macmillan, 1924) 14–16.

49. *Chicago Daily Tribune,* Jan. 21, 1872, 2; *Chicago Daily Tribune,* Jan. 19, 1872, 4.

50. *Progressive Age,* Oct. 1, 1881, 4.

51. *Progressive Age,* July 23, 1881, Oct. 8, 1881; *Ninth Census—Volume I: The Statistics of Population of the United States of America* (Washington, 1872) p. xxxiii; Margo Anderson Conk, *The United States Census and Labor Force Change: A History of Occupation Statistics, 1870–1940* (Ann Arbor: University of Michigan Press, 1978) 22–30; Blumin, *The Emergence of the Middle Class* 260–61; Stephan Thernstrom, *The Other Bostonians: Poverty and Progress in the American Metropolis* (Cambridge: Harvard University Press, 1973) 292n. Thernstrom argues that self-employed artisans had largely disappeared from Boston in 1880. That was not entirely true of Chicago, but many Chicago artisans believed their status was undermined if not fast disappearing.

52. For a full discussion of the fire and its after-effects on the social order and social conflicts in the city, see Sawislak, *Smoldering City*.

CHAPTER TWO

1. U.S. Manuscript Census, 1880, Cook County Tract Books, Cook County Treasurer's Office, Chicago; *Third Biennial Report of the Bureau of Labor Statistics of Illinois* (Springfield: H. W. Rokker, 1884) 358–62, 331–33. Records from Holy Family parish suggest that three of the Brophy children were born to Bernard's first wife, Annie Bremner. See Records of the Visit to the Holy Family Parish, 1880, 76, Loyola University Archives, Chicago. Thanks to Ellen Skerrett for finding this information.

2. Stephan Thernstrom, *Poverty and Progress: Social Mobility in a Nineteenth Century City* (New York: Atheneum, 1970); Gail Radford, *Modern Housing for America: Policy Struggles in the New Deal Era* (Chicago: University of Chicago Press, 1996) 8–10; Robert G. Barrows, "Beyond the Tenement: Patterns of American Urban Housing, 1870–1930, *Journal of Urban History* 9 (1983) 395–420; Michael J. Doucet and John C. Weaver, "Material Culture and the North American House: The Era of the Common Man, 1870–1920," *Journal of American History* 72 (1985) 561–64.

3. All of the data about the Brophy family and their neighbors comes from the U.S. Manuscript Censuses of 1880 and 1900 and from Chicago city directories for the period. Information about the type and size of their houses was gleaned from fire insurance maps, Robinsons for 1886 and Sanborn for 1911, in the CHS collections. Information about building sales and loans comes from the city's tract books in the Cook County Treasurer's Office. Earnings and spending for bread peddlers like Brophy were reported in the *Third Biennial Report of the Bureau of Labor Statistics of Illinois* (Springfield: H. W. Rokker, 1884) 358–62.

4. U.S. Manuscript Census, 1880; Tract Books. Rinehardt's name is spelled "Rinehard" in the census. Similar uses of property rights in housing can be seen along the streets bordering the packinghouses southwest of the city. See James R. Barrett, *Work and Community in the Jungle: Chicago's Packinghouse Workers, 1894–1922* (Urbana: University of Illinois Press, 1987) 104–5; "The Back of the Yards Area," unsigned typed manuscript, 4–5, University of Chicago Settlement Collection, box 1, folder 2, CHS.

5. St. Clair Drake and Horace R. Cayton, *Black Metropolis: A Study of Negro Life in a Northern City* (New York: Harcourt, Brace, 1945) 47; Bessie Louise Pierce, *A History of Chicago*, vol. 3, *The Rise of a Modern City, 1871–1893* (New York: Alfred A. Knopf, 1957) 11; Homer Hoyt, *One Hundred Years of Land Values in Chicago: The Relationship of the Growth of Chicago to the Rise of Its Land Values, 1830–1933* (Chicago: University of Chicago Press, 1933) 97; Cook County Tract Books. Thomas Lee Philpott argues that racial segregation was near complete by 1900. Philpott, *The Slum and the Ghetto: Immigrants, Blacks, and Reformers in Chicago, 1880–1930* (New York: Oxford University Press, 1978) 118–35.

6. Christopher Robert Reed, *"All the World Is Here!" The Black Presence at the White City* (Bloomington: Indiana University Press, 2000) 15, 91–92; *Black's Boot Book* (Chicago: Celerity Press, 1906) 54. The Cherrys, as Reed notes, were part of what Drake and Cayton identified as the "respectable" class among Chicago's African-American population, not the elite or "refined," but also not the "riff raff." They were working class in terms of income, aspirations, education, and location of their home. Reed, *"All the World Is Here!"* 80–98; Drake and Cayton, *Black Metropolis* 543–46.

7. Agnes Sinclair Holbrook, "Map Notes and Comments," in *Hull-House Maps and Pa-*

pers: A Presentation of Nationalities and Wages in a Congested District of Chicago (New York: T. Y. Crowell, 1895) 15–19; Philpott, *The Slum and the Ghetto* 136–43.

8. Christine Meisner Rosen, *The Limits of Power: Great Fires and the Process of City Growth in America* (New York: Cambridge University Press, 1986) 173; *Report of the Committee on Tenement Houses of the Citizens Association of Chicago* (Chicago: Geo. K. Hazlitt, 1884) 34–38, CHS.

9. Robinson's Fire Insurance Map, 1886, CHS; Pierce, *A History of Chicago* 3:50–56; Elias Colbert and Everett Chamberlin, *Chicago and the Great Conflagration* (Chicago: J. S. Goodman, 1871) 205; Edith Abbott, *The Tenements of Chicago, 1908–1935* (Chicago: University of Chicago Press, 1936) 93.

10. For maps of the city including residential and industrial districts see Rosen, *The Limits of Power* 173; Hoyt, *One Hundred Years of Land Values* 106, 114, 115.

11. Abbott, *The Tenements of Chicago* 92–100.

12. Abbott, *The Tenements of Chicago* 93; Lyman Bridges Company, *Illustrated Catalogue: Lyman Bridges Building Materials and Ready-Made Houses* (Chicago: Rand McNally, 1870). Real estate advertisements in the *Chicago Daily Tribune* included descriptions of the number of rooms in cottages and two-story houses available for rent or sale throughout the 1880s. Another source for the size of buildings offered for sale is the *Real Estate and Building Journal*. See, for example, the journal, May 29, 1886, 325. For somewhat later designs see Fred T. Hodgson, *Hodgson's Low Cost American Homes: Perspective Views and Floor Plans of One Hundred Low and Medium Priced Houses* (Chicago: Frederick J. Drake, 1904). For a full description of cottage designs and construction materials and techniques see Joseph C. Bigott, *From Cottage to Bungalow: Houses and the Working Class in Metropolitan Chicago, 1869–1929* (Chicago: University of Chicago Press, 2001) 20–53.

13. Pierce, *A History of Chicago* 3:55–56; Humbert S. Nelli, *Italians in Chicago, 1880–1930: A Study in Ethnic Mobility* (New York: Oxford University Press, 1979) 32–34; Agnes Sinclair Holbrook, "General Comments," in *Hull-House Maps and Papers* 5–8; Robert S. Hunter, *Tenement Conditions in Chicago: Report by the Investigating Committee of the City Homes Association* (Chicago: City Homes Association, 1901) 22–36; Abbott, *The Tenements of Chicago* 92. For a literary treatment of this, see Theodore Dreiser, *Sister Carrie* (New York: Oxford University Press, 1991) 10–11.

14. Hunter, *Tenement Conditions in Chicago* 70; "Interior of slum room," ICHi 32524, undated photograph, CHS; *Chicago's Dark Places: Investigations by a Corps of Specially Appointed Commissioners* (Chicago: Craig Press, 1891) 23–29.

15. Thomas J. Suhrbur, "The Economic Transformation of Carpentry in Late-Nineteenth-Century Chicago," *Illinois Historical Journal* 81 (1988) 113–18. On owner-built housing in northern cities see Richard Harris, "Self-Building in the Urban Housing Market," *Economic Geography* 67 (1991) 1–21. Harris comments that owner-built housing was less common in Chicago than "elsewhere because entrepreneurs were providing ready-made houses to a mass market." Harris, "Chicago's Other Suburbs," *Geographical Review* 84 (1994) 402–3.

16. Hunter, *Tenement Conditions of Chicago* 105–8; *Fifth Biennial Report of the Bureau of Labor Statistics of Illinois* (Springfield: Springfield Printing, 1888) 359–91; Citizen's Association Report, 1884, 34–38, CHS; Jane Addams, *Twenty Years at Hull-House* (New York: Penguin, 1961) 210–11. Even in 1920, indoor plumbing in many workers' cottages and two-flats was minimal. Radford, *Modern Housing for America* 25.

17. For similar credit systems in St. Louis, see Eric Sandweiss, *St. Louis: The Evolution of an American Urban Landscape* (Philadelphia: Temple University Press, 2001) 103.

18. Tract books rarely list a bank as providing a mortgage loan for this period. See also Lizabeth Cohen, *Making a New Deal: Industrial Workers in Chicago, 1919–1939* (New York: Cambridge University Press, 1990) 76–77. Cohen says that immigrants and their children rarely used commercial banks for savings or check cashing before WWI.

19. F. Cyril James, *The Growth of Chicago Banks* (New York: Harper & Brothers, 1938) 292. Homer Hoyt notes that until the World's Fair of 1893, there was only one bank outside the city's downtown business district and that was in the stockyards area. Hoyt, *One Hundred Years of Land Values in Chicago* 226. See also Report of the U.S. Immigration Commission, 37:216, quoted in Cohen, *Making a New Deal* 391. The commission noted that inconvenient hours in American commercial and state banks and their intimidating atmosphere tended to discourage immigrants from using them.

20. Snowden, "Mortgage and American Urbanization, 1880–1890," *Journal of Economic History* 48 (1988) 278. Before 1870, interest rates in Illinois were "extremely rigid," set at 10 percent, the maximum allowed under state law. By 1872, however, loans were available at 8 percent and during the years after the panic in 1873, rates went as low as 6 percent. James, *The Growth of Chicago Banks* 497–98.

21. Seymour Dexter, *A Treatise on Co-operative Savings and Loan Associations* (New York: D. Appleton, 1889) 59–60; *Chicago Daily Tribune*, March 25, 1883. On Polish immigrants and building and loan societies see Edward R. Kantowicz, "Polish Chicago: Survival through Solidarity," in *The Ethnic Frontier*, Melvin G. Holli and Peter d'A. Jones, eds. (Grand Rapids: William B. Eerdmans, 1977) 185.

22. Dexter, *A Treatise on Co-operative Savings and Loan Associations* 16–40, 59–60; Cohen, *Making a New Deal* 76; Victor Green, *For God and Country: The Rise of Polish and Lithuanian Ethnic Consciousness in America, 1860–1910* (Madison: State Historical Society of Wisconsin, 1975) 54–58.

23. S. E. Gross (firm), *Illustrated Catalogue of S. E. Gross' lots, houses, cottages* (Chicago: S. E. Gross, 1889), GP. For more on Gross, see chapter 5.

24. *Fifth Biennial Report of the Bureau of Labor Statistics of Illinois* (Springfield: Springfield Printing, 1888) 388–89.

25. Hoyt, *One Hundred Years of Land Values in Chicago* 119; Pierce, *A History of Chicago* 3:239; *Industrial Chicago*, vol. 2, *The Building Interests* (Chicago: Goodspeed, 1891) 514.

26. For a full account of the strike see: Pierce, *A History of Chicago* 3:240–54; James Ford Rhodes, "The Railroad Riots of 1877," *Scribners Magazine*, July 1911, 87; *Chicago Daily Tribune*, July 21–25, 1877; *Inter Ocean*, July 20–24, 1877. Angered by the police attacks on protesting workers in July 1877, labor leaders demanded the creation of "a special armed force" more sympathetic to the working classes. When some labor organizations began to maintain drill corps, labor leaders engaged in a debate over whether the corpsmen should be armed. The Illinois legislature resolved the conflict in 1879 with legislation that severely restricted the activities of the drill corps.

27. Hoyt, *One Hundred Years of Land Values in Chicago* 124; Illinois Bureau of Labor Statistics, Second Biennial Report, 1882, 288, 351.

28. That the foreign born were willing to take on debt, sometimes two or three loans at a time, suggests another distinction between the foreign born and their Yankee-bred neighbors. The late nineteenth-century economist Richard T. Ely notes the aversion to debt among New England farmers: "Where I was brought up, this creed was so applied that we looked upon a mortgage on a farm or a home as something of a stigma." Richard T. Ely, *Ground under Our Feet: An Autobiography* (New York: Macmillan, 1938) 5. As late as 1923, a pamphlet issued by the Department of Commerce and designed

to encourage home ownership reassured potential buyers that "borrowing money to buy a home is no disgrace." *How to Own Your Home: A Handbook for Prospective Home Owners*, prepared by John M. Gries and James S. Taylor, 2nd ed. (Washington: U.S. Government Printing Office, 1931) 4.

29. Kenneth A. Snowden, "Mortgage Rates and American Capital Market Development in the Late Nineteenth Century," *Journal of Economic History* 47 1987) 677. Snowden mentions the use of second and third mortgages to pay "current expenses," which he calls "calamitous mortgage[s]."

30. That Rachel Brophy got a job as a typist suggests she stayed in school at least through the eighth grade. The job, which probably paid more than a factory job or domestic service, would, however, not have led to much of a promotion or long-term increases in income, at least not enough even to sustain herself outside of her father's home. Louise Montgomery's 1913 study of teenage girls living near the stockyards found that few office workers, including stenographers and typists, earned enough to acquire the clothing or status of the middle classes. Montgomery, *The American Girl in the Stockyards District* (Chicago: University of Chicago Press, 1913) 35–53.

31. Amy·Dru Stanley, *From Bondage to Contract: Wage Labor, Marriage, and the Market in the Age of Slave Emancipation* (New York: Cambridge University Press, 1998) 144–45. The Illinois Bureau of Labor Statistics surveyed Chicago's families in 1882 and reported a significant gap between men's average wages and the minimum costs of subsistence. A year later in a study of over two thousand Illinois households, the bureau found that a family of four or five persons needed $550 per year to survive and that men's wages averaged only $525.27. Illinois Bureau of Labor Statistics, *Second Biennial Report* (1883) 288–89; Illinois Bureau of Labor Statistics, *Third Biennial Report* (1884) 137, 331–33, 255, 269, 370, 357.

32. *Report to the Common Council of the Chicago Relief and Aid Society* (1884) 4–6, CHS. For contemporary debates about the value of the wage, see Stanley, *From Bondage to Contract* 154–62.

33. *Report to the Common Council of the Chicago Relief and Aid Society* (1884) 4. For a theory of risk in an entirely different context see Mary Douglas and Aaron Wildavsky, *Risk and Culture: An Essay on the Selection of Technical and Environmental Dangers* (Berkeley: University of California Press, 1982) 187–98.

34. James, *The Growth of Chicago Banks* 449; Hoyt, *One Hundred Years of Land Values in Chicago* 130.

35. *Real Estate and Building Journal*, May 13, 1876; Hoyt, *One Hundred Years of Land Values in Chicago* 118.

36. Hoyt, *One Hundred Years of Land Values in Chicago* 118.

37. *Real Estate and Building Journal*, June 3, 1876.

38. *Chicago Daily Tribune*, July 28, 1878.

39. *Chicago Daily Tribune*, Feb. 14, 1875.

40. The Illinois state legislature, following the lead of New York, Tennessee, and several other states, passed legislation in 1841 that gave the mortgagor one year to "redeem his property." Lawrence M. Friedman, *A History of American Law*, 2nd ed. (New York: Simon & Schuster, 1985) 247; Paul Goodman, "The Emergence of Homestead Exemption in the United States: Accommodation and Resistance to the Market Revolution, 1840–1880," *Journal of American History* 80 (Sept.1993) 470–97.

41. Similar patterns of low home ownership rates among African-Americans in Detroit yielded a similar outcome. See Thomas Sugrue, *The Origins of the Urban Crisis: Race and Inequality in Postwar Detroit* (Princeton: Princeton University Press, 1996) 33–36.

42. U.S. Manuscript Census, 1880; Chicago Commission on Race Relations, *The Negro in Chicago: A Study of Race Relations and a Race Riot* (Chicago: University of Chicago Press, 1922) 111; Drake and Cayton, *Black Metropolis* 176–77. Among the categories listed in the U.S. manuscript census, the household-by-household survey of the nation's residents, were race, place of birth, employment, and relationship to other household members. It is therefore possible—by scrolling through reels of the census on microfilm—to get a general picture of where Chicagoans of different races and nationalities lived. Drake and Cayton argue that before World War I, black Chicagoans typically were grouped in enclaves within districts of European immigrants. Nevertheless, they quote several people who remember living next door to "white neighbors" at the turn of the century.

43. Addams, *Twenty Years at Hull-House* 82; John Modell and Tamara K. Hareven, "Urbanization and the Malleable Household: An Examination of Boarding and Lodging in American Families," *Journal of Marriage and the Family* 35 (1973) 467–79.

44. Construction costs fell between 1870 and 1894, but began to rise in the mid-1890s, just as wages, relative to housing costs, began to fall. From 1895 to 1914, the cost of residential construction increased by 50 percent while the overall rise in consumer prices rose just 20 percent. Radford, *Modern Housing for America* 8–12; Doucet and Weaver, "Material Culture and the North American House" 561–77; U.S. Manuscript Census, 1910. See also Carolyn S. Loeb, *Entrepreneurial Vernacular: Developers' Subdivisions in the 1920s* (Baltimore: Johns Hopkins University Press, 2001) 144–49; Clifford Edward Clark Jr., *The American Family Home, 1800–1960* (Chapel Hill: University of North Carolina Press, 1986); Barrows, "Beyond the Tenement: Patterns of American Urban Housing, 1870–1930" 398–400.

CHAPTER THREE

1. *Chicago Daily Tribune*, Sept. 20, 1874, 10. Tenement housing was not considered a problem in Chicago until the mid-1870s. Journalist James Parton, on a visit to Chicago in 1867, wrote "In all of Chicago there is not one tenement house. Thrifty workmen own the homes they live in, and the rest can still comfortably hire a house." Parton's assessment was probably inaccurate, but his claims likely represented the views of many Chicagoans. *Atlantic Monthly*, March 1867, 338–39.

2. RDH 1879–1889, Harold Washington Municipal Library Special Collections, Chicago.

3. Scholars have long highlighted Progressive Era efforts to establish federal and state regulation of industrial working conditions. Few, however, have noted that housing was among the earliest targets for government intervention. See, for example: Allen F. Davis, *Spearheads for Reform: The Social Settlements and the Progressive Movement, 1890–1914* (New York: Oxford University Press, 1967); Michael Katz, *Poverty and Policy in American History* (Philadelphia: University of Pennsylvania Press, 1983); Molly Ladd-Taylor, *Mother-Work: Women, Child Welfare, and the State, 1890–1930* (Urbana: University of Illinois Press, 1994); Sonya Michel and Seth Koven, "Womanly Duties: Maternalist Politics and the Origins of Welfare States in France, Germany, Great Britain, and the United States, 1880–1920," *American Historical Review* (1990) 1076–108.

4. Elizabeth Blackmar makes a similar argument about housing reform in mid-nineteenth-century New York City. Blackmar, *Manhattan for Rent, 1785–1850* (Ithaca: Cornell University Press, 1989) 207–12.

5. Reformers would later take on this persona. In New York City, the Danish photographer Jacob Riis and the housing reformer Robert DeForest had presented their work

as that of explorers exposing impoverished sections of the city. Explaining this genre of urban literature, which appeared in both the American and British press, Judith Walkowitz suggests that the journalist-explorer produced a map of the urban scene by separating the known from the foreign sections of the city. See Judith Walkowitz, *City of Dreadful Delight: Narratives of Sexual Danger in Late-Victorian London* (Chicago: University of Chicago Press, 1972); Anne McClintock, *Imperial Leather: Race, Gender, and Sexuality in the Colonial Contest* (New York: Routledge, 1995).

6. *Chicago Daily Tribune*, Sept. 20, 1874. Many similar articles were published in the *Tribune*. See, for example: *Chicago Daily Tribune*, Oct. 22, 1879; April 10 and Aug. 7, 1881; Oct. 21, 1882; Feb. 16, June 12, and July 8, 1883. The *Chicago Daily News* published a series on tenements, "How the Poor Live," *Chicago Daily News*, Jan. 4, 12, 14, 21, 30, Feb. 2, 9, 23, 1884. For a slightly later but similar discussion of tenement residents, see *Chicago's Dark Places: Investigations by a Corps of Specially Appointed Commissioners* (Chicago: Craig Press, 1891) 16–17, 23–29. See also Perry Duis, *Challenging Chicago: Coping with Everyday Life, 1837–1920* (Urbana: University of Illinois Press, 1998) 98.

7. *Chicago's Dark Places* 25.

8. *Chicago Daily Tribune*, Sept. 20, 1874. The reporters' language seems to prefigure the use of "racial degradation" as an explanation for social problems that was widely used in the 1890s. See McClintock, *Imperial Leather* 48. According to the census, there were small numbers of immigrants from Italy living in Chicago in the 1870s. That, I believe, supports my contention that the reporter's explanation of tenement residents' poverty had little to do with actual nationalities of Chicago residents. Thomas A. Guglielmo, *White on Arrival: Italians, Race, Color, and Power in Chicago, 1890–1945* (New York: Oxford University Press, 2003) 16–21. Guglielmo distinguishes between color and race, noting that Italian immigrants, while described as a separate race were also defined as white. Further, the language of race biology was not unique to Chicago nor was it applied only to European immigrants. See Nayan Shah, *Contagious Divides: Epidemics and Race in San Francisco's Chinatown* (Berkeley: University of California Press, 2001) 21–22; Howard Markel, *Quarantine: East European Jewish Immigrants and the New York City Epidemics of 1892* (Baltimore: Johns Hopkins University Press, 1997). The claim that immigrants were responsible for the spread of contagious disease was not new either. Lemuel Shattuck, a physician and reformer, had blamed immigrants for disease in Boston in his widely read *The Report of the Sanitary Commission of Massachusetts, 1850* (Cambridge: Harvard University Press, 1948). See also Barbara Gutmann Rosenkrantz, *Public Health and the State: Changing Views in Massachusetts, 1842–1936* (Cambridge: Harvard University Press, 1972) 16–23; Martin V. Melosi, *The Sanitary City: Urban Infrastructure in America from Colonial Times to the Present* (Baltimore: Johns Hopkins University Press, 2000) 62–63.

9. Elizabeth Blackmar, "Accountability for Public Health: Regulating the Housing Market in Nineteenth-Century New York City," in *Hives of Sickness: Public Health and Epidemics in New York City*, David Rosner, ed. (New Brunswick: Rutgers University Press, 1995) 47; Lawrence M. Friedman, *A History of American Law*, 2nd ed. (New York: Simon & Schuster, 1985) 413.

10. Sander Gilman, ed., *Degeneration: The Dark Side of Progress* (New York: Columbia University Press, 1985) xiv. See also Gilman, *Difference and Pathology: Stereotypes of Sexuality, Race, and Madness* (Ithaca: Cornell University Press, 1985); Nancy Stepan, "Race and Gender: The Role of Analogy in Science," *Isis* 77 (1986) 261–77; Stepan, *Idea of Race in Science: Great Britain, 1880–1960* (Hampton, CT: Archon Books, 1982).

11. *Chicago Daily Tribune*, Sept. 20, 1874.

12. *Progressive Age,* Oct. 1, 1881, 4.

13. *Progressive Age,* March 5, 1881, 2.

14. *Plumber and Sanitary Engineer,* June 1878, 138; *Progressive Age,* Oct. 1, 1881, 4.

15. *Progressive Age,* March 5, 1881, 2.

16. Robin Einhorn's analysis of property records shows that more than a third of wage laborers owned property valued at $1,000 or less in 1870. Those buildings were most likely single-family houses, although some may have been two-family houses. In the 1890s, there was an increase in the number of skilled wage laborers who owned buildings that were subdivided and would then house three or more households. Einhorn, *Property Rules: Political Economy in Chicago, 1833–1872* (Chicago: University of Chicago Press, 1991) 249–56.

17. *Progressive Age,* Dec. 17, 1881, 4.

18. *Progressive Age,* March 5, 1881, 2; *Chicago Daily Tribune,* Jan. 30, 1881.

19. On the rise of the sanitary reform movement see, for example: John Duffy, *The Sanitarians: A History of American Public Health* (Urbana: University of Illinois Press, 1990); Maureen Ogle, *All the Modern Conveniences: American Household Plumbing, 1840–1890* (Baltimore: Johns Hopkins University Press, 1996); Richard A. Meckel, *Save the Babies: American Public Health Reform and the Prevention of Infant Mortality, 1850–1929* (Baltimore: Johns Hopkins University Press, 1990) 1–39; Margaret Garb, "Health, Morality, and Housing: The 'Tenement Problem' in Chicago," *American Journal of Public Health* (2003) 1420–30.

20. The appellate courts ruled in 1889 that a landlord cannot be held responsible for the condition of the premises. "A landlord does not insure that nothing exists touching the premises in question that will interfere with the health or comfort of his tenant nor is he bound to repair unless the lease so provides." *Neil McCoull v. S. Herzberg,* Appellate Courts of Illinois, First District Vol. 33 (1889) 542–46.

21. RDH 1886.

22. *History of Medicine and Surgery in Chicago* (Chicago: Biographical Publishing, 1922) 344; *Sanitary History of the Board of Health of the City of Chicago* (Chicago: Bulletin Printing, 1874) 11, reel 1, 62–64, NYPL.

23. Arthur R. Reynolds, "Three Chicago and Illinois Public Health Officers," *Bulletin of the Society of Medical History of Chicago,* August 1912, 89–104.

24. *Kimball v. Ill. ex. rel. H. W. Jones,* in *Reports of Cases at Law and in Chancery Argued and Determined in the Supreme Court of Illinois,* Norman L. Freeman, ed. (Chicago: E. B. Myers, 1869) 45:297–301.

25. Report of the Board of Health for the City of Chicago, 1871, 1872, 1873, and 1874, 21.

26. Russell, *History of Medicine and Surgery in Chicago* 79.

27. Report of the Board of Health, 1874 and 1875, 16.

28. "Library for Chester Center," *Republican* (Chester, MA) (1906).

29. *Republican* (Chester, MA) (1906); *Journal of American Medical Association* 54 (1910) 1229; Russell, *History of Medicine and Surgery in Chicago* 100. While in Paris, De Wolf studied with Armand Trousseau and Auguste Nelaton. Trousseau was the "brilliant pupil" of Pierre Bretonneau, who studied typhoid fever and diphtheria, arguing that both were contagious. Nelaton was a famous surgeon in Paris. *Dictionary of American Medical Biography,* Howard A. Kelly and Walter L. Burrage, eds. (Boston: Milford House, 1971) 324–25.

30. James H. Cassedy, *Medicine in America: A Short History* (Baltimore: Johns Hopkins University Press, 1991) 64–65; Harold M. Hyman, *A More Perfect Union: The Impact of*

the Civil War and Reconstruction on the Constitution (New York: Knopf, 1973) 320; Suellen Hoy, *Chasing Dirt: The American Pursuit of Cleanliness* (New York: Oxford University Press, 1995) 29–38, 59–61. On the complex class interests of those working with the Sanitary Commission, see George M. Fredrickson, *The Inner Civil War: Northern Intellectuals and the Crisis of the Union* (Urbana: University of Illinois Press, 1993) 98–112.

31. *Republican*, 1906; *Dictionary of American Medical Biography*, Howard A. Kelly and Walter L. Burrage, eds. (Boston: Milford House, 1971) 324–25; *Journal of American Medical Association* 53 (1910) 1229.

32. Isaac D. Rawlings et al., *The Rise and Fall of Disease in Illinois* (Springfield: Schepp & Barnes, 1927) 327; *Chicago Inter-Ocean*, July 23, 1889.

33. RDH 1885, 122.

34. Melosi, *The Sanitary City* 103–5; Thomas Neville Bonner, *Medicine in Chicago: 1850–1950: A Chapter in the Social and Scientific Development of a City* (New York: Stratford Press, 1957) 25–26; Erwin H. Ackerknecht, *A Short History of Medicine*, rev. ed. (Baltimore: Johns Hopkins University Press, 1982) 177–78; Donald L. Miller, *City of the Century: The Epic of Chicago and the Making of America* (New York: Simon & Schuster, 1996) 430; Cassedy, *Medicine in America* 76–86.

35. Rawlings et al., *The Rise and Fall of Disease in Illinois* 344.

36. Oscar C. DeWolf, *Asiatic Cholera: A Sketch of its History, Nature, and Preventive Management* (Chicago: American Book, 1885) 9.

37. Melosi, *The Sanitary City* 103–16; Cassedy, *Medicine in America* 78; RDH 1879–80.

38. Chicago City Council Proceedings, 1881 and 1882, quoted in Bessie Louise Pierce, *A History of Chicago*, vol. 3, *The Rise of a Modern City, 1871–1893* (New York: Alfred A. Knopf, 1957) 54; *Chicago Daily Tribune*, Oct. 22, 1879, 8.

39. RDH 1881–82, 4.

40. In 1884, the New York court of appeals had ruled that a law banning cigar making in a tenement dwelling violated the cigar makers' rights to labor. The court's decision, based on the freedom to contract for work, similarly placed the tenement in a legal category that linked it to production and separated it from the single-family home. See *In re Application of Paul*, 94 N.Y. 496 (1884).

41. Several builders took their claims to court, asserting that the department had overstepped its legal authority, but the courts repeatedly ruled in favor of the department. RDH 1887, 6; Robert W. DeForest, "Tenement House Regulation," in *The Tenement House Problem, Including the Report of the New York State Tenement House Commission of 1900*, vol. 1, edited by Robert W. DeForest and Lawrence Veiller (New York: Macmillan, 1903) 84.

42. RDH 1883–84, 18; RDH 1885, 80.

43. RDH 1887.

44. RDH 1877, 12; *Chicago Daily Tribune*, Oct. 22, 1879, 8; Isaac D. Rawlings et al., *The Rise and Fall of Disease in Illinois* (Springfield: State Department of Public Health, 1927) 2:330.

45. RDH 1877, 22.

46. RDH 1874–75, 91. Pierce, *A History of Chicago* 3:54, asserts, "Not until 1880 did a municipal ordinance give the Department of Health the right to inspect and regulate sanitary conditions even in places of employment." But according to the board's yearly reports, sanitary inspectors were inspecting tenement housing as early as 1875.

47. *People ex rel Barmore v. Robertson*, 302 Ill. 422; 134 N.E. 815 (1922). In this case, the court ruled that the city's commissioner of health lacked the authority to quarantine

Barmore because the state legislature had not given quarantine powers to the city's board of health. The court, however, ruled that Illinois state health officials, who had affirmed the quarantine, had the legal authority to do so.

48. *Chicago Daily Tribune*, Jan. 30, 1881. The *Tribune* reported on a meeting of the Chicago Labor Union, which claimed to represent "all trades."

49. Richard Schneirov, *Labor and Urban Politics: Class Conflict and the Origins of Modern Liberalism in Chicago, 1864–97* (Urbana: University of Illinois Press, 1998) 88–89; Miller, *City of the Century* 441–49; RDH 1883–84, 36.

50. RDH 1882, 6.

51. RDH 1885, 72.

52. RDH 1882, 47–48.

53. RDH 1882, 47.

54. Schneirov, *Labor and Urban Politics* 441–9; RDH 1886; *Chicago Daily Tribune*, Jan. 30, 1881.

55. *Report of the Committee on Tenement Houses of the Citizens Association of Chicago* (Chicago: Geo. K. Hazlitt, 1884) 7; RDH 1883–84, 21–22; Margaret Crawford, *Building the Workingman's Paradise: The Design of American Company Towns* (New York: Verso, 1995) 37–43. Elizabeth Blackmar offers a full account of the market relations of housing, arguing that the reformers' emphasis on health obscured the underlying causes of the housing problem in antebellum New York. Obviously, a similar phenomenon occurred in 1880s Chicago. Blackmar, *Manhattan for Rent* 260–62.

56. *Chicago Daily Tribune*, Oct. 22, 1879, 12. For background on Angell, see Geo. T. Angell, *Autobiographical Sketches and Personal Recollections* (Boston: American Humane Education Society) 37–39, 65. There was similar public debate over regulating milk in the late nineteenth century. See Meckel, *Save the Babies* 43–63.

57. *Chicago Daily Tribune*, Oct. 22, 1879, 12.

58. *Tugman v. Chicago*, 78 Ill. 405 (1876). Grounded in two distinct legal issues, the court's ruling dismantled the board's authority to regulate business in the city. In balancing the public welfare against the rights of private individuals to engage in business enterprises, the court asserted that municipal officials had illegally "discriminated" in favor of existing businesses by preventing new, and likely competing, slaughterhouses from locating in the city. The court implicitly allowed business interests to prevail, ruling that the Department of Health, as an appointed body, lacked the authority to issue legislation. In delegating lawmaking powers to the board, the state legislature had rendered the people of Chicago subject to government by a body "they had no voice in electing. This," the jurists concluded, "would be repugnant to the theory of our government." The Illinois court's decision was in line with a host of state court decisions issued in the late nineteenth century. These decisions gradually shifted the balance of legal authority toward protecting corporate interests, rejecting government regulations designed to protect public health.

59. Blackmar, "Accountability for Public Health" 45.

60. For the nearly eight years of legal battles over slaughterhouse regulations see Rawlings et al., *The Rise and Fall of Disease in Chicago* 336; RDH 1878.

61. *Chicago Daily Tribune*, Oct. 22, 1879, 4.

62. *Chicago Daily Tribune*, Oct. 27, 1879, 4.

63. *Chicago Daily Tribune* Oct. 27, 1879, 4.

64. *Chicago Daily Tribune*, April 19 and May 23, 1889; Pierce, *A History of Chicago* 3:364–66. Cregier was elected with the support of organized labor, some socialists, and urban reformers. Gruenhut, the tenement inspector, had written much of the Demo-

cratic Party's platform and kept his job with the Health Department after the election. It is not entirely clear why Cregier forced De Wolf out, but the *Chicago Daily Tribune*, admittedly anti-Cregier, suggested that the new mayor distributed jobs to his labor supporters. Schneirov, *Labor and Urban Politics* 280–83.

CHAPTER FOUR

1. Robert Hunter, *Tenement Conditions in Chicago: Report by the Investigating Committee of the City Homes Association* (Chicago: City Homes Association, 1901) 12.
2. Hunter, *Tenement Conditions in Chicago* 104. For statistics on the cost of construction of the drainage, sewage, and water systems see Louis P. Cain, *Sanitation Strategy for a Lakefront Metropolis: The Case of Chicago* (DeKalb: Northern Illinois University Press, 1978). Yearly reports for the Board of Public Works and later the Sanitary District of Chicago provide year-by-year cost and construction figures.
3. Joel A. Tarr, "Sewerage and the Development of the Networked City in the United States, 1850–1930," in *Technology and the Rise of the Networked City in Europe and America*, Joel A. Tarr and Gabriel Dupuy, eds. (Philadelphia: Temple University Press, 1988).
4. For some excellent studies of the introduction of sewer and water systems and the rise of the public health movement, see: Nelson Manfred Blake, *Water for the Cities: A History of the Urban Water Supply Problem in the United States* (Syracuse: Syracuse University Press, 1956); John Duffy, *The Sanitarians: A History of American Public Health* (Urbana: University of Illinois Press, 1990); Charles Rosenberg, *The Cholera Years* (Chicago: University of Chicago Press, 1962); Martin V. Melosi, *The Sanitary City: Urban Infrastructure in America from Colonial Times to the Present* (Baltimore: Johns Hopkins University Press, 2000). On the impact of indoor plumbing on labor within the home, see: Maureen Ogle, *All the Modern Conveniences: American Household Plumbing, 1840–1890* (Baltimore: Johns Hopkins University Press, 1996) 94; Susan Strasser, *Never Done: A History of American Housework* (New York: Pantheon Books, 1982) 92–94; Sam Bass Warner, Jr., *The Private City: Philadelphia in Three Periods of Its Growth* (Philadelphia: University of Pennsylvania Press, 1968) 107–8.
5. Melosi, *The Sanitary City* 95; Warner, *The Private City* 107–8.
6. Cain, *Sanitation Strategy for a Lakefront Metropolis*, xi. Chicago was built on a swamp and faced drainage and water problems long before city officials set out to build a sewerage system. Unlike coastal cities, which early in their growth had to seek fresh water from nearby rivers and streams, Chicago bordered a large body of fresh water. Lake Michigan provided early settlers with drinking water and a convenient place for dumping waste. As the city grew, Chicagoans risked polluting their water supply. Cain notes that the question facing the city's decision makers throughout the nineteenth century was how to allocate a natural resource, lake and river water, between two production processes, water supply and waste removal.
7. Cain, *Sanitation Strategy for a Lakefront Metropolis* 37–40; Strasser, *Never Done* 86–96; Robin Einhorn, *Property Rules: Political Economy in Chicago, 1833–1872* (Chicago: University of Chicago Press, 1991) 134.
8. Bessie Louise Pierce, *The History of Chicago*, vol. 3, *The Rise of a Modern City, 1871–1893* (New York: Alfred A. Knopf, 1957) 320. For more on mid-nineteenth-century urban sanitation and epidemics see Alan M. Kraut, "Plagues and Prejudice: Nativism's Construction of Disease in Nineteenth and Twentieth-Century New York," in *Hives of Sickness: Public Health and Epidemics in New York City*, David Rosner, ed. (New Brunswick: Rutgers University Press, 1995) 67; Duffy, *The Sanitarians*; Elizabeth Blackmar, "Ac-

countability for Public Health: Regulating the Housing Market in Nineteenth-Century New York City," in *Hives of Sickness* 49–55; Sylvia Noble Tesh, *Hidden Arguments: Political Ideology and Disease Prevention Policy* (New Brunswick: Rutgers University Press, 1988) 25–32; Tarr, "Sewerage and the Development of the Networked City in the United States, 1850–1930."

9. Einhorn, *Property Rules* 14; Cain, *Sanitation Strategy for a Lakefront Metropolis* 5–10.

10. Chicago Board of Water Commissioners, *Ninth Semi-Annual Report* (Chicago: City of Chicago, 1856) 10–15, CHS.

11. *Industrial Chicago*, vol. 2, *The Building Interests* (Chicago: Godspeed, 1891) 305–15.

12. Einhorn, *Property Rules* 135; Homer Hoyt, *One Hundred Years of Land Values in Chicago: The Relationship of the Growth of Chicago to the Rise of Its Land Values, 1830–1933* (Chicago: University of Chicago Press, 1933) 483.

13. Quoted in Ann Durkin Keating, *Building Chicago: Suburban Developers and the Creation of a Divided Metropolis* (Columbus: Ohio State University Press, 1988) 40; Chicago Public Works, *Third Annual Report* (Chicago: City of Chicago, 1864) 5.

14. Board of Water Commissioners, *Ninth Semi-annual Report for the Year 1864*, 7. A similar disparity in the laying of water and sewer lines occurred in St. Louis. See Katherine T. Corbett, "The Politics of Sewers in Nineteenth-Century St. Louis," in *Common Fields: An Environmental History of St. Louis*, Andrew Hurley, ed. (St. Louis: Missouri Historical Society Press, 1997) 107–25.

15. Keating, *Building Chicago* 75–78.

16. Board of Public Works, *Thirteenth Annual Report for the years 1873/74* (Chicago: City of Chicago, 1874) 4, Harold Washington Municipal Library.

17. Cain, *Sanitation Strategy for a Lakefront Metropolis* 23–32; *Twenty-Third Annual Report of the Department of Public Works to the City Council of the City of Chicago for the Fiscal Year Ending Dec. 31, 1898* (Chicago: P. F. Pettibone & Co., 1899) 215; Louis P. Cain, "Raising and Watering a City: Ellis Sylvester Chesbrough and Chicago's First Sanitation System," *Technology and Culture* 13 (1972) 354–56; Melosi, *The Sanitary City* 96–97.

18. Eugene P. Moehring, *Public Works and Patterns of Urban Real Estate Growth in Manhattan, 1835–1894* (New York: Arno, 1981) 87–95; Tarr, "Sewerage and the Development of the Networked City in the United States, 1850–1930" 164.

19. E. S. Chesbrough, *Chicago Sewerage: Report of the Results of Examinations Made in Relation to Sewerage in Several European Cities, in the Winter of 1856–7* (Chicago: Board of Sewerage Commissioners, 1858) 87–91; *Report and Plan of Sewerage for the City of Chicago, Illinois adopted by the Board of Sewerage Commissioners December 31, 1855* (Chicago: Charles Scott, 1855) 15–16; Einhorn, *Property Rules* 139; Frank J. Piehl, "Chicago's Early Fight to 'Save Our Lake,'" *Chicago History* 5 (1976–77) 225. Wooden housing could be raised fairly inexpensively. Raising brick buildings proved a technological problem, ultimately solved by a young migrant from upstate New York, George Pullman, who developed a method for raising stores and banks without disrupting business. He made a fortune with the process.

20. *Chicago Daily Tribune*, June 22, 1884, 11; *Report of the Committee of the Citizens' Association on the Main Drainage and Water Supply of Chicago* (Chicago, 1885) 10–11; J. H. Rauch, "The Sanitary Problems of Chicago, Past and Present," *Public Health: Reports and Papers* 4 (1880) 11; Melosi, *The Sanitary City* 97. Extension of the intake pipe for water was expected to solve some of the problems of sewage mixing with lake water, but did little to correct the sewage disposal problem.

21. RDH 1877; Richard Schneirov, *Labor and Urban Politics: Class Conflict and the Origins of Modern Liberalism in Chicago, 1864–97* (Urbana: University of Illinois Press, 1998) 48.

22. Einhorn, *Property Rules* 141; Hoyt, *One Hundred Years of Land Values in Chicago* 92. Studies of public works in Detroit in the 1890s, where special assessments financed both sewers and street paving, show that working-class home owners did reject both types of improvements to save money to pay their home loans. See: Olivier Zunz, *The Changing Face of Inequality: Urbanization, Industrial Development, and Immigrants in Detroit, 1880–1920* (Chicago: University of Chicago Press, 1982) 174.

23. *Report of the Department of Public Works for the years 1873/74*; Einhorn, *Property Rules* 141; RDH 1881, 5. See also Department of Public Works reports for the 1880s.

24. *Chicago Daily Tribune*, March 1, 1882.

25. *Report of the Committee of the Citizens' Association on the Main Drainage and Water Supply of Chicago.* For complaints about the quality of the city's water and demands for new pumping works see, for example, *Chicago Daily Tribune*, Sept. 8, 1879, Nov. 15, 1880, March 10, 1881, March 1, 1882, March 25, 1883, and July 6, 1888.

26. Chicago Common Council Proceedings, 1894–95, 809; *Hull-House Maps and Papers* 5; Pierce, *A History of Chicago* 3:55.

27. Walter L. Newberry estate, financial records, NL.

28. Hunter, *Tenement Conditions in Chicago* 8.

29. Keating suggests that this shift in the conception of plumbing facilities occurred in the 1850s and 1860s, but there is little evidence to trace the specific timing of the change. Still, it's clear that by the 1880s, builders were advertising houses with indoor plumbing and treating plumbing as an amenity. Keating, *Building Chicago* 40.

30. Hoyt, *One Hundred Years of Land Values in Chicago* 92, 112.

31. Hoyt, *One Hundred Years of Land Values in Chicago* 92, 112. The location of public baths, promoted by housing reformers in the 1890s through the early twentieth century and typically surrounded by the poorest neighborhoods, reveals the increasing distinctions between neighborhoods of housing with indoor plumbing and those without. E. R. Pritchard, "Chicago's Free Public Baths," RDH 1905, 217–21; Maureen A. Flanagan, *Seeing with Their Hearts: Chicago Women and the Vision of the Good City, 1871–1933* (Princeton: Princeton University Press, 2002) 42–43.

32. *Chicago Daily Tribune*, June 22, 1884, 14.

33. Keating, *Building Chicago* 58; Hoyt, *One Hundred Years of Land Values in Chicago* 91, 94. On the development of the North Shore see: Michael H. Ebner, *Creating Chicago's North Shore: A Suburban History* (Chicago: University of Chicago Press, 1988).

34. *Chicago Daily Tribune*, April 20, 1873, May 18, 1873, March 25, 1883; *Real Estate and Building Journal*, May 31, 1873, 10.

35. *Chicago Daily Tribune*, April 20, 1873. I am grateful to Elizabeth Blackmar for clarifying this point.

36. Keating, *Building Chicago* 61–62; *Chicago Daily Tribune*, Feb. 17, 1877, and March 25, 1883; Perry R. Duis, *Challenging Chicago: Coping with Everyday Life, 1837–1920* (Urbana: University of Illinois Press, 1998) 74. For a description of the patronage system and corruption in the Common Council see Lincoln Steffens, *The Shame of the Cities* (New York: Hill and Wang, 1993) 162–95.

37. Robey Street was renamed Damen in 1927. See also James R. Barrett, *Work and Community in the Jungle: Chicago's Packinghouse Workers, 1894–1922* (Urbana: University of Illinois Press, 1987) 79. Ileen A. DeVault notes a similar disparity of home ownership rates among skilled working-class households, both immigrant and African-Americans, and the less skilled, less educated working classes in Pittsburgh. DeVault, *Sons and Daughters of Labor: Class and Clerical Work in Turn-of-the-Century Pittsburgh* (Ithaca: Cornell University Press, 1990) 90.

38. Pierce notes that as the West Side became increasingly crowded after the fire and the city provided few sanitary services, "the better-to-do inhabitants moved away at the first opportunity, leaving to newly arrived immigrants a legacy of dilapidation and filth." Pierce, *A History of Chicago* 3:56.

39. Mary McDowell, "City Waste," in *Mary McDowell and Municipal Housekeeping: A Symposium*, Caroline Miles Hill, ed. (Chicago: Millar, 1938) 2.

40. Keating, *Building Chicago* 61; Hoyt, *One Hundred Years of Land Values in Chicago* 91; Hilda Satt Polacheck, *I Came a Stranger: The Story of a Hull-House Girl* (Urbana: University of Illinois Press, 1989) 71.

41. Fannie Barrier Williams, "Social Bonds in the 'Black Belt' of Chicago," *Charities* 15 (Oct. 7, 1905) 40–44, quoted in William M. Tuttle, Jr., *Race Riot: Chicago in the Red Summer of 1919* (New York: Atheneum, 1970) 161–62. Even *Fortune* magazine editors recognized this problem in their 1932 study of housing conditions on Chicago's Black Belt, an analysis of rental dwellings built in the early teens. *Housing America* (New York: Harcourt, Brace, 1932) 151–53.

42. Hoyt, *One Hundred Years of Land Values in Chicago* 216; Allan H. Spear, *Black Chicago: The Making of a Negro Ghetto, 1890–1920* (Chicago: University of Chicago Press, 1967) 12; James R. Grossman, *Land of Hope: Chicago, Black Southerners, and the Great Migration* (Chicago: University of Chicago Press, 1989) 137–39; Alzada P. Comstock, "Chicago Housing Conditions, VI: The Problems of the Negro," *American Journal of Sociology* 18 (1912) 241–57; Sophonsiba P. Breckenridge, "The Color Line in the Housing Problem," *Survey* 29 (1913) 575–76; Tuttle, *Race Riot* 160–63. Many residents complained to Comstock that landlords refused to make necessary repairs or provide adequate plumbing facilities, as required by the 1902 law.

43. Ebner, *Creating Chicago's North Shore* 51–53; Sam Bass Warner, Jr., *Streetcar Suburbs: The Process of Growth in Boston, 1870–1900* (Cambridge: Harvard University Press, 1962); Kenneth T. Jackson, *Crabgrass Frontier: The Suburbanization of the United States* (New York: Oxford University Press, 1985) 87–94, 118–120.

44. John Rauch, *A Report . . . on the Necessity of an Extension of the Sewerage of the City* (Chicago: Ottaway, Brown & Colbert, printers, 1873); Rauch, "The Sanitary Problems of Chicago, Past and Present" 11–13.

45. Ebner, *Creating Chicago's North Shore* 65; Keating, *Building Chicago* 74–76; S. E. Gross (firm), *Illustrated Catalogue of S. E. Gross' Lots, Houses, Cottages* (Chicago: S. E. Gross, 1889), GP. For one day's example of builders' advertisements selling indoor plumbing and health, see *Chicago Daily Tribune*, July 8, 1888, 20. Similar advertisements appeared regularly in the paper in the late 1880s. Colleen Browne Kilner, *Joseph Sears and His Kenilworth: The Dreamer and the Dream* (Kenilworth: Kenilworth Historical Society, 1969) 119–20.

46. Rauch, *A Report on the Necessity of an Extension of the Sewerage* 18–19; RDH 1885, 18. Edith Abbott commented that lack of sewers more than any other cause resulted in poor health. Abbott, *The Tenements of Chicago, 1908–1935* (Chicago: University of Chicago Press, 1936) 36. Tuttle notes that as late as 1925, infant mortality rates of black Chicagoans were twice those of whites, a result, most likely, of a lack of sewers and indoor plumbing in the city's black neighborhoods. Tuttle, *Race Riot* 145.

47. Hoyt, *One Hundred Years of Land Values in Chicago* 96–98.

48. Howard Eugene Wilson, "Mary E. McDowell and Her Work as Head Resident of the University of Chicago Settlement House, 1894–1904," unpublished dissertation, University of Chicago, 1927, 39–42; Herbert E. Phillips, "Mary McDowell as We Knew Her in the Yards," in *Mary McDowell and Municipal Housekeeping: A Symposium*, Caro-

line Miles Hill, ed. (Chicago: Millar, 1938) 120; McDowell, "City Waste" 2; James R. Barrett, *Work and Community in the Jungle: Chicago's Packinghouse Workers, 1894–1922* (Urbana: University of Illinois Press, 1987) 68.

49. Jane Addams, *Twenty Years at Hull-House* (New York: Penguin, 1961) 281–85; Wilson, "Mary E. McDowell and Her Work" 36–37; McDowell, "City Waste" 1–6.

50. RDH 1894; RDH 1907, 35–37; Addams, *Twenty Years* 211.

51. RDH 183–85; Wilson, "Mary E. McDowell and Her Work" 94–95.

52. RDH 1894, 183–89.

53. B. W. Richardson, president of the British Medical Association, quoted in Harriette Plunkett, *Women, Plumbers, and Doctors, or, Household Sanitation* (New York: D. Appleton, 1885) 10; Ogle, *All the Modern Conveniences* 99–103.

54. Keating, *Building Chicago* 52–53; Ruth Schwartz Cowan, *More Work for Mother: The Ironies of Household Technology from the Open Hearth to the Microwave* (New York: Basic Books, 1983); Strasser, *Never Done*; Jeanne Boydston, *Home and Work: Housework, Wages, and the Ideology of Labor in the Early Republic* (New York: Oxford University Press, 1990).

55. Pierce, *History of Chicago* 3:309.

56. Cowan, *More Work for Mother* 65–66; Strasser, *Never Done* 112.

57. Lucy Maynard Salmon, *Domestic Service* (New York: Macmillan, 1897) 13–15, 200–203. For more on domestic servants see Faye E. Dudden, *Serving Women: Household Service in Nineteenth Century America* (Middletown, CT: Wesleyan University Press, 1983); David Katzman, *Seven Days a Week: Women and Domestic Service in Industrializing America* (New York: Oxford University Press, 1978).

58. Sears, Roebuck & Co., 1897 catalogue, 134, 682–83.

59. Salmon, *Domestic Service* 199; Strasser, *Never Done* 116–17.

60. Polacheck, *I Came a Stranger* 73. See also Alice Kessler-Harris, *Out to Work: A History of Wage-Earning Women in the United States* (New York: Oxford University Press, 1982) 119–21. Strasser argues that indoor plumbing accentuated the class differences that were developing throughout the nineteenth century. Strasser, *Never Done* 86.

61. George E. Waring, *The Sanitary Drainage of Houses and Towns* (New York: Hurd and Houghton, 1876) 427; Ogle, *All the Modern Conveniences* 102–4, 143.

62. Plunkett, *Women, Plumbers, and Doctors* 204.

63. Catharine Beecher and Harriet Beecher Stowe, *The American Woman's Home: or, Principles of Domestic Science, Being a Guide to the Formation and Maintenance of Economical, Healthful, Beautiful and Christian Homes* (New York: J. B. Ford, 1869) 38; Plunkett, *Women, Plumbers, and Doctors* 109–10.

64. Ogle, *All the Modern Conveniences* 140–41. Ogle notes that until about 1890, domestic advice givers debated the "relative merits of porcelain or metal fixtures, of wooden cabinetwork or porcelain stands," with most settling on the more expensive but considerably less sturdy porcelain. In the 1880s, American potters still relied almost entirely on handwork rather than mechanized production, and import duties added to the price of porcelain fixtures. Sven Beckert, writing about New York City, notes that indoor plumbing became just one design feature of the new, standardized bourgeois home, a feature that linked the homes of the lower middle classes to those of the elite. Beckert, *The Monied Metropolis: New York City and the Consolidation of the American Bourgeoisie, 1850–1896* (New York: Cambridge University Press, 2001) 260–61.

65. Plunkett, *Women, Plumbers and Doctors* 97; Ogle, *All the Modern Conveniences* 123–24; Strasser, *Never Done* 94.

66. Ellen H. Richards, *Sanitation in Daily Life* (Boston: Whitcomb & Barrows, 1907) 3 and

234 / Notes to pp. 115–119

passim. On the founding of the Home Economics Association, see Kessler-Harris, *Out to Work* 117–18.

67. T. J. Jackson Lears argues that comfort, particularly within the family home, had become another mark of "respectability," of middle-class status. Comfort was a sign of progress, so widely celebrated by late nineteenth-century Americans. Indoor plumbing, along with a host of new consumer goods for the home, made "comfort" possible. See Lears, *No Place of Grace: Antimodernism and the Transformation of American Culture, 1880–1920* (New York: Pantheon, 1981) 11; Daniel Boorstin, *The Americans: The Democratic Experience* (New York: Random House, 1973) 332–36, 346–58; Daniel Horowitz, "Frugality or Comfort: Middle-Class Styles of Life in the Early Twentieth Century," *American Quarterly* 37 (1985) 239–59; Horowitz, *The Morality of Spending: Attitudes toward the Consumer Society, 1875–1940* (Baltimore: Johns Hopkins University Press, 1985) 100–102.

CHAPTER FIVE

1. Kenneth T. Jackson, *Crabgrass Frontier: The Suburbanization of the United States* (New York: Oxford University Press, 1985) 79–81, 85. By the 1880s, the *Tribune* was attributing Riverside's failure to its having gained a "malaria-and-the-ague reputation—which it did not deserve." *Chicago Daily Tribune*, Nov. 22, 1885.

2. On the incorporation of home construction businesses see: Helen Corbin Monchow, *Seventy Years of Real Estate Subdividing in the Region of Chicago* (Evanston: Northwestern University Press, 1939) 119–32. Suburban development in and around Chicago is somewhat complicated by the fact that the city annexed many early suburbs in 1889. In addition, many early students of the city's suburbs tended to ignore city or suburban town boundaries and to equate suburban housing with dwellings of native-born white middle-class people. See Helen R. Jeter, *Trends of Population in the Region of Chicago* (Chicago: University of Chicago Press, 1927); Charles E. Merriam, "The Metropolitan Region of Chicago," in *Chicago: An Experiment in Social Science Research*, T. V. Smith and Leonard D. White, eds. (Chicago: University of Chicago Press, 1929) 78–89.

3. The working-class ethos of home ownership did not disappear, but rather growing numbers of middle-class buyers were drawn into the house-buying market, and home ownership acquired a distinct meaning for those buyers. On the persistence of working-class home ownership see: Becky Nicolaides, *My Blue Heaven: Life and Politics in the Working-Class Suburbs of Los Angeles, 1920–1965* (Chicago: University of Chicago Press, 2002); Richard Harris, *Unplanned Suburbs: Toronto's American Tragedy, 1900–1950* (Baltimore: Johns Hopkins University Press, 1996); Harris, "Chicago's Other Suburbs," *Geographical Review* 84 (1994) 394–410; Kevin David Kane and Thomas L. Bell, "Suburbs for a Labor Elite," *Geographical Review* 75 (1985) 319–34.

4. Perry Duis, *Challenging Chicago: Coping with Everyday Life, 1837–1920* (Urbana: University of Illinois Press, 1998) 32–37; Bessie Louise Pierce, *A History of Chicago*, vol. 3, *The Rise of a Modern City, 1871–1893* (New York: Alfred A. Knopf, 1957) 51; *Chicago Daily Tribune*, July 6, 1888, 4. For examples of lease agreements see Walter L. Newberry Papers, financial records, NL. On the importance of urban transportation systems and infrastructure in suburban growth see: Sam Bass Warner, Jr., *Streetcar Suburbs: The Process of Growth in Boston, 1870–1900* (Cambridge: Harvard University Press, 1962); Jon Teaford, *City and Suburb: The Political Fragmentation of Metropolitan America, 1850–1970* (Baltimore: Johns Hopkins University Press, 1979).

5. Colleen Browne Kilner, *Joseph Sears and His Kenilworth: The Dreamer and the Dream* (Kenilworth: Kenilworth Historical Society, 1969) 119–20.

6. *Chicago Daily Tribune*, April 4, 1883, and Jan. 6, 1884. See also Daniel Bluestone, "Chicago's Mecca Flat Blues," *Journal of the Society of Architectural Historians* (1999) 382–83; C. William Westfall, "From Homes to Towers: A Century of Chicago's Best Hotels and Tall Apartment Buildings," in *Chicago Architecture, 1872–1922*, John Zukowsky, ed. (Chicago: Art Institute of Chicago, 1993) 266–89; Duis, *Challenging Chicago* 83–85.

7. Mary Brewster Laflin to Josephine and Louis Laflin (undated) 1886. box 1, folder 4, March 21, 1887, May 17, 1886, George H. Laflin Collection, CHS.

8. Morton J. Horwitz, *The Transformation of American Law, 1870–1960* (New York: Oxford University Press, 1992) 145–167; Martin J. Sklar, *The Corporate Reconstruction of American Capitalism, 1890–1916* (New York: Cambridge University Press, 1988) 47–53. Sklar dates the beginning of the shift in the forms of property to the landmark Supreme Court decision in *Santa Clara v. Southern Pacific Railroad* (1886), but capitalists were responding to shifting investment opportunities even before the courts and legislators confronted the issue. See also Thorstein Veblen, *The Theory of Business Enterprise* (New York: C. Scribner's Sons, 1904); John R. Commons, *Legal Foundations of Capitalism* (New York: Macmillan, 1924); Horwitz, "Santa Clara Revisited: The Development of Corporate Theory," *West Virginia Law Review* 88 (1985) 209–10. On postemancipation debates over the boundaries of the market and the new commodification of the family home, see Amy Dru Stanley, *From Bondage to Contract: Wage Labor, Marriage, and the Market in the Age of Slave Emancipation* (New York: Cambridge University Press, 1998) 138–74.

9. *Real Estate and Building Journal*, Sept. 4, 1880, 128.

10. Monchow, *Seventy Years of Real Estate Subdividing* 59–66. On the impact of the return to the gold standard, see Nell Irvin Painter, *Standing at Armageddon: The United States, 1877–1919* (New York: W. W. Norton, 1987) 85–89.

11. Homer Hoyt, *One Hundred Years of Land Values in Chicago: The Relationship of the Growth of Chicago to the Rise of Its Land Values, 1830–1933* (Chicago: University of Chicago Press, 1933) 100; Kenneth T. Jackson, *Crabgrass Frontier* 79–81; Jerome D. Fellman, "Pre-building Growth Patterns of Chicago," *Annals of the Association of American Geographers* 47 (1957) 74.

12. *Real Estate and Building Journal*, July 3, 1880, 68.

13. Hoyt, *One Hundred Years of Land Values in Chicago* 66; Fellman, "Pre-building Growth Patterns in Chicago" 74. In 1860, 70 percent of the population lived within two miles of the downtown area. The population within a four-mile radius of State and Madison was 112,000; within a two-mile radius, 79,000. For studies that place significant emphasis on the impact of commuter rail lines on suburban development see: Sam Bass Warner, Jr., *Streetcar Suburbs: The Process of Growth in Boston, 1870–1900* (Cambridge: Harvard University Press, 1962); Jon Teaford, *City and Suburb: The Political Fragmentation of Metropolitan America, 1850–1970* (Baltimore: Johns Hopkins University Press, 1979).

14. Fellman, "Pre-building Growth Patterns in Chicago" 62–67.

15. Ann Durkin Keating, *Building Chicago: Suburban Developers and the Creation of a Divided Metropolis* (Columbus: Ohio State University Press, 1988) 16–20; Donald L. Miller, *City of the Century: The Epic of Chicago and the Making of America* (New York: Simon & Schuster, 1996) 282–85.

16. *Real Estate and Building Journal,* July 3, 1880, 68; *Chicago Times,* Oct. 1880 quoted in Monchow, *Seventy Years of Real Estate Subdividing* 2; *Real Estate and Building Journal,* Aug. 7, 1880.
17. *Real Estate and Building Journal,* Sept. 4, 1880, 129, Oct. 2, 1880, 169.
18. Monchow, *Seventy Years of Real Estate Subdividing* 56–59.
19. Until after the turn of the century, those who purchased stock certificates were known as proprietors, referring to their partial ownership of the corporation. Not until the early twentieth century were stockholders referred to as "investors," a term that distanced them from the company and reflected their passive ownership status. See: James Treat Carter, *The Nature of the Corporation as a Legal Entity* (Baltimore: M. Curlander, 1919) 160; Horwitz, "Santa Clara Revisited" 207.
20. Robert Herrick, *The Memoirs of an American Citizen* (New York: Macmillan, 1905) 346. John R. Commons wrote of a series of federal and state court decisions in the late 1880s and 1890s, "The definition of property is changed from physical things to the exchange-value of anything . . . One is physical objects, the other is marketable assets." Quoted in Sklar, *The Corporate Reconstruction of American Capitalism* 50.
21. For more on republican ideology and proprietorship in urban crafts see Elizabeth Blackmar, *Manhattan for Rent, 1785–1850* (Ithaca: Cornell University Press, 1989); Sean Wilentz, *Chants Democratic: New York City and the Rise of the American Working Class, 1788–1850* (New York: Oxford University Press, 1984); Eric Foner, *Free Soil, Free Labor, Free Men: The Ideology of the Republican Party before the Civil War* (New York: Oxford University Press, 1970).
22. For more on the cult of domesticity and the emergence of an ideology of separate spheres see Jeanne Boydston, *Home and Work: Housework, Wages, and the Ideology of Labor in the Early Republic* (New York: Oxford University Press, 1990); Linda K. Kerber, *Women of the Republic: Intellect and Ideology in Revolutionary America* (Chapel Hill: University of North Carolina Press, 1980); Kathryn Kish Sklar, *Catharine Beecher: A Study in American Domesticity* (New Haven: Yale University Press, 1973); Alice Kessler-Harris, *Out to Work: A History of Wage-Earning Women in the United States* (New York: Oxford University Press, 1982). For an analysis of wage labor relations within the home see Blackmar, *Manhattan for Rent* 110–13.
23. David Schuyler, *Apostle of Taste: Andrew Jackson Downing, 1815–1852* (Baltimore: Johns Hopkins University Press, 1996); Margaret Marsh, *Suburban Lives* (New Brunswick: Rutgers University Press, 1990) 6–8; Joan Burbick, *Healing the Republic: The Language of Health and the Culture of Nationalism in Nineteenth-Century America* (New York: Cambridge University Press, 1994).
24. *Real Estate and Building Journal,* Aug. 7, 1880, 92.
25. *Real Estate and Building Journal,* Oct. 16, 1880, 192.
26. The first University of Chicago was founded by Senator Stephen Douglas in 1857; it folded in 1886. Robin F. Bachin, "Old University of Chicago," in *The Encyclopedia of Chicago,* James R. Grossman, Ann Durkin Keating, and Janice L. Reiff, eds. (Chicago: University of Chicago Press, 2004) 845.
27. Letter from S. E. Gross to Mrs. Elizabeth Gross, dated June 2, 1881, GP, folder 78B; Emily Clark and Patrick Ashley, "The Merchant Prince of Cornville," *Chicago History* (Dec. 1992) 4–26; Emily Clark, "Own Your Own Home: S. E. Gross, the Great Domestic Promoter," in *The American Home: Material Culture, Domestic Space, and Family Life,* Eleanor McD. Thompson, ed. (Winterthur, DE: Henry Francis Du Pont Winterthur Museum, 1996); Gwendolyn Wright, *Moralism and the Model Home: Domestic*

Architecture and Cultural Conflict in Chicago, 1873-1913 (Chicago: University of Chicago Press, 1980) 41-44.

28. Alfred Theodore Andreas, *History of Chicago* (New York: Arno, 1975) 3: 78-83, 172-74; Richard Schneirov and Thomas J. Suhrbur, *Union Brotherhood, Union Town: The History of the Carpenters' Union of Chicago, 1863-1987* (Carbondale: Southern Illinois University Press, 1988) 2-9.

29. In his tenth annual catalogue, Gross wrote, "The [construction] material is purchased in large quantities . . . thus better enabling me to build and sell a house for less money." S. E. Gross, *Tenth Annual Catalogue* (Chicago, 1891) 4, GP; *Chicago Daily Tribune,* April 4, 1908, 9. Richard Harris tracks a similar emergence of businessmen-builders, or "merchant-builders," in Toronto. Harris, *Unplanned Suburbs: Toronto's American Tragedy, 1900-1950* (Baltimore: Johns Hopkins Press, 1996) 186-87.

30. S. E. Gross (firm), *The Gross Cottage and Subdivisions* (Chicago: S. E. Gross, 1884), GP; S. E. Gross (firm), *Illustrated catalogue of S. E. Gross' Lots, Houses, Cottages* (Chicago: S. E. Gross, 1889), GP.

31. Andreas, *History of Chicago from the Earliest Period to the Present Time* 3:83. *Real Estate and Building Journal,* Jan. 29, 1881, 45, commented, "Two or three gentlemen are building homes on lots in the suburbs on easy payments, for both land and house, and they have every reason to be encouraged to keep doing. A man can, in this way, become owner of a house and lot of his own, by paying installments but little heavier than monthly rent. It is a rare chance when a home can be obtained in this way." See also *Real Estate and Building Journal,* May 1, 1886, 261; *Chicago Daily Tribune,* July 1, 1888, 20.

32. S. E. Gross (firm), *Illustrated Catalogue of S. E. Gross' Lots, Houses, Cottages,* GP; *Progressive Age,* April 23, 1881; *Chicago Daily Tribune,* July 3, 1882; *Real Estate and Building Journal,* May 1, 1886, 261; *The Carpenter,* March 1885; Richard Schneirov, *Labor and Urban Politics: Class Conflict and the Origins of Modern Liberalism in Chicago, 1864-97* (Urbana: University of Illinois Press, 1998) 146.

33. *Industrial Chicago,* vol. 2, *The Building Interests* (Chicago: Goodspeed, 1891) 357-62; Thomas J. Suhrbur, "The Economic Transformation of Carpentry in Late-Nineteenth-Century Chicago," *Illinois Historical Journal* 81 (1988) 113-15; Michael J. Doucet and John C. Weaver, "Material Culture and the North American House: The Era of the Common Man, 1870-1920," *Journal of American History* 72 (1985) 570-72; Gwendolyn Wright, *Moralism and the Model Home: Domestic Architecture and Cultural Conflict in Chicago, 1873-1913* (Chicago: University of Chicago Press, 1980) 93-96.

34. Suhrbur, "The Economic Transformation of Carpentry" 115; *Progressive Age,* Aug. 27, 1881, 5; Doucet and Weaver, "Material Culture and the North American House" 574-76.

35. GP, box 78B. Gross was not the only businessman-builder to appeal to the working-class desire for home ownership. The *Progressive Age* featured advertisements from several other builders, selling lots and cottages on monthly payments. See, for example, the West Chicago Land Company advertisements, "Homes for Mechanics," D. H. Small's advertisements, "Homes for Workingmen," *Progressive Age,* July 30, 1881, 5, 8.

36. Other businessman-builders also sought to bridge this market, though not with such elaborate marketing campaigns as Gross used. See the article on the E. A. Cummings & Co. July 4 picnic, *Chicago Daily Tribune,* July 5, 1888, 2. Builders in late nineteenth-century Detroit offered similar payment plans and used similar advertising strategies.

See: Olivier Zunz, *The Changing Face of Inequality: Urbanization, Industrial Development, and Immigrants in Detroit, 1880–1920* (Chicago: University of Chicago Press, 1982) 162–65.

37. Anne McClintock makes a similar argument about soap advertisements in England. Anne McClintock, *Imperial Leather: Race, Gender, and Sexuality in the Colonial Contest* (New York: Routledge, 1995) 207–10.

38. S. E. Gross, *A Home Primer for Young and Old* (Chicago: S. E. Gross, c. 1888), GP; Marsh, *Suburban Lives* 83–87; T. J. Jackson Lears, *No Place of Grace: Antimodernism and the Transformation of American Culture, 1880–1920* (New York: Pantheon, 1981) 11.

39. On the shift from production oriented culture to consumption see: Lears, *No Place of Grace* 28; Daniel Rodgers, *The Work Ethic in Industrial America, 1850–1920* (Chicago: University of Chicago Press, 1978) 99–108; Alfred D. Chandler, *The Visible Hand: The Managerial Revolution in American Business* (Cambridge: Harvard University Press, 1977); John F. Kasson, *Civilizing the Machine: Technology and Republican Values in America, 1776–1900* (New York: Penguin, 1977).

40. Catharine Beecher and Harriet Beecher Stowe, *The American Woman's Home* (Hartford: Stowe-Day Foundation, 1975) 23–42; Marsh, *Suburban Lives* 16–17.

41. Mary Brewster Laflin to Louis and Josephine Laflin (undated letter, 1886), George H. Laflin Collection, box 1, folder 4, CHS.

42. The plan for the parks originated with a group of real estate developers lead by Hyde Park developer Paul Cornell, who was determined to enhance the value of his South Side holdings with a public park modeled on the New England countryside where he was raised. In 1867, Cornell submitted a bill to the state legislature to create a South Parks Commission, which would tax property and float bonds for the purpose of buying and improving parkland in the Hyde Park area. A descendent of the first settlers of Rhode Island and cousin of Ezra Cornell, founder of Cornell University, Paul Cornell used his friendship with some of the state's leading public officials to promote his plan. He spent the winter of 1867–68 in Springfield steering the bill through the legislature. When the bill was voted down in a referendum of South Side residents, Cornell formed an alliance with real estate interests in the West and North Divisions and launched a publicity campaign for a citywide system of parks. A revised park bill became law in 1869, creating three independently chartered park commissions armed with powers of eminent domain and financed by city and state money. Cornell got himself appointed to the South Side park board, persuading his colleagues to hire Olmsted and Vaux, who were in Chicago planning Riverside, to design the south parks system. See Duis, *Challenging Chicago* 110–25; Miller, *City of the Century* 285.

43. On the importance of landscape to the middle-class ideal of the suburb see: Jackson, *Crabgrass Frontier*; Marsh, *Suburban Lives* 14; Wright, *Moralism and the Model Home* 26.

44. *Progressive Age*, Jan. 7, 1882.

45. *Progressive Age*, Jan. 7, 1882; *Chicago Daily Tribune*, July 1, 1888, 20, and July 6, 1888, 4.

46. S. E. Gross (firm), *Illustrated Catalogue of S. E. Gross' Lots, Houses, Cottages* 18, GP; *Knights of Labor*, Oct. 19, 1889, and Oct. 11, 1901; *Chicago Daily Tribune*, July 1, 1888, 20; S. E. Gross, *Tenth Annual Illustrated Catalogue* 47, GP.

47. C. C. Landt & Co. advertisement, CHS, real estate collection, folder 72a; *Chicago Daily Tribune*, June 10, 1888; S. E. Gross, *Tenth Annual Catalogue*, GP.

48. Kilner, *Joseph Sears and His Kenilworth* 147, 201.

49. This was part of what Margaret Marsh calls "masculine domesticity." Marsh, *Suburban Lives* 74–83; Lears, *No Place of Grace* 104–7; E. Anthony Rotundo, "Body and Soul:

Changing Ideals of Middle-Class Manhood, 1770–1920," *Journal of Social History* 16 (1983) 32.

50. S. E. Gross (firm), *Illustrated Catalogue of S. E. Gross' Lots, Houses, Cottages*, GP; *Chicago Globe* Dec. 22, 1889, 6.

51. *Rights of Labor*, April 26, 1890.

52. Richard Sennett, *Families against the City: Middle Class Homes of Industrial Chicago, 1872–1890* (Cambridge: Harvard University Press, 1970) 45–50; Theodore Dreiser, *Sister Carrie* (New York: Oxford University Press, 1991) 26–46; S. E. Mary Brewster Laflin to Louis and Josephine Laflin, May 17, 1886, George H. Laflin collection, CHS, box 1, folder 2; GP, folder 78B. Gross's clipping file contains a series of articles on women who are happier married than single, and how husbands should assert control over the household, including one titled "Marriage and Some Rules for Happiness."

53. Letter (undated) from Susan B. Anthony to Emily Maudevf Gross, Susan B. Anthony Collection, CHS; J. C. Gross to S. E. Gross, Nov. 30, 1886, GP, box 78B; *Chicago Record-Herald*, April 4, 1908, 5.

54. *Chicago Journal*, April 21, 1909; *Chicago Inter-Ocean*, April 21, 1909.

55. A. E. H., *The House That Lucy Built: or A Model Landlord* (Samuel E. Gross, 1886), GP.

56. A. E. H., *The House That Lucy Built* 36.

57. GP, financial records; Theodore Dreiser, *Jenny Gerhardt* (New York: Penguin, 1989) 326–34.

58. Dreiser, *Jenny Gerhardt* 326–34.

59. Hoyt, *One Hundred Years of Land Values in Chicago* 195.

60. Hoyt, *One Hundred Years of Land Values in Chicago* 165; *Chicago Daily Tribune*, April 21, 1889.

61. *Chicago Daily Tribune*, June 15, 1890.

62. *Real Estate and Building Journal*, April 4, 1891; *Chicago Daily Tribune*, May 17 and July 25, 1891; Hoyt, *One Hundred Years of Land Values in Chicago* 174–76.

63. *Real Estate and Building Journal*, April 4, 1891. Hoyt comments, "In the general rush and feverish scramble in so many sections of the city and the surrounding suburbs, the seven thousand vacant houses in the near West Side were lightly passed by." Hoyt, *One Hundred Years of Land Values in Chicago* 172.

64. James R. Barrett, *Work and Community in the Jungle: Chicago's Packinghouse Workers, 1894–1922* (Urbana: University of Illinois Press, 1987) 63; Howard Eugene Wilson, "Mary E. McDowell and Her Work as Head Resident of the University of Chicago Settlement House, 1894–1904," unpublished dissertation, University of Chicago, 1927, 40–42; Fred T. Hodgson, *Hodgson's Low Cost American Homes: Perspective Views and Floor Plans of One Hundred Low and Medium Priced Houses* (Chicago: Frederick J. Drake, 1904). Working-class families continued to pursue home ownership and to buy single-family houses, but their version of the home ownership ideal was gradually eclipsed by the middle-class households to whom Gross and others appealed.

65. Humbert S. Nelli, *Italians in Chicago, 1880–1930: A Study in Ethnic Mobility* (New York: Oxford University Press, 1970) 204–6; Abbott, *The Tenements of Chicago* 81–84; Paul Frederick Cressey, "Population Succession in Chicago, 1898–1930," *American Journal of Sociology* 56 (1938) 59–69; Arnold Hirsch, *Making the Second Ghetto: Race and Housing in Chicago, 1940–1960* (Chicago: University of Chicago Press, 1983) 187–89.

CHAPTER SIX

1.   Howard Eugene Wilson, "Mary E. McDowell and Her Work as Head Resident of the University of Chicago Settlement," unpublished dissertation, University of Chicago, 1927; Caroline Miles Hill, ed. *Mary McDowell and Municipal Housekeeping: A Symposium* (Chicago: Millar, 1938).

2.   Jane Addams, *Twenty Years at Hull-House* (New York: Penguin Books, 1961) 100; Addams, McDowell, and the Chicago reformers were part of a national movement, working on a municipal and sometimes state level, to bring together domestic reform, public health, urban improvements and notions of Americanization and citizenship. See, for example, Paul Boyer, *Urban Masses and Moral Order in America, 1820–1920* (Cambridge: Harvard University Press, 1978); Gwendolyn Wright, *Moralism and the Model Home: Domestic Architecture and Cultural Conflict in Chicago, 1873–1913* (Chicago: University of Chicago Press, 1980); Jean Bethke Elshtain, *Jane Addams and the Dream of American Democracy: A Life* (New York: Basic Books, 2002); Robert B. Fairbanks, *Making Better Citizens: Housing Reform and the Community Development Strategy in Cincinnati, 1890–1960* (Urbana: University of Illinois Press, 1988); John Comaroff and Jean Comaroff, "Homemade Hegemony," in *Ethnography and the Historical Imagination* (Bolder: Westview Press, 1992); Nayan Shah, *Contagious Divides: Epidemics and Race in San Francisco's Chinatown* (Berkeley: University of California Press, 2001); Regina Morantz, "Making Women Modern: Middle-Class Women and Health Reform in Nineteenth-Century America," *Journal of Social History* 10 (1977) 490–507; Michael McGerr, *A Fierce Discontent: The Rise and Fall of the Progressive Movement in America, 1870–1920* (New York: Free Press, 2003).

3.   Louise Montgomery, *The American Girl in the Stockyards District* (Chicago: University of Chicago Press, 1913) 3–4. This was not a preindustrial version of the home or of the family moved to the city; instead, residents used their homes to adapt to an urban industrial environment. The neighborhood in the early 1890s was bounded by Thirty-ninth Street to the north, Fifty-first Street to the south, Halsted Street to the east, and Western Avenue to the west.

4.   James R. Barrett, *Work and Community in the Jungle: Chicago's Packinghouse Workers, 1894–1922* (Urbana: University of Illinois Press, 1987) 73–77; Rick Halpern, *Down on the Killing Floor: Black and White Workers in Chicago's Packinghouses, 1904–54* (Urbana: University of Illinois Press, 1997) 7–43.

5.   Robert Hunter, *Tenement Conditions in Chicago: Report by the Investigating Committee of the City Homes Association* (Chicago: City Homes Association, 1901) 12; Barrett, *Work and Community in the Jungle* 15–17.

6.   Barrett, *Work and Community in the Jungle* 16–19, 87–91; Halpern, *Down on the Killing Floor* 23–30.

7.   Edith Abbott, *The Tenements of Chicago, 1908–1935* (Chicago: University of Chicago Press, 1936) 59–61; Charles B. Ball, "The New Tenement in Chicago," *Charities and Commons* 17 (Oct. 1906) 90–96; Thomas Lee Philpott, *The Slum and the Ghetto: Immigrants, Blacks, and Reformers in Chicago, 1880–1930* (New York: Oxford University Press, 1978) 102–3.

8.   Stewart Manuscript Census, 1905; Barrett, *Work and Community in the Jungle* 71–73. The Stewart Manuscript Census of 1905, a door-to-door survey of 284 families, was conducted for the U.S. Commissioner of Labor, Ethelbert Stewart. Enumerators canvassed nine streets, apparently surveying households of the three largest nationality groups in the neighborhood: Poles, Lithuanians, and Bohemians. Little is known about the criteria for selecting the households, but it seems the survey was an attempt

to enumerate a cross-section of the neighborhood's residents. The original copies of the Stewart census are in the Ethelbert Stewart Miscellany, Records of the Bureau of Labor Statistics at the National Archives and Record Service, Washington. A photocopy of the census is at the CHS. For more on the survey, see Barrett, *Work and Community in the Jungle* 281–82.

9. "The Back of the Yards Area," unsigned typed manuscript, 4–5 University of Chicago Settlement Collection, CHS, box 1, folder 2; Stewart Manuscript Census, 1905; Barrett, *Work and Community in the Jungle* 104–5; Mary McDowell, "Standard of Living Civic Frontiersmen," unpublished manuscript [1914?], MC, box 3, folder 13. Margaret F. Byington found similarly high levels of home ownership and of aspirations for home ownership among the Eastern European immigrants living in Homestead, Pennsylvania, in 1907–8. Like the settlement workers in Chicago, Byington was struck by the sacrifices low-wage immigrants were willing to make to achieve home ownership. Byington, *Homestead: The Households of a Mill Town* (Pittsburgh: University of Pittsburgh Press, 1974) 57–62.

10. It is not clear whether the children of foreign-born parents left Packingtown and purchased houses in other neighborhoods or whether they remained in the parents' homes, although evidence suggests both occurred. What is clear is that significant numbers of recent immigrants, often the lowest-paid workers, owned their dwellings.

11. Abbott, *Tenements of Chicago* 363–73; Barrett, *Work and Community in the Jungle* 104–5; Upton Sinclair, *The Jungle* (New York: Signet New American Library, 1960) 44. Among the native-born were both wage laborers and salaried managers. There are no available statistics separating the native-born working classes from the middle classes. But few among the middle classes lived within the boundaries of Packingtown.

12. Sinclair, *The Jungle* 168–89; Barrett, *Work and Community in the Jungle* 68–70.

13. The average number of people per dwelling in Chicago increased steadily between 1870 and 1910, then fell between 1910 and 1920. In 1870, an average of 6.7 people lived in each dwelling in the city, in 1880 the average was 8.2, in 1890 the average was 8.6, in 1900 the average was 8.8, in 1910 the average was 8.9, and in 1920 the average was 8.0. Robert G. Barrows, "Beyond the Tenement: Patterns of American Urban Housing, 1870–1930," *Journal of Urban History* 9 (1983) 409.

14. McDowell, "Standard of Living Civic Frontiersmen"; McDowell, "Housing," unpublished manuscript (1921) 1, MC, box 3, folder 14.

15. McDowell, "The Young Girl in Industry," unpublished manuscript (n.d.) 2, MC, box 3, folder 15; *Chicago's Dark Places: Investigations by a Corps of Specially Appointed Commissioners* (Chicago: Craig Press, 1891) 17; Montgomery, *The American Girl in the Stockyards District*; Joanne J. Meyerowitz, *Women Adrift: Independent Wage Earners in Chicago, 1880–1930* (Chicago: University of Chicago Press, 1988) 1–21.

16. Montgomery, *The American Girl in the Stockyards District* 3–4, 8–9; Florence Kelley, "Wage-Earning Children," in *Hull-House Maps and Papers* (New York: T. Y. Crowell, 1895) 72. Stephan Thernstrom found a similar phenomenon, the sacrifice of education for home ownership, in Newburyport, Massachusetts. See: Thernstrom, *Poverty and Progress: Social Mobility in a Nineteenth Century City* (New York: Atheneum, 1970).

17. Montgomery, *The American Girl in the Stockyards District* 3–4.

18. Mary McDowell, "Labor—The Great Strike," unpublished manuscript (ca. 1914) 1–2, MC, box 3, folder 15; Barrett, *Work and Community in the Jungle* 128–30. The 1894 strike marked a beginning for racial conflict in the packinghouses as the packers hired black "scabs" to fill the positions of striking workers, sparking racial conflict over jobs for the first time. Halpern, *Down on the Killing Floor* 30–31.

19. *Chicago Daily Tribune,* July 9, 1894; Barrett, *Work and Community in the Jungle* 74, 130. See also *Chicago Daily Tribune,* July 4, 1894, 5.

20. Mary McDowell, "Labor—The Great Strike," unpublished manuscript, MC, box 3, folder 15.

21. Harold L. Swift, "Mary McDowell As We Knew Her in the Yards," in Hill, *Mary Mc-Dowell and Municipal Housekeeping* 117.

22. Wilson, "Mary E. McDowell and Her Work" 33–44.

23. Residents of Hull-House, *Hull-House Maps and Papers* (Arno, 1970) 202; Steven J. Diner, "Social Workers and Blacks in the Progressive Era," in *Compassion and Responsibility,* Frank R. Breul and Steven J. Diner, eds. (Chicago: University of Chicago Press, 1980) 229; Philpott, *The Slum and the Ghetto* 80. Philpott notes that McDowell established the University of Chicago settlement without consultation from Packingtown residents and included none of her neighbors on its board of directors. Louise De-Koven Bowen, for example, was the granddaughter of one of the city's earliest white settlers and the wife of a silk manufacturer and banker. She worked closely with Addams and was the treasurer at Hull House from 1894 to 1935. She inherited a substantial fortune both from her father and later from her husband and donated over one million dollars to Hull House.

24. Wilson, "Mary E. McDowell and Her Work" 44. Perhaps, as Philpott notes, they set their agenda to conform to the demands of donors, who could have destroyed the settlement houses by withdrawing funds. But that was not the case entirely. McDowell supported workers' efforts to organize even with opposition from the packers. Hull House did turn down a $20,000 donation from a donor (unnamed) who "was notorious for underpaying the girls in his establishment and concerning whom there were even darker stories." Addams, *Twenty Years* 106–7; Philpott, *The Slum and the Ghetto* 80. McDowell's sentiments about settlement house work were echoed by many others, including Graham Taylor, who launched Chicago Commons in 1894. See Taylor, *Pioneering on Social Frontiers* (Chicago: University of Chicago Press, 1930) 277–330.

25. Residents, *Hull-House Maps and Papers;* Alice O'Connor, *Poverty Knowledge: Social Science, Social Policy, and the Poor in Twentieth-Century U.S. History* (Princeton: Princeton University Press, 2001) 3–24.

26. McDowell, "Housing."

27. McDowell, "Housing" 1–2; Wilson, "Mary E. McDowell and Her Work" 33–44; Mary McDowell, "Life and Labor," unpublished manuscript (1914), MC, box 3, folder 15.

28. McDowell, "Standard of Living," unpublished manuscript (1914), MC, box 3, folder 13. Addams comments on the problem of inadequate government regulation of public health repeatedly. Though McDowell never effectively organized voters or challenged the authority of the ward's alderman, Addams did move into formal politics by registering and organizing voters to challenge the Nineteenth Ward alderman. See, for example, Addams, *Twenty Years* 219–25. For more on late nineteenth-century women's use of politics see: Paula Baker, "The Domestication of Politics: Women and American Political Society, 1780–1920," *American Historical Review* 89 (1984):620–47; Kathryn Kish Sklar, *Florence Kelley and the Nation's Work: The Rise of Women's Political Culture, 1830–1900* (New Haven: Yale University Press, 1995).

29. Addams, *Twenty Years* 225–26.

30. McDowell, "Standard of Living"; Addams, *Twenty Years* 209.

31. Addams, *Twenty Years* 225–26. Just north of the Hull House district, Graham Taylor and volunteers at Chicago Commons also were organizing neighborhood improvement associations. See Taylor, *Pioneering on Social Frontiers* 298–300; Louise C. Wade,

Graham Taylor: Pioneer for Social Justice, 1851–1938 (Chicago: University of Chicago Press, 1964).

32. McDowell, "Housing" 1.

33. Elizabeth Blackmar, *Manhattan for Rent, 1785–1850* (Ithaca: Cornell University Press, 1989) 110–19; John Modell and Tamara K. Hareven, "Urbanization and the Malleable Household: An Examination of Boarding and Lodging in American Families," *Journal of Marriage and the Family* 35 (1973) 467–79. As Dolores Hayden has shown in her remarkable study of "materialist feminists," there was significant debate among feminists, architects, and housing reformers over the design and function of the family home in the late nineteenth century. Hayden, *The Grand Domestic Revolution: A History of Feminist Designs for American Homes, Neighborhoods, and Cities* (Cambridge: MIT Press, 1991).

34. *Report of the Committee on Tenement Houses of the Citizens' Association of Chicago* (Chicago: Geo. K. Hazlitt, 1884) 7.

35. *Rights of Labor*, April 29, 1893, 2; James Gilbert, *Perfect Cities: Chicago's Utopias of 1893* (Chicago: University of Chicago Press, 1991) 131–68. See also: Stanley Buder, *Pullman: An Experiment in industrial Order and Community Planning, 1880–1930* (New York: Oxford University Press, 1967).

36. Philpott, *The Slum and the Ghetto* 46–47; Margaret Crawford, *Building the Workingman's Paradise: The Design of American Company Towns* (New York: Verso, 1995) 37–43; *Progressive Age*, Jan. 28, 1882, 4. Though labor leaders were critical of Pullman's plan in the early 1880s, in April 1893, just a little more than a year before the strike, the *Rights of Labor* published an admiring profile of Pullman and his "model" community. *Rights of Labor*, April 29, 1893, 1.

37. *Report of the Committee on Tenement Houses of the Citizens' Association of Chicago* (Chicago: Geo. K. Hazlitt, 1884) 7.

38. Northwestern University Settlement Circular, no. 6 (June 1896) 5, NL; "Bad Tenements: Chicago's Need of Radical Reform," *Chicago Commons*, Feb. 1897, 1–3; program of conference on improvement of housing conditions, sponsored by Chicago Improved Housing Association and Chicago Architectural Club, March 20–26, 1900, Graham Taylor Papers, NL; Philpott, *The Slum and the Ghetto* 90–94.

39. Philpott, *The Slum and the Ghetto* 96–97.

40. See (all in MC, box 1, file 14): "Model Tenement House"; Allen B. Pound to Mary McDowell, May 20, 1912; Clarence Buckingham to Mary McDowell, June 24, 1912; N. B. Higbie to J. J. O'Connor, July 26, 1912. See also Maureen A. Flanagan, *Seeing with Their Hearts: Chicago Women and the Vision of the Good City, 1871–1933* (Princeton: Princeton University Press, 2002) 89–96. Flanagan argues that male reformers were more likely to seek market-oriented approaches to housing problems, while women reformers sought government funding for model tenements. It is not clear that the divisions among housing reformers were entirely along gender lines, but reform groups dominated by business leaders tended, at least after 1900, to promote the use of government regulation to stabilize property values and regulate land uses rather than seeking direct investment in housing.

41. City Club Committee on Housing Conditions chairman to the City Club board of directors, April 15, 1915, City Club Collection, box 16, folder 3, CHS; George E. Hooker to Frederick Pischel, March 14, 1916, City Club Collection, box 17, folder 3, CHS. Attached to the latter was a report to New York's Board of Estimate titled "Commission on Building Districts."

42. Flanagan, *Seeing with Their Hearts* 89–98; Taylor, *Pioneering on Social Frontiers* 292. To

some extent, the housing reformers' campaign was fueled by changing ideas about children and child rearing circulating among educated Americans in the late nineteenth and early twentieth centuries. No longer seen as simply small adults, children were increasingly viewed as existing in a qualitatively distinct stage of development. Theories of evolutionary biology provided the model for new theories of human development promulgated by the most influential child psychologist in the country, G. Stanley Hall. Dorothy Ross, *G. Stanley Hall: The Psychologist as Prophet* (Chicago: University of Chicago Press, 1972) 148–69. Hall briefly became the focus of a scandal in Chicago in 1899, when he gave a controversial speech before a national kindergarten teachers' convention. See Gail Bederman, *Manliness and Civilization: A Cultural History of Gender and Race in the United States, 1880–1917* (Chicago: University of Chicago Press, 1995) 77–78; Viviana A. Zelizer, *Pricing the Priceless Child: The Changing Social Value of Children* (New York: Basic Books, 1985) 3–6; Richard A. Meckel, *Save the Babies: American Public Health Reform and the Prevention of Infant Mortality, 1850–1929* (Baltimore: Johns Hopkins University Press, 1990) 47–50; Michael B. Katz, *In the Shadow of the Poorhouse: A Social History of Welfare in America* (New York: Basic Books, 1996) 120.

43. Marcus T. Reynolds, *The Housing of the Poor in American Cities* (College Park, MD: McGrath, 1969) 29.

44. Grace Abbott, "Better Homes for America" 1, Regenstein Library, University of Chicago, special collections; Reynolds, *The Housing of the Poor in American Cities* 29; Hunter, *Tenement Conditions in Chicago* 51.

45. Abbott, "Better Homes for America" 1.

46. *Chicago's Dark Places* 16; Addams, *Twenty Years* 210.

47. Hunter, *Tenement Conditions in Chicago* 62, 70. The merging of a language of health with morality was common among middle-class reformers in other late nineteenth-century cities. See, for example, Shah, *Contagious Divides* 110–18; Mariana Valverde, *The Age of Light, Soap, and Water: Moral Reform in English Canada, 1885–1925* (Toronto: McClelland and Stewart, 1991); Martha H. Verbrugge, *Able-Bodied Womanhood: Personal Health and Social Change in Nineteenth Century Boston* (New York: Oxford University Press, 1988); Nancy J. Tomes, *The Gospel of Germs: Men, Women, and the Microbe in American Life* (Cambridge: Harvard University Press, 1998).

48. Mary McDowell, "Housing" 1; Louise DeKoven Bowen, *The Colored People of Chicago: An Investigation made for the Juvenile Protective Association* (Chicago: Juvenile Protective Association, 1913) 11; *The Housing Problem in Chicago* (Chicago: Commercial Club [ca. 1905–10]), CHS.

49. McDowell, "Housing" 5.

50. Bowen, *Colored People of Chicago* 4; Abbott, "Better Homes for America" 2. Concern about overcrowding and the resulting loss of family privacy was apparent in reformers' studies of other cities and towns. See Byington, *Homestead* 140–43.

51. Poor and laboring families rarely, if ever, complained to social investigators about a lack of family privacy. Indeed, the word "privacy" rarely appears in quotations from investigators' interviews with poor families. On privacy as a new and largely bourgeois concept in late nineteenth-century America see Rochelle Gurstein, *The Repeal of Reticence* (New York: Hill and Wang, 1996).

52. Charles S. Duke, *The Housing Situation and the Colored People of Chicago* (Chicago, 1919) 11; Hunter, *Tenement Conditions in Chicago* 70. In the mid-1910s, there were three settlement houses located in largely African-American neighborhoods, and one set on the border between a black and white working-class neighborhood. The

settlement houses were supervised by interracial boards of directors and generally staffed by young African-American women. White settlement house workers and urban investigators were among the founding members of the Chicago Urban League in 1916. Addams, Bowen, McDowell, and Celia Parker Woolley, a white founder of the interracial Frederick Douglass Center settlement, were league members. Their involvement reflects their growing concern over the poverty and poor housing conditions in African-American neighborhoods. Although the Urban League offered black Chicagoans services that social workers already provided the immigrant poor, it said almost nothing about racial segregation of residential neighborhoods until 1919. Diner, "Social Workers and Blacks in the Progressive Era" 239–40; Charles S. Duke, *The Housing Situation and the Colored People of Chicago* (Chicago, 1919) 13.

53. Lawrence Veiller, *Housing Reform: A Handbook for Practical Use in American Cities* (New York: Charities Publication Committee, 1910) 101.

54. Lucy Maynard Salmon, *Domestic Service* (New York: Macmillan, 1897) 13–15; Steven Mintz and Susan Kellogg, *Domestic Revolutions: A Social History of American Family Life* (New York: Free Press, 1988) 123–25; Jane Addams, *Democracy and Social Ethics* (New York: Macmillan, 1902) 108.

55. Mary Brewster Laflin to Louis and Josephine Laflin, March 21, 1887, George H. Laflin Collection, CHS, box 1, folder 2.

56. Gurstein, *The Repeal of Reticence* 18. Gurstein argues that a fully articulated version of privacy emerged in response to the rise of mass circulation newspapers, reform debates about sexual hygiene, and the emergence of the realism as a literary style. The earliest discussions of privacy came in response to invasive journalism. See Louis Brandeis and Samuel Warren, "The Right to Privacy," *Harvard Law Review* 4 (1890) 195; E. L. Godkin, "The Rights of the Citizen: To His Own Reputation," *Scribner's Magazine* (July 1890) 65. Godkin, however, linked an abstract right to privacy to the family dwelling.

57. Jane Addams, *Democracy and Social Ethics* (Cambridge: Harvard University Press, 1964) 116–19.

58. Sklar, *Florence Kelley* 191–92.

59. Addams, *Twenty Years* 82.

60. Montgomery, *The American Girl in the Stockyards District* 3.

61. Abbott, *The Tenements of Chicago* 384–87.

62. Montgomery, *The American Girl in the Stockyards District* 60.

63. Montgomery, *The American Girl in the Stockyards District* 3–4; Florence Kelley, "Wage-Earning Children," in *Hull-House Maps and Papers* (New York: T. Y. Crowell, 1895) 72.

64. *Bailey v. Illinois*, 190 Ill. 29 (1901).

65. Abbott, *The Tenements of Chicago* 60; Francis H. McLean, "Tenement-House Reform in Chicago—Progressive Measure Before the City Council This Week," *Charities* 9 (Dec. 20, 1902) 617–18; Philpott, *The Slum and the Ghetto* 102.

66. "The Municipal Lodging House," *Cooperation* 1 (Dec. 28, 1901) 1–2; Nels Anderson, *The Hobo: The Sociology of the Homeless Man* (Chicago: University of Chicago Press, 1923) 28–30; Philpott, *The Slum and the Ghetto* 98–102.

67. Edith Abbott, *The Tenements of Chicago, 1908–1935* (Chicago: University of Chicago Press, 1936) 344, 361–62; Mintz and Kellogg, *Domestic Revolutions* 131.

68. Barrett, *Work and Community in the Jungle* 100–101. Barrett argues that the war, with the drop in European immigration, led to the "collapse" of the boarding system. He suggests that the entrance of married women into wage work in the packinghouses was a means of replacing the income brought in by boarders.

246 / Notes to pp. 175–180

69. Abbott, *The Tenements of Chicago* 341–60; Joanne J. Meyerowitz, *Women Adrift: Independent Wage Earners in Chicago, 1880–1930* (Chicago: University of Chicago Press, 1988) 74–75.

70. Philpott makes a similar point. See Philpott, *The Slum and the Ghetto* 113.

CHAPTER SEVEN

1. *Co-operation*, May 9, 1903, quoted in Steven J. Diner, "Chicago Social Workers and Blacks in the Progressive Age," in *Compassion and Responsibility: Readings in the History of Social Welfare Policy in the United States*, Frank R. Breul and Steven J. Diner, eds. (Chicago: University of Chicago Press, 1980) 228. See also "The Negro in Business and Professions," *Chicago Record-Herald* (Aug. 24, 1909) 6.

2. William M. Tuttle, Jr., *Race Riot: Chicago in the Red Summer of 1919* (New York: Atheneum, 1970) 243.

3. Monroe Nathan Work, "Negro Real Estate Holders of Chicago," M.A. diss., University of Chicago (1903) 31. Richard R. Wright, Jr., referred to Work's study in a 1908 article, commenting that only "a few typewritten copies have been made." Wright, "Recent Improvement in Housing among Negroes in the North," *Southern Workman* (Nov. 1908) 608. Among the half dozen studies of housing conditions in African-American neighborhoods published in the 1910s and 1920s, only the 1922 report from the Chicago Commission on Race Relations mentions Work's study. In addition, even those earlier studies by reformers associated with settlement houses that mentioned race stressed common class experiences over race. For example, "no attempt was made to draw final conclusions in regard to racial differences under a common American environment." Louise Montgomery, *The American Girl in the Stockyards District* (Chicago: University of Chicago Press, 1913) 2. This neglect of racial segregation in housing markets did not, however, occur in all cities. In New York, a few white reformers did study and seek to resolve the problem in the early years of the twentieth century. See, for example, Mary White Ovington, *Half a Man: The Status of the Negro in New York* (New York: Longmans, Green, 1911); Gilbert Osofsky, *Harlem: The Making of a Ghetto, Negro New York, 1890–1930* (Chicago: Ivan R. Dee, 1996) 58–67.

4. Carter G. Woodson, *A Century of Negro Migration* (Washington: Association for the Study of Negro Life and History, 1918); St. Clair Drake and Horace R. Cayton, *Black Metropolis: A Study of Negro Life in a Northern City* (New York: Harcourt, Brace, 1945) 53. The migration of black southerners to northern cities and their struggles for adequate housing and decent paying jobs has been chronicled in a wide array of scholarly works. Most, however, either assume that black people were tenants or largely ignore the property relations at the center of the struggle for decent housing. See, for example, Nicholas Lemann, *The Promised Land: The Great Black Migration and How It Changed America* (New York: A. A. Knopf, 1991); James R. Grossman, *Land of Hope: Chicago, Black Southerners, and the Great Migration* (Chicago: University of Chicago Press, 1989); Allan H. Spear, *Black Chicago: The Making of a Negro Ghetto, 1890–1920* (Chicago: University of Chicago Press, 1967); Tuttle, *Race Riot*; Thomas Lee Philpott, *The Slum and the Ghetto: Immigrants, Blacks, and Reformers in Chicago, 1880–1930* (New York: Oxford University Press, 1978). The situation in Chicago, where growing numbers of black residents faced with white resistance to black neighbors, was similar to that of other northern cities. See, for example, Osofsky, *Harlem*; Kenneth L. Kusmer, *A Ghetto Takes Shape: Black Cleveland, 1870–1930* (Urbana: University of Illinois Press, 1976); Douglas S. Massey and Nancy A. Denton, *American Apartheid: Segregation and the Making of the Underclass* (Cambridge: Harvard University Press, 1993); Andrew

Wiese, *Places of Their Own: African American Suburbanization in the Twentieth Century* (Chicago: University of Chicago Press, 2004). Thomas Sugrue writing on Detroit and Kevin Fox Gotham writing on Kansas City have uncovered significant evidence of the role of real estate entrepreneurs in shaping the racially divided housing markets of those cities. See Sugrue, *The Origins of the Urban Crisis: Race and Inequality in Postwar Detroit* (Princeton: Princeton University Press, 1996), and Gotham, *Race, Real Estate, and Uneven Development: The Kansas City Experience, 1900–2000* (Albany: State University of New York Press, 2002).

5. U.S. Manuscript Census 1900; Work, "Negro Real Estate Holders" 25; Louise DeKoven Bowen, *The Colored People of Chicago* (Chicago: Juvenile Protective Association, 1913) 13–16; Fannie Barrier Williams, "Colored Women of Chicago," in *The New Woman of Color: The Collected Writings of Fannie Barrier Williams, 1893–1918*, Mary Jo Deegan, ed. (DeKalb: Northern Illinois University Press, 2002) 67–68.

6. Spear, *Black Chicago* 11–16; Christopher Robert Reed, *"All the World Is Here!" The Black Presence at White City* (Bloomington: Indiana University Press, 2000) 85–89; Davarian Baldwin, "Chicago's new Negros: Consumer Culture and Intellectual Life Reconsidered," paper delivered at the Urban History Conference, Oct. 2002.

7. Chicago Commission on Race Relations, *The Negro in Chicago: A Study of Race Relations and a Race Riot* (Chicago: University of Chicago Press, 1922) 107–8.

8. Spear, *Black Chicago* 11–16; Wright, "Recent Improvement in Housing among Negroes in the North" 602. Fannie Barrier Williams too complained that the "good and bad," were "huddled together" in the Black Belt. Williams, "Social Bonds in the 'Black Belt' of Chicago," *Charities* 15 (Oct. 7, 1905) 40–44.

9. Philpott, *The Slum and the Ghetto* 146, 121; U.S. Manuscript Census of 1900; Drake and Cayton, *Black Metropolis* 57; Reed, *"All the World Is Here!"* 89–93.

10. Spear, *Black Chicago* 3–4; Donald L. Miller, *City of the Century: The Epic of Chicago and the Making of America* (New York: Simon & Schuster, 1996) 533–39; Perry Duis, *Challenging Chicago: Coping with Everyday Life, 1837–1920* (Urbana: University of Illinois Press, 1998) 106.

11. Quoted in Drake and Cayton, *Black Metropolis* 55; Harold F. Gosnell, *Negro Politicians: The Rise of Negro Politics in Chicago* (Chicago: University of Chicago Press, 1967) 128–29. A 1911 police commission report on vice was explicit about the department's aim of segregating vice in the Black Belt. *The Social Evil in Chicago: A Study of Existing Conditions* (Chicago: Vice Commission of the City of Chicago, 1911) 38, CHS.

12. Williams, "Social Bonds in the 'Black Belt' of Chicago" 40–41.

13. Information about property ownership in the Black Belt comes from the Cook County Tract Books and the manuscript census for 1900. See also Edith Abbott, *The Tenements of Chicago, 1908–1935* (Chicago: University of Chicago Press, 1936) 124–25.

14. Alzada P. Comstock, "Chicago Housing Conditions, VI: The Problems of the Negro," *American Journal of Sociology* 18 (1912) 246; Duke, *The Housing Situation and the Colored People of Chicago* 7–9; Abbott, *The Tenements of Chicago* 124–25.

15. Duke, *The Housing Situation* 8, 12; Abbott, *The Tenements of Chicago* 124. For a similar phenomenon in Detroit, see Sugrue, *The Origins of the Urban Crisis* 34–35.

16. By the 1910s, Binga managed or owned an estimated 1,200 dwellings along State Street near Forty-seventh and Forty-eighth Streets. Carl R. Osthaus, "The Rise and Fall of Jesse Binga, Black Financier" *Journal of Negro History* 58 (1973) 39–60; Arnett G. Lindsay, "The Negro in Banking," *Journal of Negro History* 14 (1929) 192–93; *Chicago Daily Tribune*, May 8, 1927, 20; *Broad Ax*, Dec. 25, 1909, 2; Anthony J. Binga, Sr., "Jesse Binga: Founder and President, Binga State Bank, Chicago, Illinois," *Journal of the Afro-*

American Historical and Genealogical Society 2 (1981) 146–52. See Binga's ads in, for example, *Broad Ax*, Sept. 19, 1908, 4; *Broad Ax*, Sept. 26, 1908, 2; and *Chicago Defender*, May 11, 1912, 4. Binga had acquired his investment capital largely through marriage to the daughter of the head of one of the city's most notorious gambling networks.

17. Work, "Negro Real Estate Holders" 29–31; Bowen, *The Colored People of Chicago* 11; Comstock, "Housing Conditions in Chicago" 246–47.

18. Chicago Commission on Race Relations, *The Negro in Chicago* 116; Philpott, *The Slum and the Ghetto* 149.

19. *Chicago Defender*, May 8, 1915 2.

20. Jane Addams, *Twenty Years at Hull-House* (New York: Penguin, 1961) 209–10; Edith Abbott, *The Tenements of Chicago, 1908–1935* (Chicago: University of Chicago Press, 1936) 59–61.

21. Philpott, *The Slum and the Ghetto* 150–52. Philpott describes the strategy of the white-owned realty firm, Watson and Bartlett's, which bought up thousands of parcels east of State Street. He quotes a rival realtor saying that the firm "paid about twenty-two hundred dollars on average for these dwellings and then they would sell them to the negroes for about four thousand dollars, a hundred dollars down and about forty dollars a month. The hundred dollars secured them against nonpayment and forty dollars a month netted them a good profit."

22. *Chicago Defender*, Nov. 1, 1919; *Chicago Inter-Ocean*, Aug. 18, 1900, cited in Philpott, *The Slum and the Ghetto* 151. Philpott provides a full description of the realtors' assault on Vernon Avenue.

23. Wright, "Recent Improvement in Housing among Negroes in the North" 608 Joseph A. Logsdon, "The Rev. Archibald Carey and the Negro in Chicago Politics," unpublished thesis, University of Chicago, 1961, 29.

24. Wright, "Recent Improvement in Housing among Negroes in the North" 603; Philpott, *The Slum and the Ghetto* 147–49.

25. In 1900, Work found that while 24 percent of all families in the city owned their homes, just 5 percent of black families owned their homes. Work, "Negro Real Estate Holders" 19, 14–15; *Broad Ax*, Sept. 19, 1908, 4. Black-owned business too suffered from a lack of capital available for investment, making it more difficult for entrepreneurs like Binga to buy real estate or open banks to finance black home owners. But as early as 1840, black businessmen in Cincinnati pooled capital to buy real estate and in 1868 a group in Richmond, Virginia, organized a "Home Building Fund and Loan Association," but there were few similar enterprises in other cities. J. H. Harmon, Jr., "The Negro as Local Businessman, *Journal of Negro History* 14 (1929) 123–24, 131; *Richmond Whig*, Aug. 4, 1871.

26. Wiese, *Places of Their Own* 21–22. Although there has been little research on black suburbs before World War II, there is some evidence that black and immigrant working-class people sometimes lived in small suburban communities near industrial jobs outside of other northern cities. One example is Howard's Place, a community of black and Italian brick workers just west of St. Louis. U.S. Manuscript Census, 1910, 1920, 1930.

27. Bowen, *The Colored People of Chicago* 10; Duke, *The Housing Situation and the Colored People of Chicago* 11.

28. Abbott, *The Tenements of Chicago* 125; Duke, *The Housing Situation and the Colored People of Chicago* 15.

29. *Chicago Record-Herald*, April 5, 1911, 8.

30. Work, "Negro Real Estate Holders of Chicago" 31; Joseph Kirkland, "Among the Poor

in Chicago," in *The Poor in Great Cities* (London: Kegan Paul, Trench, Trubner, 1896) 198.

31. Bowen, *The Colored People of Chicago* 12.

32. Drake and Cayton, *Black Metropolis* 57; Comstock, "Housing Conditions in Chicago" 255–56.

33. *Chicago Record-Herald*, Feb. 7, 1911, 1.

34. Duke, *The Housing Situation and the Colored People of Chicago* 14; Spear, *Black Chicago* 21; *Chicago Defender*, May 8, 1915, 2.

35. Allan H. Spear notes that the African-American class structure did not always correspond with the white class structure. Some "occupational groups that would belong to the upper lower class among whites have traditionally formed the core of the Negro middle class." See Spear, *Black Chicago* 23. Well-to-do African-American tenants were targeted as well. See, for example, *Chicago Record-Herald*, March 9, 1905, 1.

36. Spear, *Black Chicago* 21–23.

37. Fannie Barrier Williams, letter to editor, *Chicago Record-Herald*, Sept. 15, 1906, quoted in Philpott, *The Slum and the Ghetto* 155–56; *Lakeside Annual Directory for the City of Chicago 1889* (Chicago: Chicago Directory Co., 1889), University of Illinois at Chicago library; *Lakeside Annual Directory for the City of Chicago 1898* (Chicago: Chicago Directory Co., 1898), University of Illinois at Chicago library.

38. *Chicago Record-Herald*, Aug. 23, 1909, 2; *Chicago Record-Herald*, Aug. 21, 1908, 1, 4.

39. Chicago Commission on Race Relations, *The Negro in Chicago* 117–18. The entire episode is described in Spear, *Black Chicago* 22–23.

40. Osthaus, "The Rise and Fall of Jesse Binga" 28–29; Chicago Commission on Race Relations, *The Negro in Chicago* 124–29.

41. *Chicago Defender*, May 10, 1913, cited in Spear, *Black Chicago* 21; *Chicago Defender*, Sept. 20, 1913, 1.

42. The white Hyde Parkers provided an illustration of a concept that the courts had only recently begun to recognize: property was defined both by its "use-value" and its "exchange-value." Neither the courts nor contemporary scholars acknowledged the racial component of exchange value in residential property. See, for example, John R. Commons, *Legal Foundations of Capitalism* (New York: Macmillan, 1924) 11–21; Kenneth Vandevelde, "The New Property of the Nineteenth Century: The Development of the Modern Concept of Property," *Buffalo Law Review* 29 (1980) 325; Gregory S. Alexander, *Commodity and Propriety: Competing Visions of Property in American Legal Thought, 1776–1970* (Chicago: University of Chicago Press, 1997) 259–61.

43. Alexander, *Commodity and Propriety* 1.

44. *Chicago Defender*, June 22, 1912, 1; *Chicago Record-Herald*, Aug. 21, 1909, cited in Spear, *Black Chicago* 22; Chicago Commission on Race Relations, *The Negro in Chicago* 114.

45. Chicago Commission on Race Relations, *The Negro in Chicago* 3.

46. See, for example, *Buchanan v. Warley*, 245 U.S. 60; 38 S. Ct. 16; 62 L. Ed. 149 (1917).

47. Lizabeth Cohen suggests that settlement workers sought to dilute ethnic differences to organize neighborhood groups. Cohen, *Making a New Deal* (New York: Cambridge University Press, 1990) 55; Philpott, *Slum and Ghetto* 66, 75.

48. Ida B. Wells-Barnett, *Crusade for Justice: The Autobiography of Ida B. Wells*, Alfreda M. Duster, ed. (Chicago: University of Chicago Press, 1970) 250; Work, "Negro Real Estate Holders of Chicago" 31.

49. For more on Ely's life and influence on American thought see: Benjamin G. Rader, *The Academic Mind and Reform: The Influence of Richard T. Ely in American Life* (Lexington:

University of Kentucky Press, 1966); Dorothy Ross, *The Origins of American Social Science* (New York: Cambridge University Press, 1991) 102–5, 192–93; Richard T. Ely, *Ground under Our Feet* (New York: Macmillan, 1938); Alexander, *Commodity and Propriety* 323–25.

50. Richard T. Ely, "The City Housing Corporation and 'Sunnyside,'" *Land Economics* 2, no. 2 (1926) 81.

51. Marc A. Weiss, *Richard T. Ely and the Contribution of Economic Research to Home Ownership and Housing Policy* (Boston: MIT Center For Real Estate Development, 1989) 6.

52. Marc A. Weiss, *The Rise of the Community Builders: The American Real Estate Industry and Urban Land Planning* (New York: Columbia University Press, 1987) 147–59. Here, Weiss describes the evolution of FHA loan policies, but for the point about racial barriers to FHA loans, see Weiss, *Richard T. Ely* 18; Kenneth T. Jackson, *Crabgrass Frontier: The Suburbanization of the United States* (New York: Oxford University Press, 1985) 195–215.

53. *Chicago Daily Tribune*, July 7, 1919.

54. Wells-Barnett, *Crusade for Justice;* Mildred I. Thompson, *Ida B. Wells-Barnett: An Exploratory Study of an American Black Woman, 1893–1930* (New York: Carlson, 1990) 27–30, 114–16; Patricia A. Schechter, *Ida B. Wells-Barnett and American Reform, 1880–1930* (Chapel Hill: University of North Carolina Press, 2001) 11, 17–18.

55. Chicago Commission on Race Relations, *The Negro in Chicago* 2.

56. *Chicago Daily Tribune*, July 7, 1919; Tuttle, *Race Riot* 11.

57. T. Arnold Hill to L. Hollingsworth Wood (telegram dated July 29, 1919), Julius Rosenwald Papers, Joseph Regenstein Library, University of Chicago, box 6, folder 4. This account and Tuttle's account of the riot's beginning differ in several significant places. Hill, apparently spreading a widely believed rumor, claimed "whites refused to rescue" Eugene Williams or "to permit his rescue by colored people." Tuttle says there is little evidence for that claim. Tuttle, *Race Riot* 49.

58. Chicago Commission on Race Relations, *The Negro in Chicago* 1.

59. Chicago Commission on Race Relations, *The Negro in Chicago* 3, 645.

60. Chicago League on Urban Conditions among Negroes, *Annual Report* 1:10, CHS; Hill to Wood (1919).

EPILOGUE

1. Edith Elmer Wood, *The Housing of the Unskilled Wage Earner: America's Next Problem* (New York: Macmillan, 1919) 19.

2. Edward K. Spann, *Designing Modern America: The Regional Planning Association of America and Its Members* (Columbus: Ohio State University Press, 1996) 132–33; Dolores Hayden, *The Grand Domestic Revolution: A History of Feminist Designs for American Homes, Neighborhoods, and Cities* (Cambridge: MIT Press, 1991) 251, 273; Eugenie Ladner Birch, "Edith Elmer Wood and the Genesis of Liberal Housing Thought, 1910–1942," Ph.D. diss., Columbia University (1976) 30–41.

3. Wood, *The Housing of the Unskilled Wage Earner* 19.

4. Richard Plunz, *A History of Housing in New York City: Dwelling Type and Social Change in the American Metropolis* (New York: Columbia University Press, 1990) 151–59; Gail Radford, *Modern Housing for America: Policy Struggles in the New Deal Era* (Chicago: University of Chicago Press, 1996) 50–51; Deanna Benson, "'Garden Homes': An Experiment in Housing the Worker in Socialist Milwaukee, 1920–1923," paper delivered at the Tenth National Conference on Planning History, Society for American City

and Regional Planning History, St. Louis, Nov. 2003. The Amalgamated Houses in the Bronx, completed in 1927, remain a limited-equity housing cooperative.

5.   Radford, *Modern Housing for America* 2–3.

6.   I want to clearly distinguish here between housing costs and land values. As Homer Hoyt shows, both land values and wages increased slowly and steadily after 1900. But the costs of constructing or purchasing a new house increased even more after about 1895. See Hoyt, *One Hundred Years of Land Values in Chicago: The Relationship of the Growth of Chicago to the Rise of Its Land Values, 1830–1933.* (Chicago: University of Chicago Press, 1933) 410.

7.   Kenneth T. Jackson, *Crabgrass Frontier: The Suburbanization of the United States* (New York: Oxford University Press, 1985) 203–218; Thomas W. Hanchett, "The Other 'Subsidized Housing': Federal Aid to Suburbanization, 1940s–1960s," in John F. Bauman, Roger Biles, and Kristin M. Szylvian, eds., *From Tenements to the Taylor Homes: In Search of an Urban Housing Policy in Twentieth-Century America* (University Park: Pennsylvania State University Press, 2000); Marc A. Weiss, *Richard T. Ely and the Contribution of Economic Research to Home Ownership and Housing Policy* (Boston: MIT Center for Real Estate Development, 1989) 18.

8.   Wood, *The Housing of the Unskilled Wage Earner* 277.